MURAL PAINTING

BY

FREDERIC CROWNINSHIELD

ILLUSTRATED

British Library Cataloguing-in-Publication Data
A catalogue record for this book is available from
the British Library

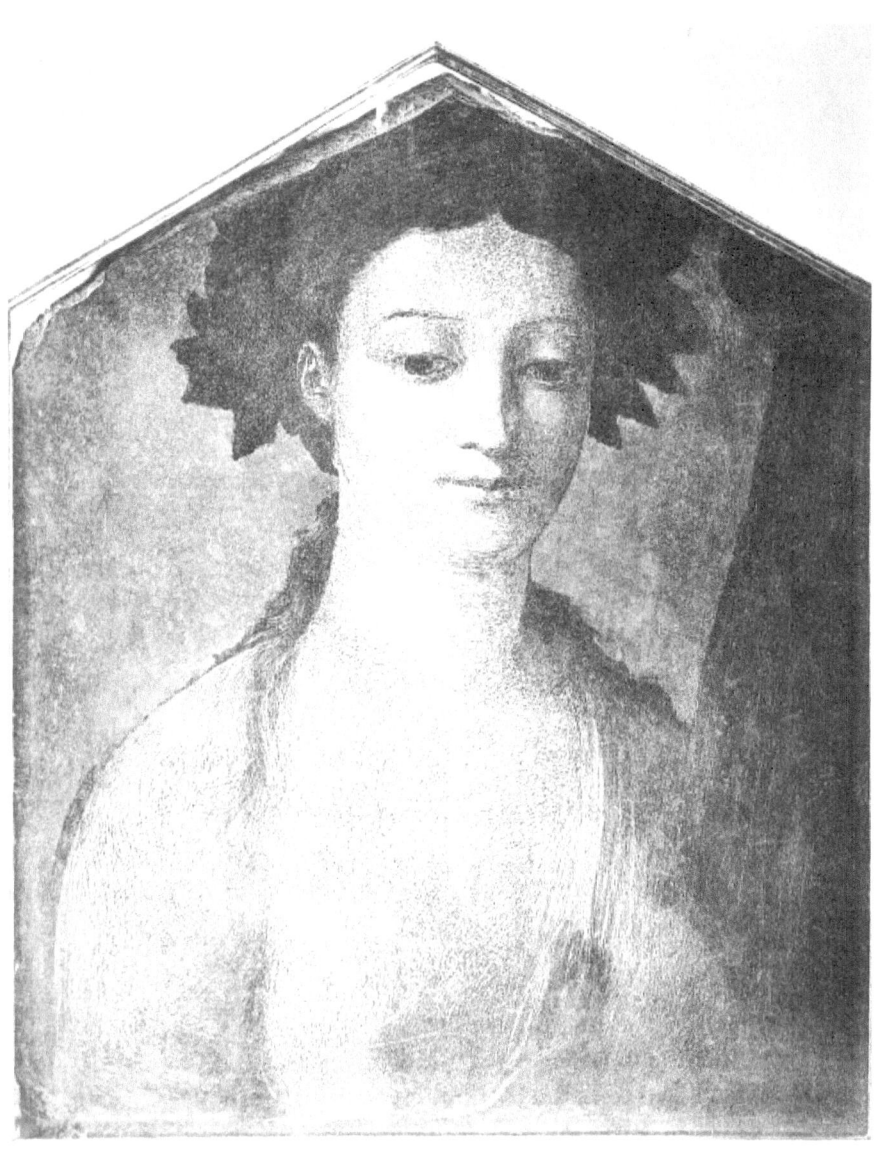

PREFACE.

THE following chapters originally appeared as "papers" in the *American Architect*. With the exception of those few verbal changes which their present and more formal garb has necessitated, together with the slight emendations and additions that time and fresh material have suggested, their substance is the same. It would have been useless to attempt to disguise their "periodical" character, which will account for the enforced and otherwise unwarrantable condensation. Had their length or subsequent publication in book-form been originally foreseen, much valuable information might have been drawn from distant sources that would have greatly enriched them both as to text and illustration. But the first intention was far more limited and modest, and when afterwards the work grew prodigiously under the inspiration of the subject, it was then too late.

The inadequacy of ordinary methods of reproduction to an intelligible exposition of the qualities peculiar to mural painting has necessarily curtailed the number of illustrations. The linear interpretation of a picture is not without value, seeing that it translates the composition, forms, and often the light and shade. For these reasons it has been utilized; but it gives no insight whatever into those technical peculiarities that differentiate one process from another: it would not tell us, for example, whether the prototype were executed in fresco, oil, or water glass; nor does it portray the actual condition of the work, a matter of the highest import. The gelatine print is the only form of reproduction that adequately conveys this information. Unfortunately, gelatine prints are expensive, and a liberal use of them would have defeated the very end in view — a perhaps over-sanguine hope that my labors may prove serviceable to artists, whose purses are rarely as plethoric as their desires. It must be borne in mind, however, that gelatine prints, even more than photographs, are apt to exaggerate the deterioration of a painting, and sometimes give a diseased and shabby appearance to a prototype that is comparatively sound.

The publication of this volume, notwithstanding its incompleteness, must be justified by the immediate importance of the subject, the vast scope for mural decoration now offered by an extraordinary building activity — an activity that is likely to continue for years — and by the very misty ideas that are entertained of its technics by architect, client, and would-be practitioner. Even an indifferent treatise at this important juncture would be better than none at all. Without further apology, therefore, I dedicate this little work most affectionately to my pupils. Should any of them, through its means, be induced to practise monumental painting, the noblest form of all pictorial expression, I shall deem myself well content.

F. C.

1886.

CONTENTS.

FULL PAGE ILLUSTRATIONS.

FIGURES IN THE TEXT.

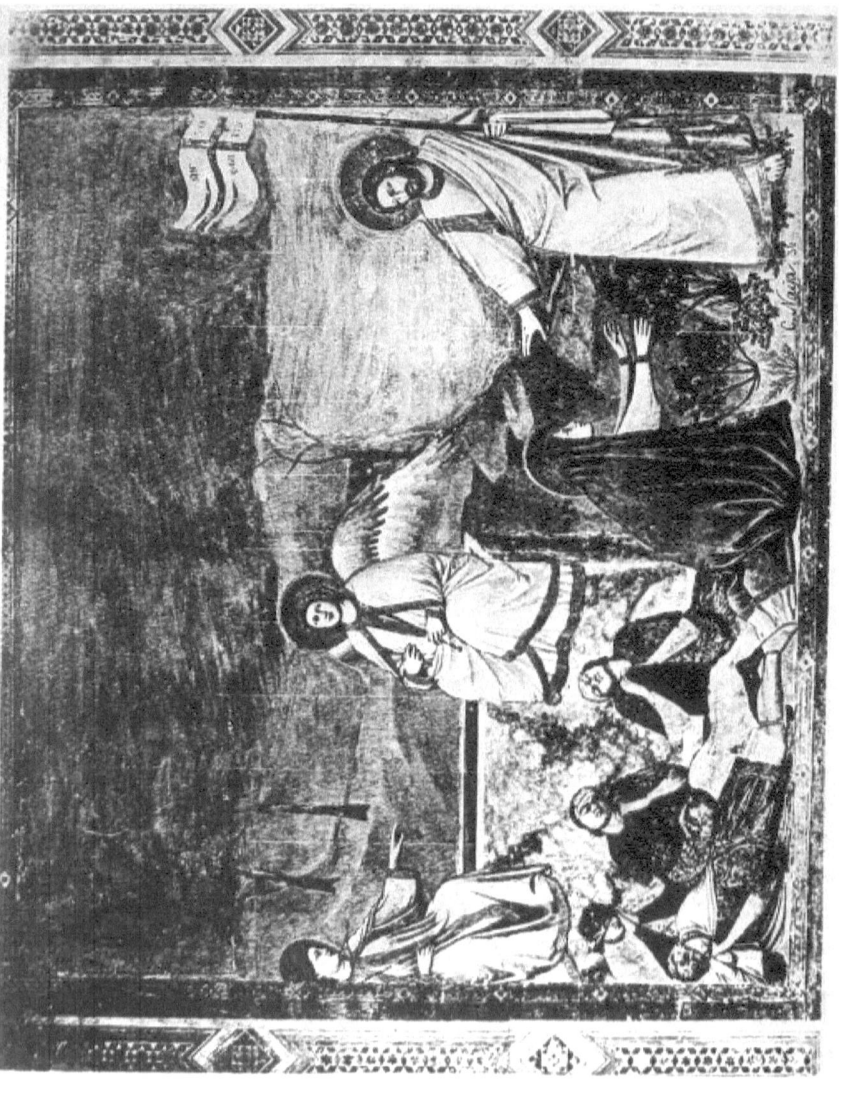

'The Resurrection' (Fresco) by Giotto (1276 - 1437.) Arena Chapel, Padua

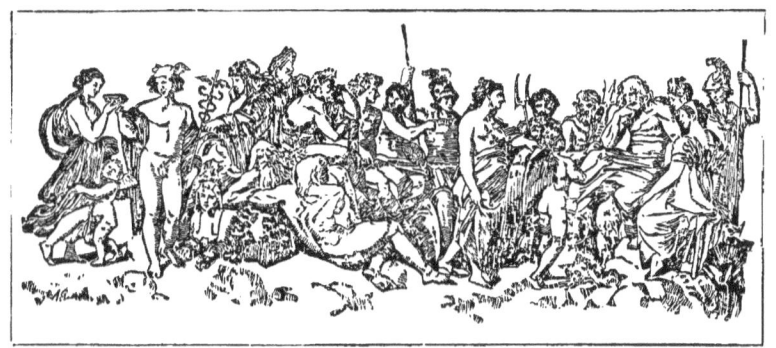

MURAL PAINTING.

CHAPTER I.

INTRODUCTORY REMARKS.

THE glories of mural painting have lately been eclipsed by the predominating popularity of its younger sister, the easel picture. The eclipse has not been total, and, given the proper impetus, its sun may yet shine with more than pristine splendor. True, the pictorial story-telling age is gone, at least for us. The A B C's of history, the quondam all-sufficient biblical narratives are no longer gleaned from temple walls; prosaic type has usurped their functions. Rising generations imbibe more copious draughts from more generous fonts. Didactical painting is no longer the principal, merely an accessory, though not a valueless one. Picture-writing is evidence of savagery. Painting has other spheres, though many deluded painters (and musicians) still cling to the story-telling idea, and try to churn out of poor paint (and sound) with a labor to which the mountain's travail is as naught, ideas that the pen of poet can jot down with a facility that must ever be their despair. From the time that man was man — and that we fain must believe was at least a million years ago—he has had a heart, and it is probable that he will continue to have one, unless the wise men of the earth evolutionize it out of him again, till this world is chilled to its marrow, and for mere warmth's sake drops into the sun. Now, at least, good mother earth is warm. Men live on her and feel. Yes, 'tis the *feeling* that is the fun of it as well as the sorrow. An unemotional entity would be about as sympathetic as the snow-man of the winter-loving urchin.

Art is the high-priest of the emotions, the great humanizer. To humanize the million is one of the problems of the day. Mural painting, above all other kinds, is for the million. Its dignity, its simplicity, its light, airy tones are wonderfully impressive, even to the uncultivated. Its mere accessibility is greatly in its favor; so too its intimacy with the structure. Mural painting is no movable exotic, but an actual part of the habitation. Art should be all-embracing. Of course there is an esoteric art, very charming to the elect, just as there is an esoteric literature; but, completely to fulfil its mission, art must be exoteric. What better vehicle for a universal, beneficent art than the wall? As for wall-space, actual and potential in this land, the brain reels to think of it. For ages custom has sanctioned the painted wall of temple, capitol and theatre; but what glorious opportunities are offered by the walls of our colossal railroad stations, our public halls, our mammoth hotels and costly restaurants, our vast stores! Paint them, and the people would be brought face to face with art in the daily routine of life, and absorb it as children absorb a foreign language. Instead of the occasional visit of a few to some remote museum of fine arts, or to a fee-exacting exhibition, there would be the effortless, expenseless communion with art at all times. Art, like religion, should be an every-day affair. Museums are oases in a Sahara of bad taste (and blessed be their founders!), but they are not enough. Of necessity they are exclusive. We ought to live with art. Beginnings, humble beginnings have already been made to decorate some of our large structures. Unfortunately these efforts have not been universally successful, owing rather to lack of practitioners and good taste than to lack of money. Yet bad taste is not infrequently better than no taste at all, since it may lead to better things. The habit of decoration once acquired, the bad will eventually be replaced by the good. That stupid negative doctrine advanced so persistently and with such puritanical priggishness by some people of so-called "good form," that a room or a house must be bare — "chaste" and "simple," they say — that "beauty must be unadorned," means artistic famine. This negative doctrine, by the way, is germane to the modern Anglo-Saxon tendency to suppress emotion. Hamerton, in a capital chapter ('Unrecognized Untruth' : Human Intercourse) remarks, "Overstatement is regarded as a vice, and understatement as a sort of modest virtue, whilst in fact they are both untruthful, exactly in the degree of their departure from perfect accuracy." The latter kind of untruth he calls the "untruthfulness by inadequacy." To establish a learned balance between the blank and ornamented spaces is the effort of all good architects and decorators. This quality, the essence of successful ornamentation, is a source of ineffable delight to the beholder.

By mural painting I do not mean geometrical design merely, or purely conventional ornament, but rather figure-work, combined perhaps with conventional ornament, or that sort of design where a free imagination seems to dominate the rule and compass, and which certainly would not be repeated indefinitely without modification. This is a somewhat lame definition — certain things never can be defined— but one, I trust, that will be felt. A repeated pattern or diaper is well enough at times, but alone in an important edifice does not suffice. It may play the part of accessory, but cannot fill the protagonist's rôle. Though there are splendid historical exceptions, it may be said that a geometrical pattern, interlacement or the like, however ingenious, unaided by the figure or other important motive from nature, tends to produce a very irritating mental effect, when, as has just been observed, it covers large spaces in important interiors. It seems to torment the brain instead of refreshing it, appealing to the imagination in a measure, but working it as mathematics work, without soothing it. How sterile, merely for an example, and starved is a theatre without the graceful, eloquent, suggestive forms of the human figure.

There are those who still believe in the oft-cited but false principle that mural figures should be treated only in outlined flat tints. They hold that modelled forms will conflict with the architecture. The proper thing to do is to make the figures, modelled or not, *look well* in their given places. If they discord with the architecture, they will surely not look well. Painters of experience would never try to make their figures "come out from the wall"—not such an easy thing, by the way, to do if they use colors and mediums suited to the work. And if by chance the figures should come a little too far forward, though it is better that they should not, would it be a very heinous offence? Would it be half so heinous as the frequent current practice of shading the ground-tone of a wall from light above to dark below, or vice-versa, so that the wall appears to topple? This question of relief will be handled in a subsequent article on the tech-nics of mural painting. After a few prefatory and somewhat erratic observations, I intend to describe technically some of the principal methods of wall-painting, and to conclude with a few observations on the personal qualifications of the painter.

It cannot be denied there are conditions that antagonize, as well as those that favor, the development of mural painting in this country. The fluctuation of wealth is against it. Fathers make a fortune; their sons dissipate it. The equal distribution of the parental prop-erty is not conducive to the maintenance of the family mansion. The denial of the rights of primogeniture means the non-erection of those stupendous monuments of family pride, the glory of their own and succeeding ages, with which every traveller is familiar. There is, moreover, a general feeling that socially we are living in a transi-tional age. No one dares to discount the future. Mighty agencies are at work that render the prolonged tenure of property a matter of doubt. Formerly a patrician built for eternity ; to-day every man is a patrician and builds for his lifetime. The concentration of art in the palaces of a lordly few is giving place to its diffusion over the whole land. In the palmiest days of Grecian art the private houses were simple, the public places resplendent. This is somewhat consol-ing. Doubtless there will always be exceptional houses dominating their neighbors, at least, till the millenium sets in. On the other hand the average house promises to be luxurious, vastly more so than the average Grecian house in the time of Pericles. There are opportuni-ties for artistic work of a high order, even in comparatively modest houses. If people would only learn to husband their resources, to con-centrate it on given points, and not to fritter it away in useless deco-ration from attic to cellar, to indulge in a little more cream and a great deal less skim-milk. It is the cream that stamps a house, pro-claiming the taste of the owner. How many a quiet façade, or plain-toned wall has been dignified by a delicately-carved moulding or a sweetly-painted frieze? People always economize at the wrong mo-ment, forgetting that the few last touches are the most telling ones. Here let it be observed, parenthetically, that though artists have always been blamed for their unbusinesslike qualities, *per contra*, in matters of taste, there is no one more unbusinesslike than the business man. So skilfully does he scheme at times to get the worst thing possible ! Bad taste is about as expensive as good taste, though the latter in the end is a more profitable investment. What fruitful property the paintings and frescoes of the fifteenth and sixteenth centuries have proved to be ! Hear what Morelli says of the Sistine Madonna : " It cost Saxony about two hundred and twenty thousand francs. What price would it now fetch, when a Murillo has been thought worth seven hundred and thirty thousand francs! None but a Rothschild could afford to buy it. If the picture were still standing in its little church of S. Sisto at Piazenza, not only would that town be more talked of and more visited than it is, but that picture alone would bring the inhabitants more gain than all they possess besides." [1] A first-class Raphael in Broadway would probably yield better dividends than the most favored railroad stock. This is an extreme case ; yet one may guess that the bar-room Bouguereau has paid handsomely. Though I cannot speak authoritively, I am inclined to think that a house with a little tasteful decoration would let better than a house with a great deal of offensive decoration, other things being equal. Again, when a building is condemned, the good things are saved.

That mammon of unrighteousness, the speculative builder, is the avowed enemy of good decoration (and of mankind). Judging from the cracked, peeling, spotted and generally demoralized walls, ceilings and stucco-work to be found in nine houses out of ten, one is tempted to dub all plasterers and builders — I don't dare to add architects — mammons of unrighteousness. Seriously, our plaster-work is disheartening, totally unfit to receive mural paintings of value. Its amelioration is well worth the earnest attention of all conscientious architects. General shabbiness ought not to supervene after a few years of use. Even paint, if properly laid on a firm ground, and in the right place, should hold for generations, to judge from the paintings that have come down to us from antiquity. Durability is a noble quality, yet held apparently in light esteem. Perishable substitutes do duty for stone, terra-cotta and the hard woods. Inferior plaster is hastily spread over flimsy, inflammable furrings. and as a consequence threatening fissures are speedily developed. This lack of durability is often disguised by upholsterers' work, that soon deteriorates. How inherent is the taste for upholstery! How people love it! Verily, the moth has its functions. Akin to the taste for upholstery is the application of incongruous and inappropriate materials to alien surfaces. It is a pleasure to feel that a design is made for the place, congenital with it; not an applied, interrupted design, that might as well have veneered anything else (interrupted designs are rarely satisfactory). Call to mind the patch-work ceilings in wall-paper scraps (how can men be so viciously ingenious!) ; the inappropriate bits of plush, often in combination with durable metals, employed ubiquitously, sometimes framing,

---

[1] *Italian Masters in German Galleries : Giovanni Morelli.*

sometimes framed; the machine-stamped designs to be cut to suit
the place — ready-made ornament "on draught," as it were.
Some of this ornament may be good, even first-rate, but sole pro-
prietorship enhances any art-product. Vulgarize a thing, and it
loses its charm. Do we feel happier when a coat identical with
our own confronts us? This feeling may be very unphilanthropic,
but it is not inartistic. If expense precludes the use of elaborate
mural painting, certainly it cannot of carefully-chosen flat tints,
relieved here and there, if necessary, by a few appropriate lines.
Wall-papers are not objectionable, if used with discretion. They
are very appropriate to cottages, and to informal or temporary
structures. Still, papers are substitutes for something better, and
those who can afford it indulge in paintings, tapestries, wood-work,
or other rich and durable materials.

The day for ecclesiastical decoration has by no means passed
away. There is less votive piety than there was in the palmy days
of *buon fresco*, and what remains expresses itself in glass rather
than in pigment, though the stained-glass window is but a phase of
mural painting. The taste for memorial windows is genuine, and
likely to wax stronger. Their rich, transparent tones are entranc-
ing, their splendor exalting. Add to this the sanctity of ages, and
an ineffable mystery, engendered partly by the radiation of the
blending tones, partly by the maze of leaded lines, and we have
the *raison d'être* of a beautiful and legitimate form of church decoration. The blond, I might almost say heavenly, tones of fresco
if well-lighted, are extremely happy in churches. In a dome, for
instance, how aerial they are. Care must be taken to avoid a clash
with the windows; but paintings clash less with stained glass than
one would suppose, so totally different are they in quality of color,
and so overpowering is that of the glass. In churches dimly lighted
by "storied windows richly dight," paintings are superfluous, for
the reason that they are practically invisible. Clear glass is always
more favorable to them; yet the combination is frequently desirable. Then the stained glass should neither be so clear, even, or
thin, as to shed colored rays on the walls, nor so dark as to obfus-
cate the decorations. Painter and glazier can rarely work together
in a church, seeing that its decoration is slowly accumulated. Where
they can, mutual enhancement of their work should be the result.
Mosaics are the most suitable accompaniment to colored glass, but
expense precludes their general adoption.

Not long since the interior of the average Protestant church
was but little better than a barn, the natural result of Puritanism.

Every day we are emancipating ourselves from the outward expression — austere and hungry — of that sturdy faith. Worshippers crave sympathy, geniality, less bare wall, more emotion, and — art. At least, so I heard some orthodoxly-minded deacons observe one day, while working unseen in a dimly-lighted dome. A church, to be popular, must be attractive; the preacher must have a becoming background — so, at least, the deacons said. Under whatever forms religion may manifest itself, whatever may be the tenets of the day and place, or however modified by modern ideas, in the broadest sense of the word man will always be religious. These broader, more human, less-encumbered beliefs might well seek expression on the wall. They have not yet been treated. Even the old ideas can be repeated *ad infinitum* without wearying, if they be rendered with modern feeling. That love of ecclesiastical grotesqueness, the offspring of mediæval insufficiency, is very stupid. Some think that a painter must have the faith of an Angelico to limn an angel. Not a bit of it. The faithless Perugino painted exquisite angels; Raphael, the divine Raphael, was a courtier of pagan Leo the Tenth. To believe in your saints and angels *artistically* is the requisite — to fancy celestial forms and try to realize them. It is not necessary to believe in their actualities. It suffices to be inspired by the subject, and one can be inspired without being a bigot. The poet does not give credence to the legends and myths he celebrates in verse. He has a clear vision of them and a certain temporary fictitious belief. Too much faith may hamper a creative mind. Even in his orthodox days, the poor, good old painter and author, Cennino Cennini (1437) must have been sorely circumscribed by his very conciliatory attitude towards the saints, who never rescued him from a wretched death in a debtor's cell. The painter-monks of Mt. Athos are still painting twelfth-century pictures after the recipe of Panselinos, so enslaved are they by tradition. Superstition would be as great a drawback to art to-day as aruspicy would be to military science. Fancy a Von Moltke consulting the entrails!

CHAPTER II.

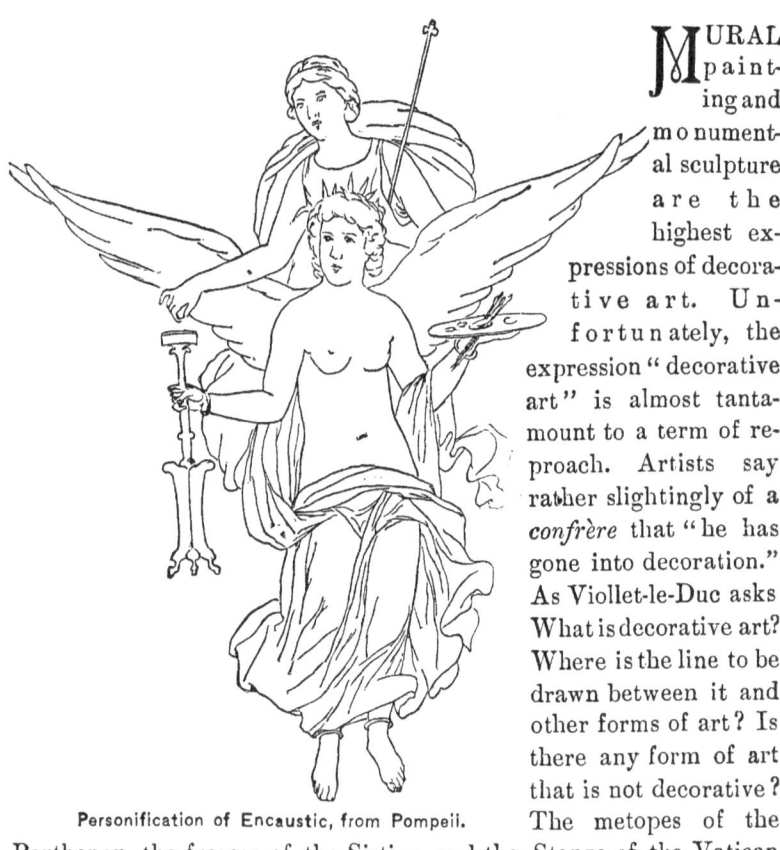

Personification of Encaustic, from Pompeii.

MURAL painting and monumental sculpture are the highest expressions of decorative art. Unfortunately, the expression "decorative art" is almost tantamount to a term of reproach. Artists say rather slightingly of a *confrère* that "he has gone into decoration." As Viollet-le-Duc asks What is decorative art? Where is the line to be drawn between it and other forms of art? Is there any form of art that is not decorative? The metopes of the Parthenon, the frescos of the Sistine, and the Stanze of the Vatican are examples of so-called decorative art; yet it may be presumed that Phidias, Michael Angelo, and Raphael would be somewhat surprised, were they to return among us, not to find themselves in "smart" artistic society. Does a picture or a statue cease to be decorative when it is executed for no particular place? Does it cease to be decorative

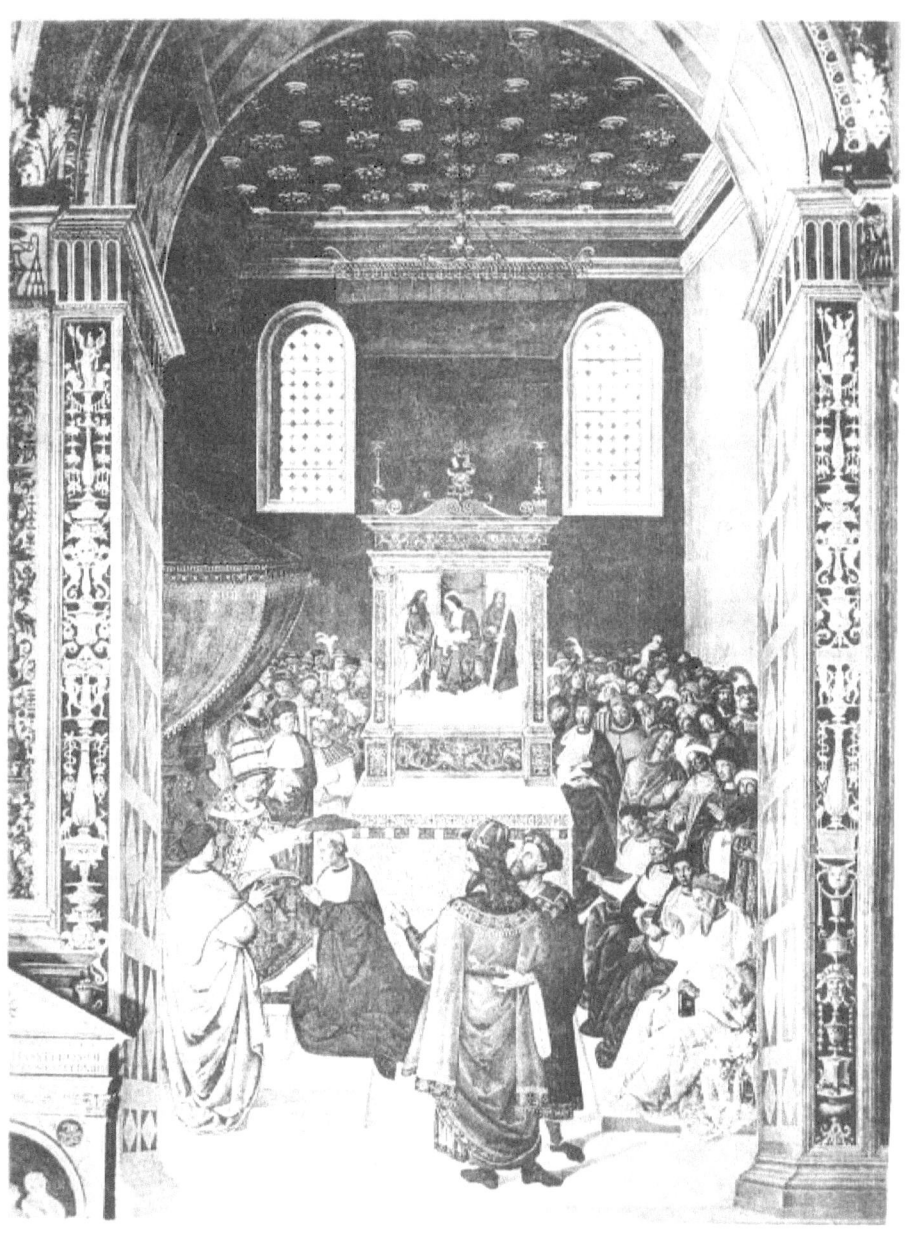

'Æneas Piccolomini created Cardinal by Pope Calixtus III' (Fresco)
by Pinturicchio (1454-1513). Library, Siena.

when it is portable? Is there any particular charm in portability? Portability has its advantages. A man can decamp at short notice with all his household gods; but certainly no one has ever eulogized art for this reason. Has any artist ever discovered a system of painting or sculpture universally adaptable to the ever-varying conditions of light and place? If any one has been so ingenious, he must have locked the secret up in his own consciousness. Is the ulterior destination of easel pictures, then, ignored by the painter? In the majority of cases it would seem so, unless the picture be painted to order for a given place. The poor mural painter — or monumental sculptor— has to bother his brains very much about the conditions of light and place, and to make many a reluctant sacrifice to them. Because an art takes cognizance of its environments, is it inferior to an art that trusts to luck for its setting?

Far be it from me to depreciate the easel picture in my eagerness to exalt monumental art. To do anything well is an arduous task. Comparisons between the kindred arts are not only odious and sterile, but well-nigh impossible without the bias of personal preference. Leonardo's spleen when he vaunts the superiority of painting over sculpture — owing, probably, to a grudge against Michael Angelo — is delicious reading. Hear him: " The sculptor by blows and muscle wears away the marble or superfluous stone that exceeds the figure which is enclosed within it — a very mechanical operation — in a great sweat mixed with dust and converted into mud, his face well pasted, and completely powdered with marble dust, so that he looks like a baker, and covered with minute chips, as if he had been snowed upon, and his house [is] filthy, and full of chips and stone-dust; whilst the well-dressed painter sits comfortably before his work, and manipulates light brushes and exquisite colors, adorned with garments to his taste, and his house is full of beautiful paintings," etc. His atrabiliousness entirely runs away with his style and stops. Michael Angelo's tirade against oil painting was unworthy of him; but when he waxed old, and approaching death mellowed his austere temperament, he kindly and fairly writes to Benedetto Varchi, estimating by request the comparative supremacy of painting and sculpture : " . . . . then painting and sculpture may be considered equal, and this being admitted, it follows that no painter should undervalue sculpture, nor should any sculptor depreciate painting." [1]

It has been said that all good painting comes from the wall. (Almost to a man the " big ones " have painted on, or for, the wall.) This may be a somewhat superlative statement, but there is

---

[1] *Life of Michael Angelo:* Charles Heath Wilson.

a germ of truth in it. In its higher phases mural painting is an excellent antidote to the vagaries of fashion, being intolerant of impertinent eccentricities and egotistical extravagances. It must be dignified and appropriate, as well as free from all ephemeral picturesqueness. Wouldn't art gain something were the painters of the easel picture to take a hint from their mural brethren, and consider the final destination of their work? The ultimate resting-place of a picture cannot be predicted with certainty; yet it is fair to assume that the majority of paintings, if they be of moderate size, will eventually hang in a dwelling-house. As a matter of fact, many painters — too many, it is to be feared — whilst incubating, are thinking very much more of the next important exhibition than of the quiet little nook where perchance their creation will find itself, feebly lighted and at close quarters with the family.

Exhibitions are useful disseminators of art. To the public they are beneficent teachers; to the artists themselves, while they are undeniably of great advantage as criterions of comparative merit, they are also fraught with grave danger. As for the concomitant system of medals and prizes, it is enough "to drag angels down." Let them be relegated to the domain of the schoolboy; there are worthier prizes for the artist than medals and red ribbon — the great prizes of life, honor and success, not to mention the mere joy of creation. This prize system is just beginning to take root here; let us eradicate it ere it is too late. In other countries it has tarnished many brilliant names. Great men have belittled themselves in their scramble for rewards. Jurymen have first bedizened their own button-holes and then bedecked their henchmen. Intrigues and enmities quite as crafty and fierce as those of the political arena are rampant in the lists of art. The Olympic games were favorable to the development of symmetry and heroic action. Perfect Greek met perfect Greek in nerve and limb-testing struggle; and a simple garland of wild olive sufficed to immortalize the mightiest. Had these games been semi-annual, instead of quadrennial, with interludes of the Nemean, Pythian and Isthmian, they would soon have degenerated into "go-as-you-please" matches, with vulgar belts and purses to allure equally vulgar champions. The present mania for exhibitions is fast lowering them to the level of the show, and in many cases to the pecuniary advantage of the showmen. That picture-dealers should speculate in art is just and natural. There is no humbug about their calling. But there is a vast amount of humbug underlying the self-sacrificing manifestoes of the benevolent art-agent. If exhibitions are great picture marts, let it be frankly acknowledged:

there is no sin in it, and art is degraded by the lie. But pray, gen-tlemen, dispense with the solicitous cant about the welfare of the American public.

There remains one more observation to be made about exhibitions (having little, apparently, to do with mural painting, save indirectly), and that is their distracting influence on the younger artists, not to mention the older. "One must be seen to be appreciated," they say; "but *côute que côute*, one must be seen." Either motive or technique must be noisy, so that those who run may read. This is frequently the key-note to production, and what a key-note to sonnet or epic! How can any heartfelt song be attuned to it? At times it would seem as though the whole artistic world were "Salon"-struck, insular England excepted, be it said to her credit. The spaciousness and garish light of a gallery exact a very different handling from the quiet light of home, where, by the way, a picture can choose its neighbors without elbowing them.

The mental attitude of the prospective exhibitor is unhealthy. Un-harassed concentration and personal inspiration are requisite for the evolution of an idea. There is a temptation to force a note for an exhibition, or to sacrifice personality to a fashion set by some hero of the hour. An artist must be very self-reliant or unreceptive not to lose his head; very confident and shrewd to glean the few whole-some hints that will strengthen his own expression without stealing the soul of his brother-artist. The mural painter is a perpetual exhibitor. He exhibits naturally, not artificially; he paints for a given place under definite conditions. He is not obliged to whistle to the passer-by, nor is he bothered by whistling neighbors. He is himself, when left to his own resources. When left to his own resources! Could he only assert himself with the haughty stubborn-ness of Michael Angelo, who rode rough-shod over popes! If popes, too, were equally complaisant! "I said to the pope," writes Buan-arroti concerning the Sistine, "that to represent the Apostles only it would prove a poor thing; he asked me why. I said to him, because they were poor also. Then he gave me a new commission that I should do what I pleased. . ."

A comparatively limited experience has verified the opinion — which may be erroneous, seeing that it is well-nigh impossible to sub-stantiate a generalization without very extended researches — that the attitude of educated people in matters of taste is far less defer-ential to professional judgment in this than in other countries, and relatively far more deferential to the *ex cathedra* utterances of the other professions. Taste is apparently too obvious to admit of cultivation, and personal preferences suffice. However this may be, the attitude of the profession, and the architectural profession as well, is too yielding. Talk earnestly, sensibly, firmly to a man of common-sense and an impression will be made, unless his will is adamantine. Firmness and tact work marvels. Clients can exercise a great deal of taste under professional advice. The primary conditions they impose, the man they select to work out these conditions, and the decision of the many alternatives that are presented to them, all imply personal taste. In cases involving professional science an architect should be absolute. From the first he should work with a view to mural paintings, if there are to be any. The mural painter has to take things as he finds them. He is generally summoned at the last moment, when it is too late to choose his grounds. He has to make the best of faulty conditions. Pigments must be applied to half-dried and inferior plaster. Why? Because the client is in a hurry, or because the architect has not personally tested the plaster and its application, or because the paintings have been suggested at the eleventh hour. The architects are doing much, through their associations, to strengthen and dignify their position. Would that the decorators would follow their example instead of cutting each others' throats. The relations between architect, client and decorator are, to say the least, very trying. Theoretically, when employed by the architect, the decorator does not recognize the client. Actually it is very different. Not infrequently he finds himself between two fires, and in his efforts to please two masters pleases none.

It is to be regretted that there is no department in our larger schools of art where mural painting is taught. The regular academic fig-ure-work, though necessary, is not enough. It should be supplemented not only by a course of elementary architectural and decorative forms, but by instruction in the monumental treatment of figures, as well as by lectures on walls and plaster, on the chemistry of colors, their deterioration under climatic, solar or gaseous influences, in fact, on all the mechanical part of decorative art. Greatly to their disad-vantage our artists know almost nothing about the chemistry of colors, oils, varnishes, and their behavior under trying conditions. Pictures frequently blacken or crack in a way that is quite unaccountable. It may be owing to the ground, the vehicle, colors, or undue haste. Who can tell? Artists rely implicitly on the colormen. It is well that labor should be divided in these bustling days, and that our ma-terials should be prepared for us by others. But it is not well to del-egate all *knowledge* of them. Cennino Cennini [1437] allows "the space of six years at least" to "learn all the parts and members of the art," and six years more for the practice of it, "drawing without intermission on holydays and weekdays." If an artist is moved by the praiseworthy impulse to make a few investigations, he is forthwith confronted by a disheartening disagreement of the doctors. Here is a hap-hazard example. Indian yellow is classed by several authors among the dangerous pigments ; while Ulisse Forni, restorer of the royal galleries at Florence, describes it as a " beautiful and durable color in nowise noxious." Some of the most charming qualities in modern pictures are gained at the expense of durability ; such a quality, for instance, as texture—unless great care be observed. Where paint is unevenly and lumpily applied, it is very apt to crack, especially if the undertone be not thoroughly dry. In out-of-door work where time is an object to the artist, the undertone has very rarely time to dry properly ; recourse is then had to the doubtful expedient of powerful siccatives. Perhaps it is not known to the average painter that the rather popular palette-knife execution is more liable to crack than brush-work—the air acting on the latter more readily. Artists are daily employing methods that would have shocked the atelier-bred men of the Renaissance ; not from lack of moral sense, but from sheer ignorance of the physical laws relating to their craft. Unfortunately, unpunished offences promote this ignorance, and engender indifference, to boot. It is authoritatively said that deterioration is the logical sequence of certain evil methods. This is not always the case, the conditions environing a picture being exceedingly complex, and possibly harboring an unsuspected antidote. Yet immunity from degeneration is frequently enjoyed for a space only — time settling the account.

The ideal school for the mural painter must have been the studio of the Renaissance — Perugino's, for instance, where practice and precept were most happily combined. Great works were consummated under the eye of the pupil, himself a coadjutor when sufficiently advanced. His relations with the master were intimate, as they should be. The master was the father of the artistic family. He exacted obedience, which — if he were a man of note — was cheerfully rendered. In return the pupil was relieved of all anxiety. He was taught everything worth teaching. Instead of flitting from master to master, as students are prone to do now-a-days, bound by no tie, following their own immature judgment, he was regularly apprenticed by his parents to some reputable artist with whom he worked till maturity. Didron, in his *Manuel d'Iconographie Chrétienne,* a work to which future reference will be made, describes an interesting scene he witnessed in the atelier of Father Macarios, one of the

best Byzantine painters on Mount Athos, who still hold to the mediæval methods. Alluding to a certain Greek manuscript—a perfect thesaurus of all that a painter should know, called in fact the
'Painter's Guide,' and dating back in precept to the eleventh century—he says: "This Bible of his art was placed in the middle of
the atelier, and two of the young pupils read from it, alternately in
a loud voice, whilst the others painted as they listened." What delightful and easy co-operation!

The rigors of a trying climate would probably make short work of
any painting on the exterior of our buildings. In milder countries
even it has fared badly with frescos exposed to the open air. Would
that Giorgione had never painted on palace façades! The actinic
rays of the sun, sea-air, dampness, changes of temperature rapidly
deteriorate all pigments. It is said that successful experiments have
lately been made in Germany to render mural paintings weather-
proof by a process resembling the water-glass method, though not
identical with it. This may be so, yet one is inclined to doubt its
permanent durability. At all events time alone can guarantee it. [1]
Even the recently-discovered endolithic process, where the colors are
imbibed by the marble and incorporated with it, will not resist atmospheric deterioration. It is, however, admirably adapted to certain in-
door uses where marble is desirable, for example in a bath-room. Of
exposed vermilion, Vitruvius says, " In open places, such as peristylia
or exedræ, and similar situations whereto the rays of the sun and moon
penetrate, the brilliancy of the color is destroyed by contact with
them, and it becomes black. Thus, as it has happened to many

---

[1] This process was invented by Adolph Keim of Munich. The artists on the commission sum up their report with these remarks: " According to the foregoing
opinions, Mr. Keim has undoubtedly succeeded in providing a method of monumental painting carefully thought out, even to the smallest detail, grounded on
scientific principles, and practically verified by visible facts, which is by far to be
preferred to all methods of painting hitherto existent, and which, once recognized
for its high value, would bring about a complete revolution in all our monumental and decorative art, and which deserves the widest publication and practical
employment." [American Architect, Vol. XV, No. 429.] May this unstinted praise
be verified by time! Yet almost as handsome things were said years ago of the
stereo-chrome, or water-glass process, which has since proved perishable. For
example: " In order to test the advantages of stereochromy, proof plates were
submitted to the roughest treatment; they were exposed for weeks to rain and
frost; the ice which had formed upon them was allowed to thaw in a warm room
and this freezing and thawing process was repeated without in the slightest degree damaging the plates, whilst fresco paintings treated in the same manner
became quite friable, and crumbled to pieces;" and more in the same strain
From W. Cave Thomas's *Mural Decoration.*] Time—the true test—has scaled
off the colors submitted to the water-glass treatment. " Certain colors in particular, as ultramarine, umber and black, were observed to be always the first
to detach themselves in the form of powder, or by scaling off from the painting,
thus pointing to the fact that their destruction was not owing to any accidental
defect in the manner of their application, but to some radical unsuitability arising from the chemical conditions of the process. [American Architect, Vol. XV,
No. 429.]

others, Faberius, the scribe, wishing to have his house on the Aventine elegantly finished, colored the walls of the peristylia with vermilion. In the course of thirty days they turned to a disagreeable, uneven color; on which account he was obliged to agree with the contractors to lay on other colors. Those who are particular in this respect, and are desirous that the vermilion should retain its color, should, when the wall is colored and dry, rub it with a hard brush charged with Punic wax melted and tempered with oil; then, with live coals in an iron pan, the wall should be thoroughly heated, so as to melt the wax and make it lie even, and then rubbed with a candle and clean cloth, as they do marble statues. This practice is called καῦσις by the Greeks," [Gwilt's translation]. Its power to resist the action of acids has frequently suggested the use of wax with pigments. As observed by Vitruvius, the Greeks saturated their marble statues with it to protect them from atmospheric corrosion. It would be interesting and profitable to apply an out-of-door test to ordinary oil house-paints, either mixed with wax dissolved in turpentine, or laid on in the usual fashion with a final coat of liquefied wax and oil. The durability of paint might thus be prolonged several years, though nothing probably would adhere to our walls either externally or internally as they did to those of Vitruvius. What walls they were! It would be well for architects to familiarize their clients with his chapter on plastering. " Three sand coats and the same number of marble-dust coats ; " but the preparation of the walls and the use of wax will be treated more fully in subsequent chapters.

Mosaic is undoubtedly the best medium for exterior pictures. It is both durable and decorative. It harmonizes with stone, marble, or even brick. If the stone or marble be highly colored or polished, the mosaic may be rich and brilliant in tone. If, on the contrary, they be low-toned or dull, care must be taken to use tesseræ of quiet materials. Mosaics can be slightly deadened by using a white cement and allowing it to be visible in the interstices. Mosaic does not harmonize with painted wood. Its juxtaposition to any wood is open to criticism. Glazed encaustic tiles are also well adapted to out-of-door decoration. Our climate favors the use of color in façades. Our sun is as splendid as that of more southern climes. The reflected lights are strong; therefore it is well to accentuate architectural forms with color. Moreover, color is in keeping with our brilliant skies and foliage. In gray England or northern France it discords with the leaden atmosphere. We are just accustoming ourselves to its use. The denizen of the " brown-stone front " was somewhat shocked at first, but even he is beginning to yield. While the private citizen may prefer to present a quiet and dignified façade to the street from motives of modesty, public buildings have the right, and ought to blaze with a fair amount of splendor.

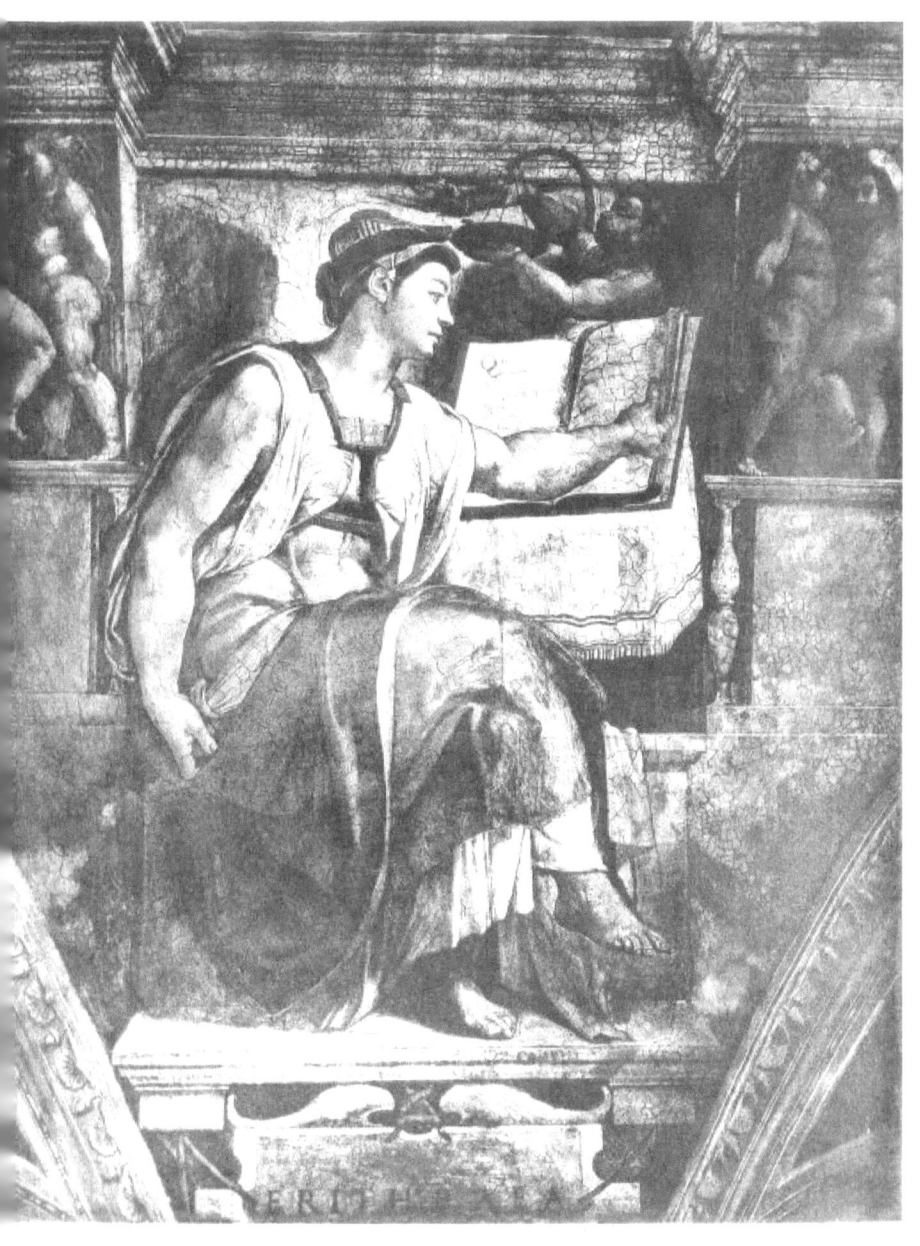

'Erythraean Sibyl' (Fresco) by Pinturicchio (1454 - 1513).
Library, Sienna.

CHAPTER III.

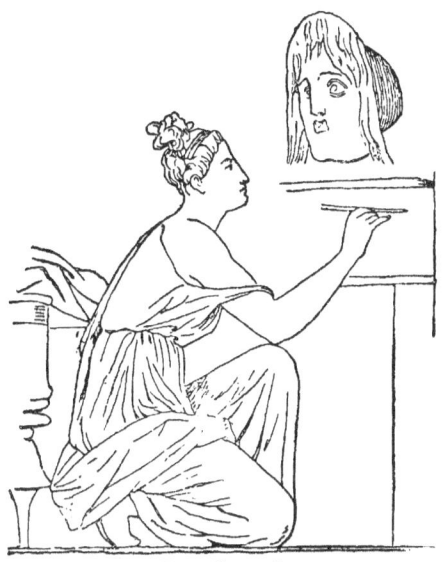

From Pompeii.

OF the various kinds of mural painting, several take their name from the vehicle with which the colors are mixed, as *tempera* or distemper, oil, and water-glass. *Fresco* — real fresco, not the s h a m palmed off as fresco — is so called because the colors are laid on *fresh* plaster. *Encaustic* implies the application of heat, either subsequent to the laying on of the colors or during the operation. There are other kinds of mural painting, but they can all be classified under these five historical heads, unless mosaic and stained glass be reckoned phases of mural painting. Though several of these methods have been employed by different peoples, and at times mutually remote, others are invariably associated with definite epochs and nations. Instances of the arch, by way of illustration, are frequent enough before the days of Rome, yet it is justly deemed a Roman method of construction, inasmuch as the Romans were the first thoroughly to develop its constructive possibilities. Thus encaustic is peculiarly a Grecian method of pictorial expression. Fresco, though practised alike by ancients and moderns, is *par excellence* the medium of the Italian Renaissance decorators. Water-glass is a modern German method.

Though several mummy - masks have been found that prove the

knowledge of encaustic painting by the Egyptians, yet this process was not developed by them till after the Macedonian conquest. Distemper was the national method. The menstruum employed was probably some flexible gum, such as tragacanth, mixed with water. Perhaps honey was at times the vehicle, as it is now for water-colors. It should be noted that their paintings have rarely cracked.[1] The colors were applied with brushes; the smaller made from reeds soaked in water till their fibres were separated; the larger from branches of the *salvadora persica.* The Egyptians tapestried their buildings with color, externally and internally, without regard to architectural lines, but rather to "immortalize the ideas that floated through their brains." The light in Egypt is intense, and there was need to emphasize the structures with color. The vibration of strong color under strong light is so great that its strength is broken, and pure tones are tolerable, where, in grayer climes, they would be insupportable. The pigments were brushed on a coat of white stucco, which enhances their brilliancy. On both outside and inside walls the decorations were first engraved or sculptured, before receiving this priming coat — which obliterated the joints of the masonry — probably to give accent and durability. In the tombs, however, where there was neither wear and tear, nor dazzling light (how little did they foresee, poor souls!), the painter worked without the concurrence of the sculptor. Yet the paintings on the sculptured grounds must have been very perishable. A sharp abrasion would detach the stucco, or a severe earthquake shock open the joints of masonry. Not being works of art, however, in one sense of the word, they could be easily repainted. Figures played a more prominent part in Egyptian mural decoration than in that of subsequent epochs. But they were decorative or hieroglyphic forms, rather than figures, as the Greeks understood them. Figures were used by the latter less abundantly, less monotonously, with more discretion and telling concentration, not to speak of artistic merit. The use of figures on ceilings was avoided by the Egyptian painters, their treatment of the human form not favoring its adoption. (In later days the problem was — and still is — terrible to solve.) "The ceilings of the temples at Thebes had generally a blue ground, upon which vultures, with their great wings outspread, floated among golden stars." All this and very much more may be found in the *History of*

---

[1] Gen. Chas. G. Loring, Curator of the Boston Museum of Fine Arts, has a fragment of stucco, dating back to the XVIIIth dynasty, from a royal tomb. It is covered with a highly polished blue substance, hard as enamel, and insoluble in water. The whole ceiling was once covered with it. We showed it to a well-known chemist, but none of us could come to a definite conclusion as to its composition

Ancient Egyptian Art, by Perrot and Chipiez, a very readable book, unencumbered by an excess of archæological baggage, so discouraging to the busy practitioner. The Greeks painted in fresco, tempera and encaustic. With them the encaustic process reached its highest development. They used it not only in flat tints to cover plain surface or sculptured ornament, but also to model the delicate undulations of the human form. Great ingenuity and learning have been displayed in the many attempts to solve the encaustic riddle. Unfortunately, the texts on which scholars rely to elucidate the process were not always written by professional men. Unfortunately, too, the scholars have in many instances been unfamiliar with the technic of painting, and have, moreover, encumbered their theories with a prodigious number of citations more flattering to their erudition than edifying to the inquirer. The most intelligible and rational account that I have yet seen is a monograph, published last year in Paris, entitled *L'Encaustique et les Autres Procédés de Peinture chez les Anciens, Histoire et Technique, par Henry Cros, Statuaire et Peintre; Charles Henry, Bibliothécaire à la Sorbonne.* After a critical examination of existing texts and monuments, they thus restore the encaustic process : (Be it understood that encaustic means a *burning in*, and that no system of wax-painting can properly be called encaustic, unless there is an application of heat.)[1]

" When the colored sticks of wax and resin have been melted over the fire, either in separate cups, or, better still, on a metallic palette with depressions for the colors, the tones are laid on the panel with a brush. Up to this point the work is rough and disunited. Now the tones are blended with the cestrum — at times red-hot. From the cooled palette, or from another set for the purpose, with (cold) wax colors, the intermediate tones can be taken with the cestrum, still hot, to give the gradations to the modelling."

From this primary process they derive three secondary processes : —

(1) " Hot-painting with colored sticks of wax and resin, softened by the addition of an oil, conveyed to the panel from a hot palette with the brush, then melted and modelled with the cestrum. The addition of oil, while facilitating the work, enables it to be finished more highly. We shall not be far out, if we see in this method the technic of the painting of Cortona."

---

[1] The ancients sometimes used the term *encaustic* synonymously with *painting*, as some moderns apply the term *fresco* to all mural painting. For clearness sake it would be better to restrict both words to their original and legitimate signification.

(2) "Cold-painting with colored sticks of wax and resin, softened by the addition of an oil, applied directly to the panel like crayons of pastel, then worked with the cestrum, just as modelling-wax is worked with the tool."

. (3) "Cold-painting with colored sticks of wax and resin, dissolved in an essential and volatile oil, and applied with the brush."

The *cestrum* (generic name *cauteria*) is a metallic instrument for modelling the wax, of which many examples are to be found in museums. The shapes are various, both to meet the needs of the

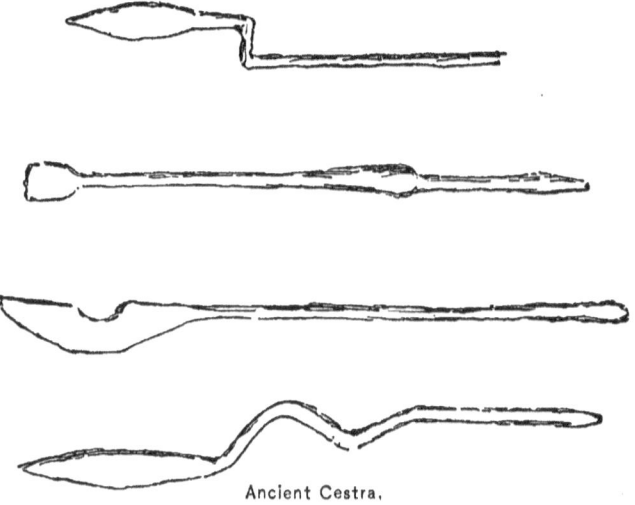

Ancient Cestra.

process and the personality of the artist — as to-day some painters prefer round brushes to flat, and *vice versa*. They were heated, in order to blend the vigorous but rough strokes of the brush, and without which the soft transitions from tone to tone could not be effected.

Reference is made above to the famous 'Muse of Cortona.' Some doubts have been cast on its antiquity; our authors, however, believe in it. It was found by a peasant in the environs of Cortona, along with several statuettes, in 1732. It is two-thirds the size of life, and is painted on slate. "The family venerated it for a long while as an image of the Virgin; but the good people, having discovered their mistake, used it to close a little window near an oven, and even cut off the two upper corners. It remained in that state till the year 1735, when the Cavaliere Tommaso Tommasi, proprietor of the estate, purchased and saved it from such barbarous treatment. Thirty years ago, Signora Louisa Bartolotti Tommasi presented it to the Etruscan Academy of Cortona." "The coloring is perfect; the drawing deliciously pure. The process is evidently encaustic — encaustic pushed to the last stage of perfection. . . . The modelling is very diversely treated. There are long marks, like crayon lines, on the drapery, the breast, the arms, the nose, brow, and ear ; the neck and throat look as if they were ironed — not the sign of a harsh mark, but that of an instrument, long or flat, according to the exigencies of the case. Is not this a sufficiently clear indication of the cestrum?"[1]

Whatever doubts may be cast on the authenticity of the celebrated muse, there are three encaustic portraits from Egypt in the British Museum, and three more in the Louvre, that are incontestably ancient. The latter represent members of the family of Pollius Soter, archon of Thebes in Hadrian's reign (A. D. 117–138.) On one of these in particular — the head of a young girl, strangely fascinating — the technic of the cestrum is clearly visible. "Sometimes long marks, as though the color came from an inexhaustible brush ; sometimes hollow hatchings, softly breaking over-defined touches, model the forms."

MM. Cros & Henry devote a chapter to their "personal practice of encaustic." As practice is more convincing and intelligible than theory, I shall give a *résumé* of their experiments.

1. *The Heater.* — Its functions are to prepare the colored sticks of wax ; to keep the palette hot for brush-work ; and to heat the cestra. The heater should be of metal or earthen-ware, and rather small. Otherwise the painter would be incommoded by the burning charcoal. To avoid the blueish fumes of oxide of carbon, preference should be given to embers (perhaps kerosene could be utilized). Its orifice should be a little more than a hand's length in diameter, and the palette should rest horizontally on its edges.

2. *The Hot Palette* — Should be a disk of tinned metal — iron or copper — on which there should be circular depressions for the colors, the centre of the palette being left free for their mixture. It should have a handle covered with wood to protect the painter's hand from heat.

---

[1] Cros & Henry, following Zannoni, do not accept the genuineness of the Cleopatra said to have been found at Hadrian's vi la. They base their doubts especially on the too evident contradictions between it and the recognized portraits of Cleopatra, not to mention "all the impossibilities." If one may judge from the steel engraving of it, by Mr. John Sartain — which is, no doubt, a faithful translation — its antiquity may well be questioned. There is not a particle of antique feeling in it, the jewelry and forms of the ornaments, as well as the treatment of the drapery, being notably unclassic in taste. On the contrary, it has considerable affinity with the feeling of the late Renaissance work.

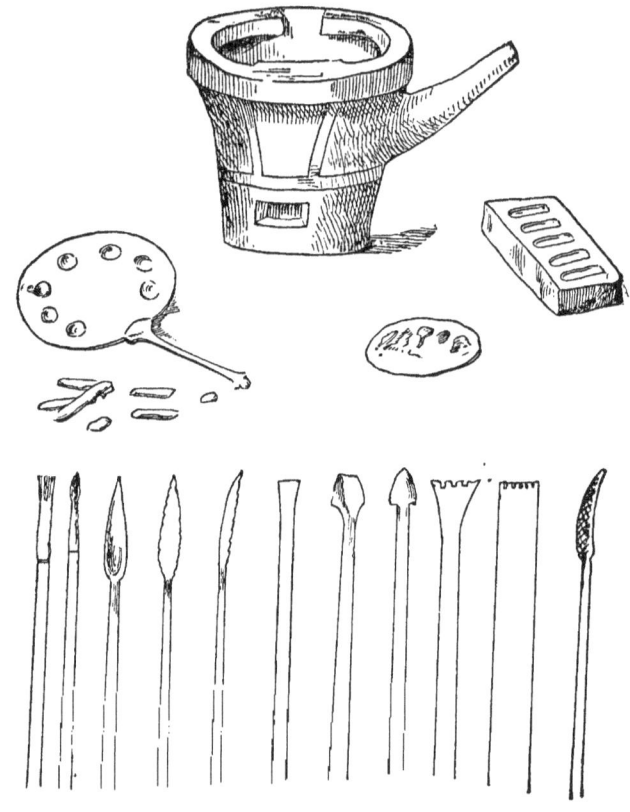

Modern Encaustic Tools.

3. *The Wax and Colors.* — Apothecary's white wax is the best. It can be used alone for preparing the colors, but it is an advantage to add to it one-half its weight of purified fine resin, called colophony — the least colored to be preferred. This addition notably economizes the wax, and far from injuring the colors imparts to them greater brilliancy and tenacity. Certain colors require more wax than others; the quantity being determined by experiment. This is the way: place a tinned (or better, enamelled) pot on a moderate fire; then put the color into it ground very fine. The color should now be stirred with half a cake of white wax. From time to time throw into this compound, liquified by the heat, as much resin as there is wax — or a trifle more if necessary. When the color is thoroughly mixed and has sufficient covering-power, it should be moulded into sticks, and subsequently placed in a color-box. The palette may be as extended in range of tone as desired.

4. *The Brushes.* — In order to paint, the colors should be melted in the depressions of the palette, and then rapidly applied with the brush.   All sorts of brushes are allowable, from the broadest bristle to the most delicate red-sable.   Care must be taken not to turn back the hairs of the brush in too hot colors, or to give them an ugly twist by pressing them too long against the over-heated palette.

5. *The Cestra.* — The brush-work, if well touched, gives a vigorous aspect to the sketch, which cannot be pushed further without the intervention of the cestra.   These are necessary to unite the tones.   As has already been observed, they are of various shapes suited to their special offices.   They should be long enough to protect the artist's hand from the heat.   An angle, at some part of their length enables the painter to see his work more easily.

6. *The Cold Palette* — Should be an oval or rectangular piece of thin wood, small enough to be held in the left hand.   The colors are to be poured on it and allowed to cool, and then to be conveyed to the panel with the heated cestra.   Encaustic is applicable to all sorts of surfaces — wood, linen primed with glue, stone, plaster, slate, and even paper.   Freedom from humidity being assured, a priming of white wax is laid on with the brush, and afterwards burnt in with a brazier or hot iron, till the pores of the ground are well filled.   Even this priming may be dispensed with, provided the subsequent painting be heavy enough thoroughly to cover the ground, so that it may be worked with the hot cestrum.

To recapitulate, we have a primary encaustic process — colors mixed with wax and resin, applied hot with a brush, and afterwards worked with a hot cestrum — and three derivative processes.

1. Similar to the primary process, but with the addition of an oil to facilitate the work.   2. Cold applications of the preceding mixture conveyed to the panel like crayons of pastel, and modelled with cold cestra.   3. Cold brush-painting with colors of wax and resin dissolved in an essential and volatile oil (such as spirits of turpentine).   These last two processes are not, strictly speaking, encaustic.   MM. Cros & Henry do not mention the final cauterization of the cold process.   This would probably be optional, though it was undoubtedly applied at times, if we are to place any credence in the ancient texts — the famous "*ceris pingere ac picturam inurere*" among others.   Not improbably, the picture was sometimes polished with fine linen — wax readily taking a polish.

Encaustic of Ships. — The colors were mixed with wax and pitch

— the latter to increase the resisting power of the former — applied
with the brush, and then passed over with large heated irons.

Encaustic of Walls. — These are first painted in distemper or
fresco, and afterwards fixed with a cauterization of wax, as both
Pliny and Vitruvius explicitly say. When the wall is thoroughly dry
it must be covered with a coat of melted Punic wax mixed with
oil, then sweated with a brazier, and finally rubbed with a candle
and fine linen which gives a lustre to the surface. We know that
the exteriors of the Greek buildings were highly colored, even when
of marble. The statues were not only cauterized for their preservation, but sometimes colored and cauterized for their embellishment.
Vitruvius tells us that the triglyphs of temples were colored blue.
The fragment of a Greek inscription, found in 1836, refers to the
workman who *burnt* the cymatium of the temple of Minerva Polias.
It is more than probable that these flat tints on marble, exposed to
atmospheric corrosion, were cauterized, just as the statues were.
Does any one ever take the trouble now-a-days to cauterize a
statue?

Great care was bestowed on the plastering. Vitruvius describes
the process at length in his well-known Seventh Book. As the
very life of mural painting depends on the preparation of the
wall, it may be well to quote one or two garbled passages from
Gwilt's translation. Wattling with reeds seems to have been an
effective precaution against cracks. " When arched ceilings are
introduced they must be executed as follows : Parallel ribs are
set up, not more than two feet apart. These ribs are fixed to the
ties of the flooring or roof with iron nails. The ribs having been
fixed, Greek reeds, previously bruised, are tied to them with cords
made of the Spanish broom. On the upper side of the arch a composition of lime and sand is to be laid, so that if any water fall from
the floor above, or from the roof, it may not penetrate." [Well-
thought of safe-guard.] " The arches being prepared and inter-
woven with the reeds, a coat is to be laid on the underside. The
sand is afterwards introduced on it, and it is then polished with
chalk or marble. . . . If stucco be used on timber partitions,
which are necessarily constructed with spaces between the upright
and cross pieces, and thence, when smeared with clay, liable to
swell with the damp, and when dry to shrink and cause cracks,
the following expedient should be used. After the partition has
been covered with the clay, reeds, by the side of each other are
to be nailed thereon with bossed nails ; and clay having been laid

over these, and another layer of reeds nailed on the former, but crossed in their direction, so that one set is nailed upright and the other horizontally; then, as above described, the sand and marble coats and finishing are to be followed up. The double row of reeds thus crossed on walls prevents all cracks and fissures." As to the plastering, "three sand coats "—besides the rough-cast—are recommended, "and the same number of marble-dust coats," the walls will then be solid and not liable to crack. This, of course, is the ideal wall. "When only one coat of sand and one of marble-dust are used, it is easily broken." But mortals were human in those days, too, for Pompeii testifies to instances of only two coats. The Greek plaster was so hard that slabs of it were cut from the ancient walls and used for tables. The ancients painted in fresco and distemper as well as in encaustic. Their frescoes will be discussed later. There is little to be said about their distemper work — which was similar to any tempera painting. The colors were tempered with a gum, or glue, or honey, egg, juice of the fig-tree, milk, or other glutinous substance, soluble in water, that serves to bind them.

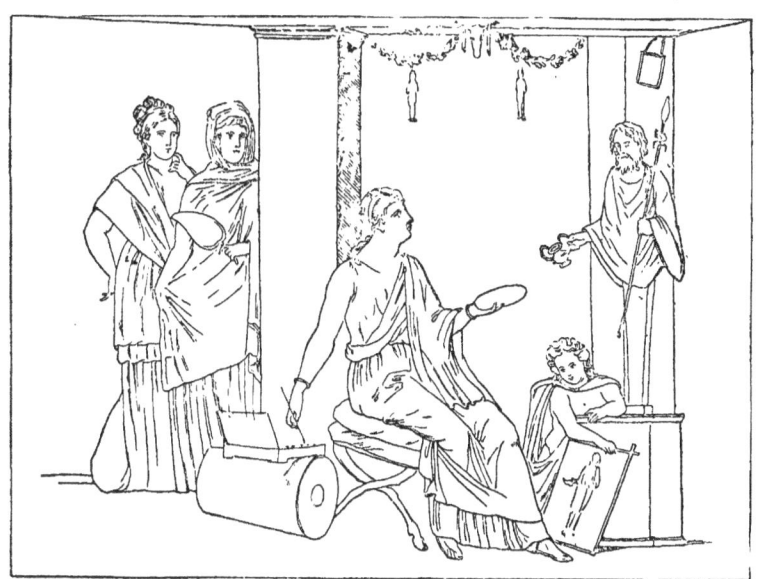

A Paintress at Work. (Pompeii.)

I shall close this chapter with an illustration from Pompeii, representing a paintress copying a Hermes of Bacchus. In her left hand she holds an oval palette, in the right the cestrum or brush (the paint-

ing is somewhat vague), which she dips into the box, the colors on
the palette being exhausted. If the cylinder contains fire, then we
have a representation of the encaustic process ; if its purpose is merely
to raise the box, we have an illustration of the cold process.

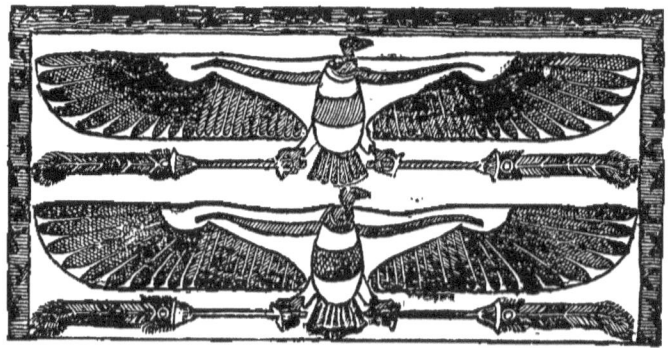

Vultures on a Ceiling.

CHAPTER IV.

THE WALL.

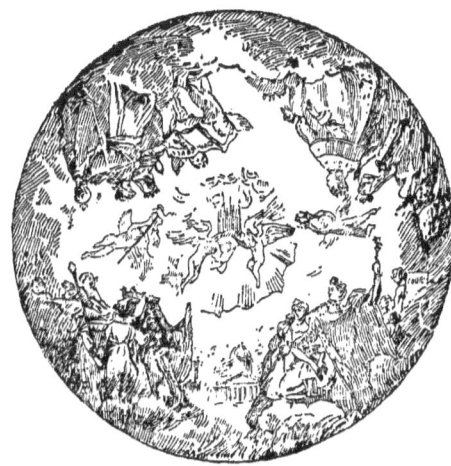

Sketch by Gros for dome of Pantheon, Paris.

FROM the encaustic painting of the ancients, described in the preceding article, the passage to modern wax - painting seems easy and natural. In order that its description may be unbroken, the preliminary and very important questions of the wall and ground will be discussed in this paper, and the process of wax-painting in the succeeding one.

That the walls and their preparation [1] should be objects of the greatest solicitude to the painter is axiomatic. Even had I the practical knowledge, it would be presumptuous to dictate methods of construction to trained architects. I can merely as a painter recall to their attention one or two principles on the observance of which the vitality of mural painting depends. In this way their interest may be sufficiently aroused to practice what has so often been preached by far wiser men than I. To their indifference, or a misplaced confidence in others, we must attribute the cracked and shabby plastering, and peeling or disintegrated paint by which the majority of structures are disfigured.

---

[1] Three excellent papers have appeared in the *American Architect*, by Charles T. Davis, entitled 'Saltpeter Exudations upon Brickwork,' I and II, [Nos. 462 and 467, Vol. XVI.], and 'Hints on Plastering,' [Nos. 488, Vol. XVII.]. There is another interesting paper from the *Builder*, entitled 'Damp Walls,' [*American Architect*, No. 372, Vol. XIII.]

Damp walls militate against mural painting of all sorts; they may be caused by : —

(1) Leakage from above.

(2) Ascension by capillary attraction from the soil.

(3) The presence of saltpetre.

(4) Condensation of moisture.

(5) Exposure of porous materials to extraordinary weather influences.

Naturally the cure for the first of these evils is to stop the leak ; but it would be well, as Vitruvius recommends, to guard against any such contingency by protecting decorated ceilings with a water-proof stratum between the paintings and roof or floor above.

Experts say that the vertical ascension of moisture by capillary attraction from the soil has been far more injurious to frescos than the horizontal penetration of damp through the perpendicular faces of the wall. To prevent the ascension of humidity various hydrofuges have been employed, such as a water-proof course of asphalt felt, or of sheet-lead covered on both sides with pitch at the third course above the level of the ground, or again, "a coating of liquid asphaltum laid on 'pretty thick, and very carefully, with a strong brush; this is then covered with coarse sand, and at the same level a projecting joint of hard asphaltum is laid to cut off completely the capillary communication of the moisture." [1]

The mystery of saltpetre, which is a frequent cause of wet walls, has hardly yet been solved. The presence of certain soluble alkalies that contribute to produce it is more frequent in some clays than in others. The lime and sand of the mortar, too, may contain its chemical constituents, which would be greedily imbibed by very porous bricks. Several preventives against the penetration of saltpetre into the plaster have been recommended: asphalt alone, or with linseed oil; resin, tarred-felt, etc. A hydrofuge of pitch and sand, to exclude damp and saltpetre from walls that are to be frescoed is an old Lombard recipe. "This composition was thrown like rough-cast against the wall, and thus afforded so strong a hold for the mortar laid on it, that in breaking through walls thus protected the mortar and hydrofuge have never been found to separate at their point of juncture." [2] But before any such application is made to the perpendicular surface of the wall, all ascension of damp from the soil must be checked by a water-proof course, if possible.

---

[1] M. Polenceau's method, quoted from *A Manual of Fresco and Encaustic Painting*, by W. B. Sarsfield Taylor. London: 1843.

[2] W. B. Sarsfield Taylor.

The condensation of moisture on cold walls is a source of danger to mural paintings. The outer walls are chiefly exposed to this precipitation of water. Ashlar walls are more liable to it than brick. A double or furred wall would probably be free from it.

Storm-exposed walls may prove conductors of damp, unless protected; but whether they be coated with paint or a vitreous glaze, or boarding, they must first be thoroughly dried and guaranteed from ascending moisture; otherwise the damp will be driven inwards. Paint applied externally is very short-lived. Unless the walls be much exposed, it is far better to apply the protecting coat on the inside.

For stone walls that are to be painted, perhaps the most efficient hydrofuge is the encaustic process. The construction of walls cannot always be controlled, or the painter may be called upon to decorate an old stone wall — of a church, for instance — to which neither furring nor pitch may be applied. Then a coat of wax and oil, or the like, well burnt in, is to be recommended.

In the year 1811 Gros was commissioned by the first Napoleon to paint the dome of the Panthéon. To quote his own words, he agreed "to represent on it — the figures being to the scale of four metres — a glory of angels bearing to heaven the shrine of St. Geneviève; below, Clovis and Clothilde his wife, founders of the first church; farther on, Charlemagne, St. Louis; and, on the opposite side, His Majesty the Emperor and Her Majesty the Empress consecrating the new church to the worship of that saint. I ask for this work the sum of thirty-six thousand francs, which is to be paid me in three instalments; to wit, twelve thousand francs on the completion of my composition and its approval by your excellency [Chevalier Denon, Director General of the Museum Napoleon] and when I am ready to paint; twelve thousand francs when my work is three-fourths done, and the last twelve thousand francs when, on the removal of the scaffold, it is open to inspection." [1]

As a preparatory measure, the interior surface of the stone was first treated with a coat of size, upon which was laid another of white lead and drying-oil. Gros did not place confidence in this preparation, and a special commission was appointed to provide a suitable ground. The commissioners were MM. Thénard and Darcet, the most eminent chemists of the day. "After making some experiments not requisite to be noticed here, they gave the preference to a

---

[1] *Les Decorations du Panthéon* (troisième article), par M. le Marquis Ph. de Chenuevières. *Gazette des Beaux-Arts*, T. XXIII, L. 284. 2d période.

composition of one part wax and three parts linseed oil, boiled with
one-tenth its weight of litharge. The absorption took place readily
by means of heat, and the liquid penetrated the experimental stone
to the depth of a quarter of an inch. The composition, as it cooled,
acquired solidity, and in from six to eight weeks it became hard."
The same process was adopted for the cupola. "By means of a
portable furnace the whole superficies was heated in successive portions (about a square yard at each heating) by moving-on the *caute-
rium* (furnace) horizontally, parallel to the wall, as such part became
sufficiently heated, and then the composition was applied with strong
brushes, when the stone was at a temperature of one hundred
degrees. The first application having been quickly absorbed, others
were repeated until the stone ceased to absorb, and as it was rather
porous, it required the heating to be repeated oftener than would
have been necessary for a stone of a closer texture; and in these
heatings care was taken that they should not be so strong as to car-
bonize the oil. At length, the stone having refused to absorb any
more *mastic* [composition,] and the surface which it covered being soon
cool, smooth and dry, it received a coat of white lead and oil well
ground together, and it was upon this preparation that the ground-
work of the distinguished artist, Gros, was painted." [1] From various
indications I should infer that these decorations were executed in an
oil medium, although there is no direct statement to that effect.
Owing to conflicting statements as to their present condition, I wrote
to a friend in Paris for accurate information. The answer, just received, is that "they are as fresh as if painted yesterday;" though
the joints in the masonry tell as dark lines here and there when
viewed very near. The paint in these places seems "to be stained,
not cracked or peeled."

The decorations shared the dynastic vicissitudes of the epoch. On
the 10th of August, 1814, Louis XVIII was substituted for Napoleon, the price being raised to fifty thousand francs. On the 31st of
March, 1815, Napoleon was reinstated, and finally Louis XVIII was
again restored, pictorially as well as politically. During these
changes Gros writes in a semi-frantic state to the minister (16 April,
1815) that unless he can command "the tranquility of a definite
work," he "will be obliged to fall back on portraiture, sorry resource
of our art and the shoal of artists called to noble undertakings."
On the completion of the painting in 1824, Gros was created a baron.
It has seemed worth while to describe at some length the condi-

---

[1] Taylor.

tions under which this decoration was painted, seeing that the
evidence (by which the conduct of similar undertakings may be
guided) is incontestable, and that it has already stood the test of
over half a century. Moreover, the unnecessary and premature
decay of William M. Hunt's mural work in the Capitol at Albany,
executed less than ten years ago, has appalled every one interested in
monumental painting, and cast a certain discredit on this noble art.
Perhaps the foregoing description may serve as an antidote. MM.
Thénard and Darcet recommend their composition (the wax, oil and
litharge) for the preparation of stucco on ceilings. It penetrates the
stucco deeply, renders it as hard as stone, and effectually wards off
damp.

When walls are constructed with a view to subsequent decoration,
all pigment-destroying agencies can be eliminated. A double wall,
with an air-space between, is a safe foundation for mural painting of
all kinds, provided that the air-space be well ventilated, and the
bondings damp-proof. The inner wall at least should be brick, but
not very soft or porous brick, from which plaster is liable to fall,
as it yields its water of hydration too quickly, even though the bricks
be thoroughly drenched before the plaster is "rendered." If the
paintings are not to be in "fresco" — which, as we shall see later,
calls for a backing of brick — iron lathing would probably be the
safest foundation. The wall behind the ironwork should be solid
and dry, and if double, so much the better. Furring and lathing of
wood are not reliable. Wattled reeds are recommended by Vitruvius
to prevent cracks, and they are still used in Germany and Italy.
Architects should familiarize themselves with the mysteries of plaster. No all-embracing rule can be formulated, owing to the varying
properties of local ingredients; but these should be thoroughly mastered. Much of the rotten and defaced plastering is undoubtedly
due to bad walls and settling foundations; but a great deal is also
attributable to an inferior quality of plaster and to hasty methods of
applying it. We know that our plaster, as a whole, is wretched,
while that of a people who flourished some two thousand years ago
(the Romans) was, and one might almost say is, excellent. The
latter carefully applied many coats of a superior compound, while
we hastily lay on but half the number of an inferior one.

Of late years so many constructive improvements and appliances
have been invented, that it is astounding to see the same old defective
methods of plastering in vogue. Apparently "common lath-and-
plaster still wins nine times out of ten." For *buon fresco* plaster

is a necessity, but *buon fresco* is a process rarely used by American decorators. Why, then, has not plaster long since been banished from first-class buildings, and its place supplied by some reliable cement? Where the need is felt, the thing needed is generally forthcoming. If reliance is to be placed on an article that recently appeared in these columns (Vol. xviii., No. 502), "Robinson's cement" would seem to be a good substitute for plaster. Its use would do away with the "pit" and all the clumsy appliances of the plasterer. The time occupied in slaking the lime and drying the successive coats would be saved. The rendering coat, mixed with sand, sets at once, and the finishing coat, with or without sand, may be applied directly, forming a homogeneous body that is very hard at the end of a few hours. It has "excellent fire-proof qualities," and "has been carefully tested for painting in several ways by a well-known London decorator, and with entirely satisfactory results, showing that it can be applied and painted upon at once, as with Keene's or Parian, or it may be left to get dry, and then painted, as within three weeks of being rendered it is thoroughly dry and ready for decoration, and will stand fine colors perfectly. With other cements, if left, the period that must elapse before they can be painted must be measured by months instead of weeks. In using it no notice need be taken of the time of year or the state of the weather." This cement can be manufactured at much less cost than any of the others. The principal cement-works of the patentees, Messrs. Joseph Robinson & Co., "are situated at Kenthill, near Carlisle (England), where they have immense deposits of the purest alabaster." [1]

Another cement worthy of notice (doubtless there are others) is the Merrit Asbestine Plaster, which has the advantage of being manufactured in this country. It is unnecessary to dilate here on its fire-proof qualities. Though not absolutely water-proof, it is vastly more so than ordinary plaster. It is made from asbestine, a mineral containing over ninety per cent of silicate of magnesium, with a small proportion of aluminum, iron and water. This is ground to a fine powder, and then mixed with caustic potash and silicate of soda. When needed for use, it is mixed with sand. It hardens in a few days to the consistency of stone, and is very adhesive, adhering even to plate-glass. Instead of a wood or wire-lathing, thin corrugated sheet-iron plates are used, nailed to ordinary, or fire-proof, furrings of pulp. The corrugations are very close, and only one-eighth of an inch deep. Of

---

[1] *American Architect*, Vol. XVIII, No. 502.

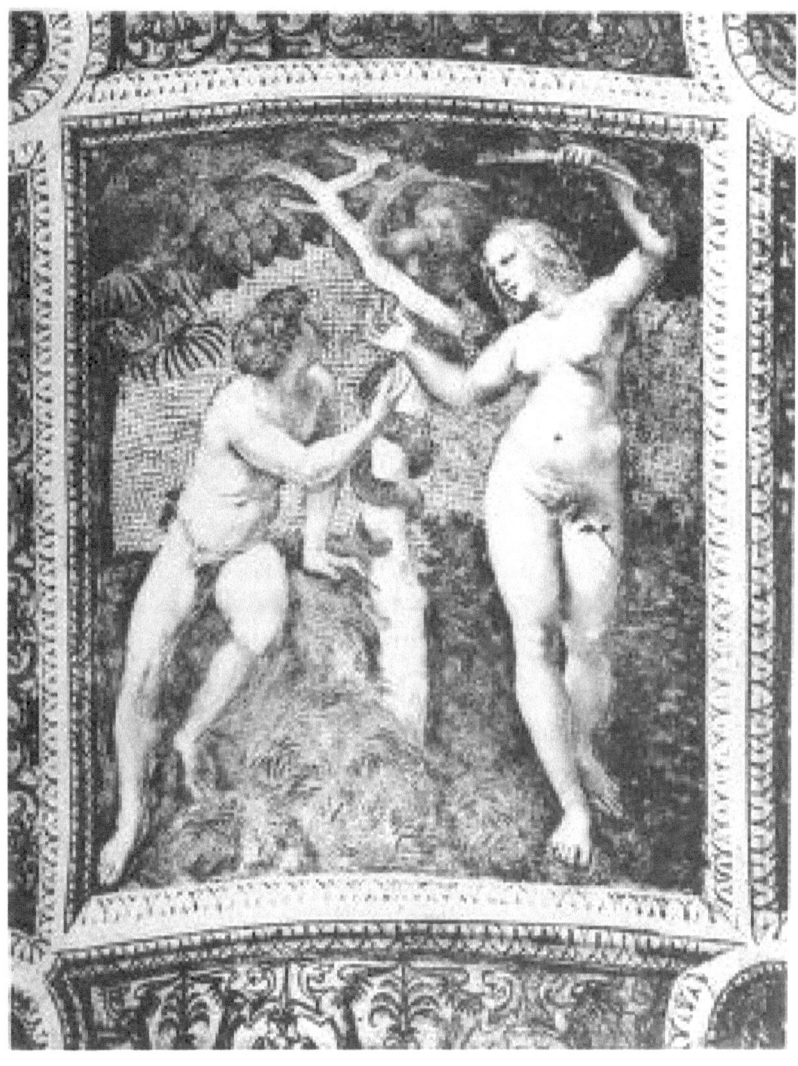

'The Temptation' (Fresco) by Raphael Sanzio (1483 - 1520). Stanze of the Vatican, Rome.

course, the plaster could be applied directly to the wall. I saw a specimen of it spread on a thin board that had warped considerably, but the plaster had not cracked. Its expense is not much, if any, greater than ordinary plaster, taking time and labor into consideration. Of its excellence as a ground for painting it is impossible yet to speak with certainty. Time alone can decide the question, notwithstanding all "claims." Several decorators have experimented on it with perfect success, first having given it a coat of suitable size.[1] It must be borne in mind, however, that some cements are liable eventually to effloresce, and act chemically on the colors. While on this particular cement, the colors might, and probably would, stand long enough for all practical purposes, could they be guaranteed for an important mural composition that is expected to last? Professor Lewis M. Norton, of the Massachusetts Institute of Technology, to whom I am indebted for much valuable information, while heartily praising the fire-proof qualities of this plaster, shared my doubts as to the durability of any superposed pigments. He feared efflorescence and chemical action. Of course these fears might never be realized. I have written at some length of these cements, hoping that good might come of it. The deplorable state of our plastering will, I trust, justify my prolixity.

---

[1] Since writing the above paragraphs on the Robinson and Merrit cements (which I prefer to leave unchanged, in the hope of stimulating the ingenious), I have conferred with Professor T. M. Clark, Professor of Architecture, Mass. Inst. of Technology. He distrusts silicate of soda, which he thinks is almost certain to cause efflorescence. Of cements in general, he writes : " I don't think any cement would be very favorable for painting, at least without particular treatment. Mixing with sand would give it key enough for paint, but there is usually more or less of an efflorescence, much slighter than that caused by silicate of soda, but which, in my experience, works under the film of paint and separates it, especially if the back of the work is exposed to any dampness. The only remedy I have ever found for this is to mix a large proportion of oil with the cement before putting it on. This nearly or quite stops the efflorescence, and might make the cement good for painting on, but very little is known about this part of the subject." Again, he writes : "Keene's cement is smooth and hard, something like plaster-of-Paris, but harder and less absorbent. I have never seen any indication of efflorescence on it which seemed to come from the cement itself. Keene's cement is rather disposed to crack. There is a process of crystallization which goes on for years in cement of the ordinary kind, and the blue efflorescence may be a product of this."

Keene's cement was used by Messrs. Sturgis & Brigham in the Boston Museum of Fine Arts for the architraves and baseboards. It has cracked in some places, and effloresced in others, where the wall is damp. Mr. Sturgis says of it : "Beware of dampness." Robert Jackson, an Englishman, (and late manager for Mr. Sturgis), who has had a large experience with Keene's cement both in England and America, would trust it as a ground for mural painting. He says that it should receive its first coat of paint before it has set. This coat should contain no lead, and the paint should be diluted in a liquid composed of three parts turpentine, one part boiled oil, with a small quantity of litharge. Owing to a disregard of these rules, the paint has often deteriorated. No oil is to be mixed with the cement. He preferred Keene's to the other cements, though he did not know from experience anything about Robinson's.

Professor Clark thinks, with me, that our plaster and methods of plastering could be greatly bettered, as will be shown in a subsequent paper.

A painter is frequently required to decorate an existing but unreliable plaster wall. When the space to be decorated is not very large the safest way is to fasten artists' canvas to it with a composition to be specified hereafter. This is a somewhat expensive method, yet worth while when the picture to be painted is valuable; not only because it ensures the painting against plaster-cracks; but also for the reason that it can be more readily detached in case of need. Canvas, moreover, is innocuous to the superposed colors; lime is not always so, unless well covered with several preparatory coats of paint. Lime saponifies oil, which quickly turns yellow in the absence of strong light. For oil paintings the regular prepared canvas as sold by colormen is suitable, but for wax-painting the unprepared material is preferable. When comparatively large surfaces are to be covered, the unprepared canvas is better even for oil painting, as it can be attached to the wall more easily and securely, the composition penetrating its meshes. The only advantage of prepared canvas is that it can be painted upon at once. The composition is apt to percolate through the meshes of the raw stuff, and should be given time to dry. It is difficult to procure wide pieces of unprepared canvas in this country. A few years ago the widest in the French market was about four metres; a greater width being desired, the canvas must be pieced. But when the wall-space to be covered is very great, this method is usually abandoned. Linen canvas is better than cotton. To fasten it to the wall demands care and patience. Trusting too much to the readiness of inexperienced artisans, I have undergone several mortifying and costly experiences. Like the making of good coffee it seems so simple and easy that almost any neophyte is willing to guarantee success. Such however, is not the case. There may be those who have succeeded with glue or paste; I have not. Blisters invariably appeared on the following day, when the prepared canvas was used for large spaces, and even the unprepared behaved badly. Small spaces present no great difficulties. It must be remembered that glue does not resist moisture. The following composition has not belied its recommendation : —

> 70 lbs. white lead.
> 2 qts. boiled oil.
> 1 pt. dammar varnish.
> 1 pt. Japan.

Doubtless other ingredients or proportions might be used; but the basis should be white lead. An unpainted wall needs a priming coat. (It would not be unwise where there is danger of damp to precede the priming coat with an encaustic or cold-wax treatment).

Then a very heavy coat of the composition should be laid on with broad, flat brushes and the raw canvas immediately applied. When this is large four or five men, at least, are needed. It should afterwards be rolled (with rollers) and smoothed with the hands for hours till it is perfectly flat. This operation exacts patience. When prepared canvas is used, a coat of the composition should be laid on the back immediately before its application to the wall. In either case the edges should be nailed, or fastened with a moulding.

It is a frequent custom to attach the canvases to a "keyed" stretcher, and then fasten it to the wall with mouldings. This is not a good method, unless the canvases are small, and the mouldings easily removed to " key up " the stretchers. Canvases are in a way barometers, shrinking or expanding according to the dryness or humidity of the atmosphere. It is almost impossible to prevent the " bellying " of stretched canvas, placed against a cold wall in damp weather, and this appearance of flabbiness is very unpleasant. The use of stretchers is undoubtedly due to the habit of painting mural pictures in the studio, a convenient and fatigue-saving habit, but antagonistic to scholarly decoration. Not only does it obtain to-day with good artists, but with the very best, and I should have great hesitancy in condemning it were I not backed by the demi-gods of the wall, when mural painting was at its zenith. The great virtue of monumental paintings lies in their harmonious relations to their surroundings. The conditions of light and shade are far too complex to be divined by the most skilful and experienced. The freaks that distance, altitude, or curvature of surface play with lines, utterly baffle human prescience. When it is considered that color is an entirely relative quality, how can its settings—settings that change with changing light— be ignored? or rather how can they be imagined in the foreign environments of the studio? On merely sentimental grounds (which are never very sure foundations it must be confessed) it seems inartistic to paint mural pictures in the studio. The studies and cartoons must necessarily be prepared in it. There is something stimulating in the expectant wall; and when that wall is vast and imposing, as it often is in church or hall, it is absolutely inspiring! Nothing is more difficult or compromising than to raise the key or change the tonality of a picture; yet studio-painted decorations must frequently be subjected to such ultra measures, or else discord with their surroundings. How tasteless to paint a ceiling in the studio, and then exhibit it on the perpendicular walls of an exhibition-room, yet this is done! On mechanical grounds there are objections to studio-painted decorations; the attachment of canvass to the wall has already been described, and it can easily be imagined that there is great danger of percolation of white-lead through the meshes of the canvas, in places where the picture may be thinly painted. Such a contingency must be guarded against by a very heavily-painted ground; but at best the rolling and unrolling of large pictures, and excessive handling demanded by the white-lead process, are very compromising.

There is a class of pictures that may be confounded with, yet are not properly mural paintings. Such, for instance, are the altarpieces, of which so many are painted by the great decorators. It was desirable that they should be movable; hence they must be regarded as easel pictures, and consequently not within the scope of this article.

CHAPTER V.

MODERN ENCAUSTIC.

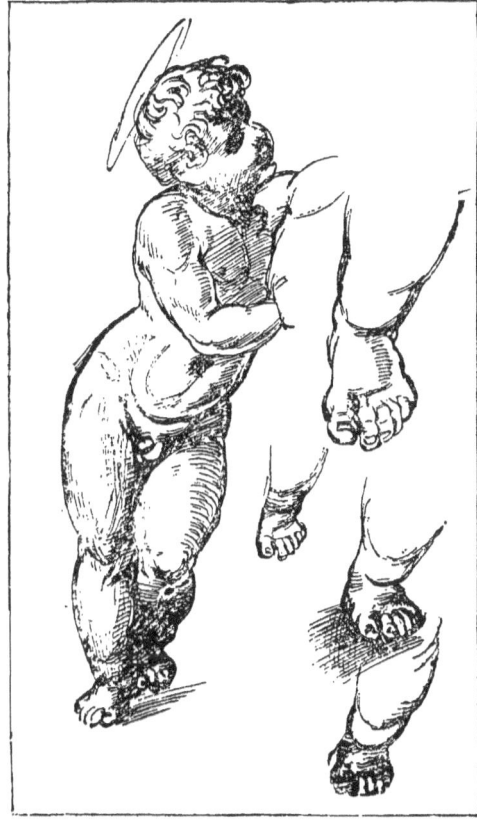

From a drawing by Raphael.

IN order to maintain the continuity of these somewhat extended and interrupted remarks on encaustic painting, as well as to refresh the memory of the reader without necessitating a reference to a preceding chapter, it will be well summarily to restate the formulas for ancient encaustic.

1. Hot painting with colored sticks of wax and resin, liquified by heat, and applied with a brush; then blended and modelled with heated *cestra.*

2. D e r i v a t i v e processes.

(*a.*) Hot painting, as above, with colored sticks of wax and resin, but softened by the addition of an oil.

(*b.*) Cold painting of wax and resin, softened by oil, and applied like crayons of pastel; then modelled with cold *cestra.* (*c.*) Cold painting with colored sticks of wax and resin, dissolved in an essential and volatile oil, then applied and finished with the brush.

Strictly speaking, the last two processes are not encaustic, seeing

that there is no " burning in." Modern wax-painting is but a vari-
ation of the last process. The media may differ, but they all have a
wax basis. Here is a medium that I have used with good mechanical
results :

> Eight sheets of apothecary's white wax — about one-half ounce each,
> One-half pound Venice turpentine,
> One quart spirits of turpentine.

The wax and Venice turpentine to be melted together, then the
spirits of turpentine to be stirred in gradually, and the whole made
to boil. If the medium be too stiff, add spirits of turpentine. It can
be kept for an indefinite time without injury. Its inventor is Mr.
F. D. Millet. It will be seen on comparison that it is composed of
substantially the same ingredients as were used by the ancients, viz.
— a resinous matter (the Venice turpentine), wax, and an essential
oil (the spirits of turpentine). Resin is merely what is left after
distilling off the volatile oil from turpentine, and gives the necessary
hardness to the medium in drying. The unctuous nature of Venice
turpentine — an oleo-resinous substance — facilitates the working of
the colors. This medium combines perfectly well with the ordinary
oil colors, or linseed oil may be added to it; but experience and in-
vestigation have led me to avoid oil on all possible occasions. It is
the darkening and destroying agent in paintings, and should be
reduced to a minimum, especially in decorative works. "Mellowing"
does them no good, though often favorable to easel pictures. Oil,
moreover, is apt to compromise the dead surface guaranteed by the
pure wax medium. It is customary to adulterate wax with spermaceti
in order to increase its whiteness. Pure wax should be asked for.

PREPARATION OF THE WALL–SURFACE OR GROUND.

The wall itself was fully discussed in the preceding paper. If it
be of a porous nature — such as stone, plaster, unprimed wood, raw
canvas, or the like — saturate it with the medium, i.e., till it ceases to
absorb, and leave it for a few days to dry. The encaustic process is
not a necessity, nor have I ever used it; but were the picture to be
painted directly on a stone ground, I should strongly recommend the
" burning-in " of the medium. First heat the wall to a temperature
of 100°, as previously described, then lay on the wax medium, re-
peating the operation if necessary. The cold stone might not absorb
the medium without heat. Another method would be to heat the medium till it flows freely, then quickly to apply it. Or, again, the heat
might be applied after the coat, or coats, of the medium, according to

the Vitruvian method. Some artists prefer a white ground to work on. In this case, lay on a coat of white lead, or zinc, ground in the medium, after the wall has been well saturated with it and allowed to dry. When the picture is to be painted on a ground of oil paint, I should advise the addition of a small amount of linseed oil to the medium, for the first painting — not subsequently — to prevent possible scaling.

THE CARTOON.

This should be carefully prepared in the studio. Extemporizing is a dangerous policy, except within definite outlines. If the figures are large, the painter loses all sense of proportion on the staging.[1] Hence the need of a cartoon drawn to the final scale. It is not essential that the cartoon should be more than outlined. Any detail of light and shade would be effaced by "pouncing," and, even if a tracing should be made from the cartoon for pouncing purposes, it would be difficult — at times impossible — so to place the cartoon that a simultaneous view might be had of it and the wall to be painted. The artist will doubtless need, on the staging, a small study of his picture and detail-drawings; but, above all, he should approach the wall thoroughly conversant with his work, and with a definite purpose. The wall is no place for vacillation or experiments.

POUNCING.

This process is almost too well known to describe. Prick the outlines of the cartoon with a large pin — the nearer the pin-holes the better. Then, on some soft linen, or muslin, pour powdered charcoal, and tie it up like a bag. The medicated charcoal sold by druggists is very fine, and well adapted for the purpose.[2] Having attached the cartoon to the wall, rub the bag freely over it. On removing the cartoon the pricked outline should be clearly visible on the wall.[3]

---

[1] A small concave reducing lens is an assistance to the painter on a staging. By its means he can get a better idea of *ensemble*, though it is never tantamount to a view of the work from a distance. I have often used both a hand-glass and a reducing lens, looking at the reflected image through the lens; this approximates more closely the distant view, but is not equivalent to it.

[2] Any fine ground color may be substituted for charcoal.

[3] Under certain conditions the stereopticon, or magic-lantern, may profitably be used for the transfer of the sketch to the wall. I am indebted to Mr. J. W. Black, of Boston, the well-known photographer, who transferred William Hunt's sketches to the capitol walls at Albany, for the following information. The study or sketch for the picture to be painted is first photographed on a glass slide suited to the stereopticon, and then, by means of the calcium-light, its image is projected on the wall magnified to the desired scale. The calcium-light is a necessity, and naturally demands a supply of gas. The stereopticon should be about twice the greatest dimension of the picture distant from it, and at right angles to a straight line drawn perpendicularly from its centre to the instrument. This is the ideal position. It can be used at a greater distance, but not much nearer. The scale of the picture can be increased or diminished by advancing or withdrawing the instrument. Studies of separate figures, if superior

MATERIALS.

It is not my object to lay down a method of painting. It is taken for granted that any one who would hazard a mural picture is already familiar with oils and water-colors, or at least distemper. Methods are, in a great measure, personal, and no words can adequately describe them. Wax-painting is not unlike oil-painting, or distemper. At the outset it will undoubtedly prove troublesome to one unaccustomed to it. Practice alone can overcome its apparent inconveniences — apparent because short lived, and eventually real conveniences. The rapid drying of the colors, for instance, is harrassing at first, but in reality very advantageous, as it permits the completion of the work in hand at a sitting, or the renewal of it the day following, without the slightest danger of subsequent cracking.

(a.) *Brushes.* These must be chosen as in oils, to suit the handling of the painter, and the size of the picture. They should be thoroughly cleaned in turpentine at the end of the day's work, and *afterwards* washed with soap and water. Soap does not remove the wax color from the brushes, nor from the hands. During the work it is frequently necessary to rinse the brushes in " turps " (I like the familiar word), to prevent clogging.

(b.) *Palette.* Any large palette will do; but I can recommend one so weighted that the great and numbing strain on the thumb can be avoided when the palette is heavily charged with color and the necessarily large palette-cups. The two dark circles represent leaden discs, which so balance the palette that its whole weight falls on the arm, and is scarcely perceptible. These discs are placed

to those in the sketch, may afterwards be substituted, or other desirable changes made. The outline cast by the stereopticon is not a sharp one, so that its use by a person unfamiliar with the drawing would be precluded. Mr. Black thinks the instrument could be perfected so as to cast a sharp outline. As the stereopticon should directly face the painting, a special staging must often be constructed. It cannot be used for vaulted or domical surfaces; nor for ceilings unless modified so as to work perpendicularly. Its expense is not great — about $3 per hour. It does away with the large cartoons — though not in fresco painting. For some reasons the enlarged cartoon is preferable, especially if executed by the artist himself. The drawing would probably gain in grandeur and accuracy. But to avoid tiresome repetitions of the same *motif*,' the artist usually delegates the enlargement of his sketch to assistants. The handling of a cartoon on a staging is somewhat awkward. Perhaps the greatest advantage offered by the use of the stereopticon is the possibility of experimenting in scale.

where they do not come in contact with the colors. They might be fastened to the underside of the palette, or another metal might be substituted. Two palettes are a convenience, and a studio-boy a necessity. Every now and then he should free the palette from the sticky and rapidly-drying colors. Cleanliness is next to godliness, and foul mixtures are not to be tolerated in mural painting.

(c.) *Palette-cups.* They should be large enough to accommodate the broad brushes, and provided with a screw top. Two are necessary — one for the medium, the other for spirits of turpentine.

(d.) *The Colors.* These should be ground in the medium by an artist's colorman. House-painters do not grind their colors fine enough. Some may be kept in tin cans or glass jars, while others should be tubed. When used in large quantities the cans, or jars, are more convenient. Personal experience suggested the making of cans with screw-covers — these answer their purpose admirably. Glass preserve-jars, with screw-tops, are not bad, but they are liable to be broken in transportation. The same colors may be used in wax as in oil painting.[1] With almost every medium, preference should be given to the earth colors. They are durable and innocuous. If the colors become too dry, add more medium; if too hard from the congelation of the wax, heat them. The more medium used, the better for the durability of the picture; but an excess of medium robs the color of its body. When it is desired to apply the colors in a semi-liquid state, dilute them in the medium and spirits of turpentine (turpentine must not be used with the whites), but better still, heat and apply them rapidly. Zinc white is to be preferred to white lead. It has not so much body, but is whiter and less injurious to the health. When more covering power is desired, use white lead for the first painting, and zinc subsequently. The most serious objections to white lead are to be found in its combination with oil, which yellows it. Sulphuretted-hydrogen gas blackens it. It would be irrelevant to discuss these questions now, because the medium is wax, not oil. They will be treated later, under oil-painting. Such, however, is the resisting power of wax to acids and certain gases, that white lead ground in oil and mixed with the wax medium remains unchanged under a stream of sulphuretted-hydrogen gas, when the same pigment without the wax turns to a deep umber, almost as dark as printer's ink. In mural-painting — especially when the medium is

---

[1] It will be seen later that certain dangerous oil pigments are perfectly safe when mixed with wax. Hence a more extended palette in the latter medium.

wax, — it is well to prepare the frequently-recurring tones before-hand, and not mix them on the palette when needed, as in easel work. In the first place, the work will thereby be more homoge-neous, and secondly, a great deal of time will be saved. Much color-mixing, while the work is in progress, impedes the flow of ideas. Foul mixtures are avoided if the supply is equal to the demand; when it is not, thinness or slovenliness is the result. Finally, the painter is independent of the uncertain light that prevails so fre-quently during mural work. Particularly for flesh, he will find it very convenient to mix and tube in sufficient quantities two or three dominant tones. A final coat of wax medium may be applied to the completed painting, so as to bind the whole together and prevent the detachment of loose particles. I say *may* be applied, for it is not always necessary,— at least I have not found it so. The painter can quickly decide whether it be requisite or not by passing his hand over the surface of the picture. If particles of color are rubbed off, apply the medium, taking great care not to disturb the under colors, which a stiff brush will do, as they are soluble in the medium — unless they are very hard. With time they become exceedingly hard, thanks to the resin. In some wax processes the final coat of medium is followed by a " burning-in " with heaters, and by a subsequent polishing. This is substantially the encaustic process for walls (previously quoted) recommended by Pliny and Vitruvius. On certain grounds, such as porous stone or plaster, this " burning-in " might be advantageous, even without the polishing. But on canvas, gold, oil-paint, or any non-absorbent substance, it would obvi-ously be useless. Cauterization causes the colors to shine slightly, even without the polishing. Though a slight shine may, at times, be desirable, inasmuch as the colors are thereby deepened, yet in nine cases out of ten the mural painter wishes to avoid gloss — the delicate, airy, and *dead* tints being the great charm of his work. *Per contra*, a polish on easel pictures, executed in wax, may be very desirable. With our modern methods of impasto for large works, the brushing might be compromised by the encaustic process. Were I to use this process at all, I should prefer to use it for the priming-coat of medium, as Gros did, not for the final coat. A final " burning-in " would undoubtedly greatly prolong the existence of out-of-door work in simple tones — hence the adoption of it by the Greeks for coloring their temples. We all know how Leonardo da Vinci spoiled his famous battle of Anghiari in the Sala del Consiglio, at Florence, by his clumsy attempts to burn it in, wishing to revive the ancient encaustic methods. "It is evident that he used wax with a solvent, and no doubt a gum to harden the mixture, for when he had finished the painting he applied heat by lighting fires upon the floor. Here was the defective part of his plan. . . . That the heat might also reach the upper portions, fuel was heaped on, and the result was that the wax melted in the lower extremity, making the colors run, to the artist's deep mortification." (Wilson's *Michael Angelo*, page 69.)

(*e*) *Lamps.* A few of these will be found necessary for dark corners. During the short days of late autumn and winter, the painter is often obliged to work continuously by artificial light. There is nothing like the electric-light, of course, which might be introduced for very elaborate and costly work, but the cases where it would be supplied are rare. When gas cannot be used, any kerosene lamp will do, provided its stand be broad and firm. A very serviceable stand was once hastily gotten up for me — one that did its duty well on a somewhat elaborate staging.

$a =$ the place for the lamp.

$b =$ the reflector.

$c =$ the handle.

The whole was made of tin.

DANGERS.

Avoid the use of turpentine with white pigments. It does not bind them sufficiently. If mixed with them freely they will crack in drying, like mud. The cure for such cracks is a heavy coat of the medium, consequently whites need more of it than the other colors. The following advice to the mural painter may seem superfluous, as being dictated by common-sense (a rare commodity), and known to every house-painter; but mural-painters are not house-painters, and have not had their practical training : —

Of all pigments, white lead is the arch poisoner; use it as little as possible. The mural-painter deals more freely with paints than his brother of the studio, and often works in combination with the house-painter; hence he runs greater risks. To avoid paint-poisoning change the working-suits frequently, and do not eat in a room where there is much fresh paint. Milk and lemonade are antidotes to lead-poisoning, alcohol favorable to it. Turpentine vapors are injurious to the lungs, and often cause faintness. Cure — ventilation. Wax paints adhere tenaciously to the hands. Soap and water do not remove them. Turpentine does, but its continued use is injurious. Other solvents, such as benzine or chloroform, carry them off; but for the dirtiest work, at least, it is well to wear gloves, as a deposit of paint under the nails is a source of danger. The body should be well protected against the damp of new buildings, churches or the like, and against the sudden transition from the heat above to the cold below. As mural painting is very fatiguing, the diet and mode of life should be as simple during the progress of the work as those of a training athlete.

Old Cennini counsels but two meals a day, "using light and good food, and but little wine." Perhaps we need more, but the quotation emphasizes the importance of simple living. As a rule, artists are unaccustomed to stagings. When undertaking mural work, they run a fair chance of breaking their necks, or at least, of an ugly fall; serious injuries have too frequently been paid as the price of carelessness. Theoretically, the mural painter works on a comfortable railed-platform,— even on a movable tower, capable of being raised or lowered at will. Practically, he often finds himself on a shaky plank or two, with both hands full. Why? Because there is neither time nor money to rig up the proper staging. He has, moreover, the almost uncontrollable desire, acquired in the studio, to walk away from his work into — space. Everything on the person that might catch on projecting planks, nails, or the like, should be carefully avoided.

ADVANTAGES OF WAX-PAINTING FOR MURAL DECORATION.

They may be summarized as follows : —

(1) Its durability. Wax resists moisture, the action of acids, and sulphuretted-hydrogen gas.[1]

(2) Its dead surface, and exquisite, airy tones. It has low-toned capabilities, too; may be polished, and even [*horresco referens !*] varnished.

(3) Its impasto, equalling that of oils, without the disadvantages of the latter.

(4) Its quick-drying qualities, that enable the painter to complete

---

[1] In answer to my inquiry, Professor Lewis K. Norton kindly writes: " There can be no doubt that wax prevents, to a certain extent, and to a very considerable degree, the action of the air, moisture and gases present in the air on pigments. Of course it would not materially hinder strong chemicals from acting upon pigments."

the work in hand at a sitting, or to continue it without fear of cracks.

OTHER METHODS.

There are other systems of wax-painting, both cold and hot, but the same principle dominates them all. The one that I have described has the immense advantage of extreme simplicity and directness. The so-called 'Spirit Fresco Painting,' invented and used with success by T. Gambier Parry, also by Sir Frederick Leighton in his mural work at South Kensington, is but another phase of wax-painting, less simple than the above, but — as is claimed — very durable. A full account of this process is contained in a pamphlet prepared by its inventor, at the request of the Committee of Council on Education, and obtainable at the South Kensington Museum. In the author's own words I will give a condensed account of it : —

"The wall must be dry. No painting materials can be durable on a damp foundation. The surface to be painted must also be perfectly dry and porous. The best is good common stucco, precisely the same as that always used for *buon fresco*. The one primary necessity is that it should be left with its natural surface, its porous quality being absolutely essential. All smoothing processes, or 'floating' with plaster-of-Paris, destroys this quality. All cements must be avoided, some of them having too hard and smooth a surface, and consequently being devoid of all key or means of attachment for colors, and others being liable to efflorescence and chemical action."

The medium and preparation of colors are described as follows : —

"Take in any multiple of these proportions, according to the quantity required for a week : —

Elemi resin (gum elemi)	2 oz.	} weight.
Pure white wax	4 oz.	
Oil of spike lavender	8 oz.	} liquid
Finest preparation of artists' copal	20 oz.	measure.

(If a stronger kind of copal is used, 18 ounces are sufficient.) With these materials, incorporated by heat, all colors, in *dry* powder, must be mixed, and the most convenient system is to do so precisely as oil-colors are mixed on a slab, and put into tubes. The colors keep in this way for many years. I have many in tubes above twenty years old, as fresh as when put there."

"To prepare the wall-surface, choose a time of dry and warm weather. Dilute the amount of medium required in once-and-a-half its bulk of good turpentine. The mixture is more effective if compounded by heat. With this wash let the surface of the wall be well saturated, the liquid being dashed against it, rather than merely washed over it. After a few days left for evaporation, mix equal quantities of pure white lead (in powder) and of gilders' whitening (common whitening being often full of large grits and too strong of lime) in the medium, *slightly* diluted with about a third of turpentine, and paint the surface thickly, and when sufficiently evaporated to bear a second coat, add it as thickly as a brush can lay it. This, when dry — for which two or three weeks may be required — produces a perfect surface, so white that colors upon it have all the internal light of *buon fresco* and the transparency of pure watercolors, and it is so absorbent that their attachment is complete.

" Paint boldly and simply as in *buon fresco;* as much as possible *alla prima,* and with much body; and use pure oil-of-spike in your dipper freely. Decision is very necessary, because, by much harassing the surface, the materials are liable to be disintegrated, the resins rise to the surface, and perfect deadness is lost. If the surface has been left for so long as to have become quite hard, wash over the part for the morning's work with pure spike-oil, to melt the surface (hence the name Spirit Fresco), and prepare it to incorporate the colors painted *into* it. If any part requires second painting the next day, do *not* wash again with spike-oil; it is liable to bring the resins to the surface, but use plenty of spike-oil in your dipper, as a water-color painter uses water. Paint rather solidly than transparently. Transparent glazing is less likely to dry dead than colors used with white lead."

" *The Rationale of the Painting* is, therefore, this: that the colors in powder, being incorporated with material identical with that which has already sunk deep into the pores of the wall-surface, and has hardened there by the evaporation of the spirit-vehicle, may be regarded as belonging to the mass of the wall itself, and not as mere superficial applications. This result is produced by the spike-oil being the one common solvent of all the materials, which turpentine is not; the moment the painter's brush touches the surface (already softened, *if necessary,* for the day's work), it opens to receive the colors, and, on the rapid evaporation of the spike-oil, it closes them in, and thus the work is done." [1]

---

[1] Here is still another medium from the *Painter;* " Copal resin may be blended with twice its bulk of turpentine, the two ingredients being kept for some time in a bottle in a warm place, after which pure white wax, melted to a creamy consistence, is added." The principle is always the same.

One of the encaustic methods, suggested by Count Caylus (1692–1765), is so simple — though designed for easel-pictures — that I cannot but quote it. With modifications it might be used for larger works on the wall.

"First. The cloth or wood designed for the picture is waxed over, by rubbing it simply with a piece of beeswax.

"Secondly. The colors are mixed up with pure water, but as these colors will not adhere to the wax, the whole ground must be rubbed over with chalk or whiting, before the color is applied.

"Thirdly. When the picture is dry, it is put near the fire, whereby the wax is melted and absorbs the colors." [1]

---

[1] *Mural or Monumental Decoration.* W. Cave Thomas. Winsor & Newton, London.

CHAPTER VI.

FRESCO is an Italian word that means fresh. Fresco painting means painting on fresh, wet plaster. *Buon fresco* means real fresco as distinguished from the false. All sorts of mural paintings, from distemper to encaustic, are indiscriminately and wrongly called frescos. This generic use of the word is as unnecessary as it is improper, and tends to create confusion. When the word fresco is used in these chapters, it will be employed in its legitimate and restricted sense, viz., to paint on fresh plaster.

I shall now endeavor to explain in a few simple words the principle of fresco painting, well knowing that the artistic mind recoils from an over-dose of the incomprehensible terminology and concise formulas in which scientists revel. If these last only knew what harum-scarum brains were ours, they might pound some useful information into them by the assumption of an extreme simplicity. As it is, we frequently run at the first discharge of the chemical battery.

Pure limestone consists of carbonic acid and lime = carbonate of lime.

The limestone is subjected to heat, the carbonic acid is expelled, and there remains lime.

If to this lime, water be added, the result will be hydrate of lime. Only a certain amount of water combines chemically with the lime, hydrate of lime being a powder. The rest of the water mixes with it mechanically.

When hydrate of lime is exposed to the air, the water is expelled by carbonic acid, and the result is again carbonate of lime, or the original limestone, chemically speaking, for practically the cohesion of limestone is never regained.

Sand is usually mixed with the liquid lime to augment its cohesiveness. The latter acts chemically, but very feebly, on the former. The mixture is chiefly mechanical.[1]

---

[1] Unfortunately, very little is really known about the reciprocal action of lime and sand. The table here appended, showing the effect of time on plaster, if

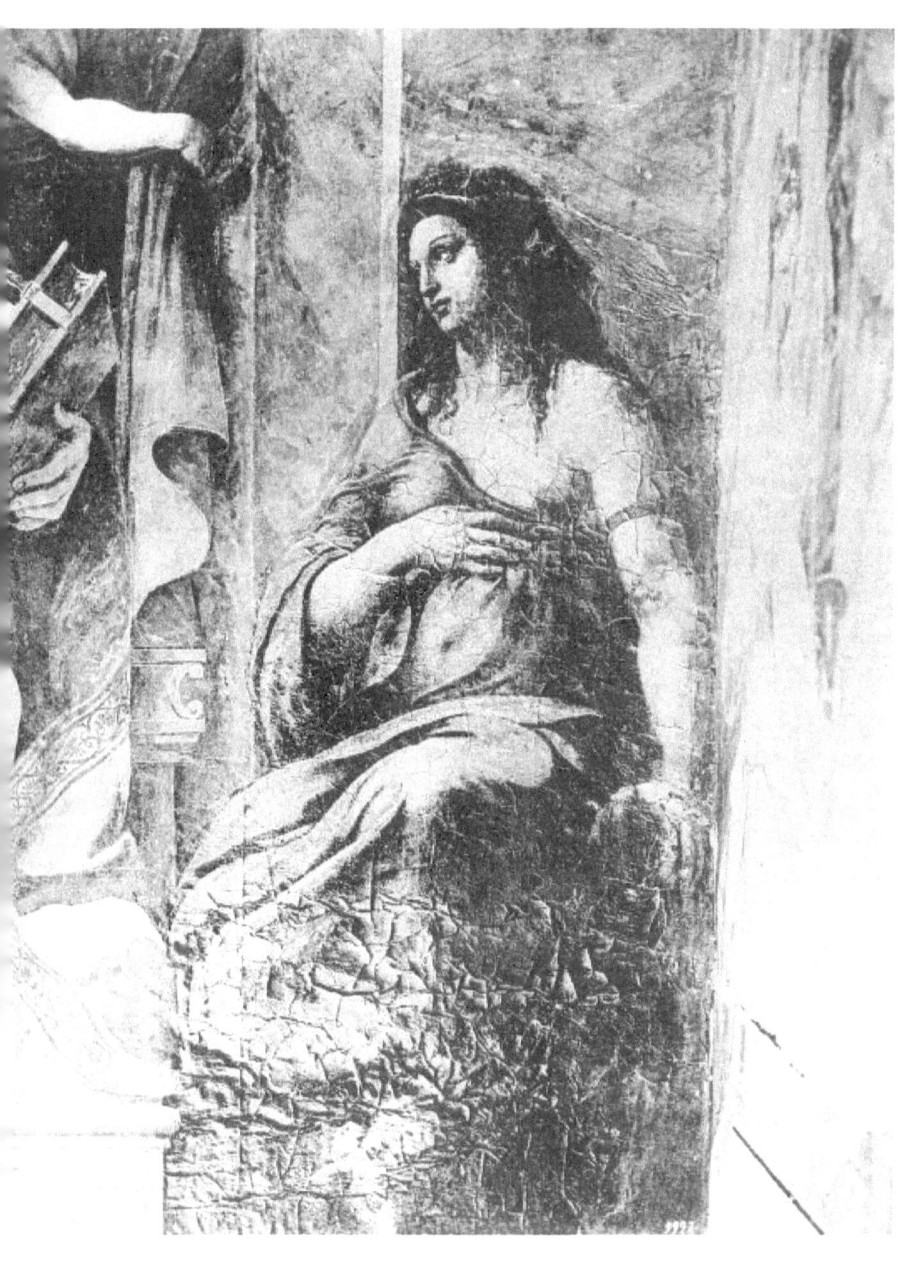

'Mansuetudo' (Oil Painting) by F. Penni, (1488?-1528), and Guilio
Romano (1492?-1546). Hall of Constantine, Stanze of Vatican.

The pigments are applied while the wet plaster is drying and har·
dening; that is, while the carbonic acid is expelling the water. The
painting must be finished before its expulsion is complete. A thin
crust of carbonate of lime will then be formed over the painting,
protecting it from water and moderate friction. If the painting be
continued after the plaster has lost the greater part of its water, no
crust will be formed, and the pigments will be deprived of their nat·
ural protection. Moreover, when dry, they will exhibit chalky
spots.

Fresco, then, is durable, not because the colors are absorbed by the
plaster, as many erroneously suppose, but because they are protected
by it chemically.

HISTORY.

The birth of fresco is unrecorded. It is certain that the Greeks
worked in it. The discussions have been long and sharp on the
methods employed by the Pompeians in their well-known mural
decorations. The best and most recent authorities decidedly pronounce them to be frescos. From personal observation I can give
no opinion, for I have no other ground on which to build a theory
than deceitful memory. One must be on the spot to arrive at a definite conclusion. While there is no good reason for doubting the

---

correct, is interesting. It will be noticed that for the first four or five hundred
years plaster gains in carbonate of lime, and that afterwards it loses in carbonate and gains in silicate. At the end of two thousand years there is very little
carbonate left. As a result, the plaster would be friable: —

COMPOSITION OF FRESH LIME MORTAR AND MORTAR HARDENED BY AGE.

From Wochenblatt f. Architekt. und Ingen. 1884; Töpfer und Ziegler Zeitung,
1884, 5, 206.

Components.	Fresh.	Age of the mortar in years.								
		1	30	100	200	3·0	600	1330	1800	2000
Carbonate of calcium......	1.5–3.2	9–10.	13.	13.4	8–13.	14.	13.6	10. 0	6–7.	5
Hydrate of cal- cium.........	11.3–8.6	4–5.5	2.	1.4	0.4–1.0	0.7	0.4	—	—	—
Lime combined with silicic acid..........	—	—	0.15	0.3	0.6–1.2	2.0	2.7	9. 0	14–16.	20
Soluble silic- ates.........:	—	—	0.35	0.5	1–2.	3.5	3.3	2. 5	1–1.5	—
Oxide of iron and soluble alumina	0.6–1.2	0.90–1.2	1.10	0.6	0.4–0.6	0.5	0.7	2. 0	2.	4
Alumina	0.1–0.8	0.95–1.0	0.55	0.7	0.1–0.6	0.7	0.3			
Sand, gypsum, magnesia, etc.	85.5–86.2	82–84.	82–83	81.8	81.4–88.	78.5	79.	75. 5	75.	70

Parts by weight.

The carbonate is formed first, then the silicate.
More will be said on the combination of sand with lime, as compared with the
mixture of lime and other ingredients, at the close of the eighth chapter, which
treats of Byzantine fresco.

authoritative statements of those who declare the paintings to be frescos pure and simple, yet one cannot blink the circumstances that tempted the less scientific to pronounce them encaustics, or frescos waxed and cauterized, the most weighty being their astounding freshness when first unearthed. Damp is disastrous to frescos, and here are paintings that have been buried some eighteen hundred years in a not over-dry region almost as fresh as when first painted. MM. Cros and Henry say that no traces of wax, save that of modern application, can be found on these pictures, with the exception of two or three fragments covered with vermilion, a color usually protected with cauterized wax and oil, as Vitruvius recommends. The highly polished surfaces that I call to mind must be the result, then, of the modern and ineffectual attempts to preserve the paintings with a coat of wax, or some other process unbeknown to me. But these things cannot be studied from a distance. Vitruvius has a great deal to say about plastering, and very little about the process of fresco painting, but enough to convince us that the usual process for mural painting in his day was fresco — even were certain unmistakable peculiarities of fresco painting wanting in the pictures that have been preserved. "When, besides the first coat, three sand-coats at least have been laid, the coat of marble-dust follows, and this is to be so prepared that when used it does not stick to the trowel, but easily comes away from the iron. Whilst the stucco is drying, another thin coat is to be laid on; this is to be well worked and rubbed, and then still another, finer than the last. Thus, with three sand-coats and the same number of marble-dust coats [not counting the rough-cast, which was allowed to dry], the walls will be rendered solid, and not liable to cracks or other defects. When the stuff is well beaten and the under coats made solid, and afterwards well smoothed by the hardness and whiteness of the marble-powder, it throws out the colors mixed therein with great brilliancy. Colors, when used on damp stucco, are very durable." (Book VII, Chap. III.) When the Italian method has been described, it will be seen to differ from that of the ancients in two respects: —

(1) Marble-dust is used by the ancients for the finishing coats, where the Italians as a rule used sand, though not infrequently marble-dust was mixed with the sand by the latter.

(2) The ancient plaster is thicker and more compact, thereby retaining its humidity for a much longer period, and enabling the painter to continue his work for several days before the formation of the crust, after which all painting must cease.

THE PROCESS.

As these papers are addressed to the professional public, the technics of fresco will be summarily described. The method is too well known to call for an elaborate statement which any hand-book of the art will furnish. A sketch, however, of the process is necessary, in order that architects and painters may judge of its adaptability to certain sites, and that comparisons may be instituted between it and other processes, with a view to modern mural undertakings. Principles will be emphasized rather than details, and the preliminary steps rather than the actual process of painting, for the latter is largely personal. It was my good fortune, a few years ago, to witness the execution of some frescos in the Campo Santo of Siena — that truly blessed spot with its monumental view over broad stretches of limitless clay-mounds, corrugated by the action of water, and backed by hazy Amiata and Santa Croce, and more distant Apennines. (No one of sensibility can ever recall those beloved, impressive Italian vistas without rhapsodizing.) Through the courtesy of Professor Franchi of the Sienese Academy of Fine Arts, I was enabled to try my hand at fresco, and to glean some practical information. Practice is so much more reliable and convincing than theory — the treatises not infrequently being written by mere compilers — that I shall give the preference to my own notes in the following statements, except, of course, when they are silent.

The Wall.—It is unnecessary to repeat what has been written at some length in a previous paper about the construction of the walls and their protection from damp. But there are a few rules of special applicability to fresco. Walls of well-dried and equally hard brick are the best. Rough stone walls are not objectionable. The plaster is liable to peel from smooth stone. Lathing is inferior to brick for perpendicular surfaces. Being exposed to the air on both sides, the plaster dries too rapidly, one of the requisites being that it should retain its moisture long enough to enable the painter to complete his allotted task. A wall of one or two bricks in thickness is preferable to a very thick one; for the latter remaining damp for a longer period, is more liable to saline efflorescence, the damp carrying the particles composing the salt to the surface. But whether thick or thin, brick or stone, the wall must be dry. A double wall with an air-space between is obviously the best. In Pompeii the painted walls were sometimes constructed of tiles placed edgewise and fastened to the outer wall by leaden cramps with a narrow space between, as a safeguard against damp. If there is any old plaster on the wall to be frescoed, it should be entirely removed, and the material of the wall laid bare. Lathing was used both in ancient and Renaissance times for ceilings, except when these were vaulted with brick. But the lathing then was much more durable than now, as has already been explained, and frequently was plastered above as well as below, thus protecting the paintings from dirt and moisture, and by retaining the humidity for a longer period enabled the frescoer to work more leisurely. Where the lathing was inferior, the frescos have paid the penalty, as, for example, those on the ceiling of the Loggie in the Vatican painted by Giovanni da Udine. With all our modern appliances, architects could undoubtedly construct a ceiling fulfilling all the conditions imposed by fresco, without having recourse to the lathing makeshift. If concrete blocks are used, they must not be too porous.

(a) *The Lime.* — A limestone free from foreign ingredients yields the best lime for fresco. After the lime has been well mixed with water till it has attained the consistency of cream, it is poured into earthen pits and kept there for at least a year, the longer the better. If too fresh, it will blister and flake off. Lime kept in this way is said to improve in consistence, and to grow milder or less caustic. It is hardly possible, however, that it should grow less caustic, for it is not exposed to the air. Though it is difficult to say why it improves by keeping, the fact that it does improve is attested by long experience — the best authority. Time alone is the true test, and though we may approximate its action by ingenious experiments, we can never exactly counterfeit it.[1] A certain amount of causticity is indispensable; otherwise the lime would lose its adhesiveness, the crust fail to form, and fresco be impossible. On the other hand, excessive causticity is to be avoided, for the crust would form too rapidly, before the painter could complete his work. Lime remains caustic till it has gained its maximum of carbonic acid, which it attracts from the atmosphere while drying. But the causticity cannot be reduced by exposing it to the air for any length of time, as it would become too hard for handling. Yet wet lime can be rendered less caustic in several ways without losing its requisite causticity.

---

[1] Perhaps the best reason for keeping the lime in pits is given by Vitruvius: "Stucco will be well executed if lime of the best quality be slaked long before it is wanted; in order that if any portion was imperfectly burned in the kiln, the action of moisture in long maceration might slake it, and reduce it to the same consistence as the rest. For if lime be used too fresh, instead of being thoroughly macerated, it will, when spread (on walls), throw out blisters, owing to the crude particles that lurk in it. These particles, not having been duly slaked, swell and destroy the smoothness of the plaster." Prof. T. M. Clark tells me that his experience corroborates this view.

One of these ways, often recommended by the old masters, is to wash it frequently in river or spring water containing carbonic acid.

(*b*) *The Plaster.*—The lime is taken out of the pit, again mixed with water till it is about as thick as milk, well strained, and the superfluous water, which rises to the surface, poured off. It has then the consistence of cream cheese, and is ready to be mixed with the sand. This must be river sand well washed and passed through a sieve. No hair is to be used. Two plasterings are necessary for fresco:—

(1) The *arriccio*, or *arricciatura*, or   rough-cast.

(2) The *intonaco*, or *intonacatura*, or   *scialbo*,   or finishing coat.

The proportion of sand to lime varies according to the richness of the lime. In Siena the rule was one part sand to one part lime, with rather more sand for the *arriccio*. Some authorities recommend two parts sand to one of lime. A good practical test for the *arriccio* is to spread the plaster on a dry, absorbing brick. If the plaster be good, little short cracks will appear. If deep, long cracks are developed, the plaster is too fat (*grasso*); in other words, there is too much lime. If no cracks make their appearance it is too poor (*magro*), too much sand. The *arriccio* should be a little less than half an inch in thickness, and applied in two or three quickly succeeding coats. Its surface should be roughened, to give a key to the *intonaco*. When it is thoroughly dry and hard, it is ready for the *intonaco*, on which the fresco is to be painted. After the *arriccio* has been saturated with water, the *intonaco* is spread in two thin coats, the whole being about one-tenth of an inch thick. Some painters mix marble-dust with the plaster for the *intonaco*, and occasionally color, to reduce its whiteness to a middle tint. The plaster is spread with a trowel or wooden float. At Siena they used both, but finished with the trowel. If the plaster be rubbed too hard, black spots injurious to the painting will appear. The surface should be so hard " as with difficulty to receive the impression of the finger." If texture be desired, it should be rubbed with a cloth, brush or the like. It sometimes happens that the plaster becomes too dry while polishing it with the trowel. In that case wet both plaster and trowel.

(*c*) *The Cartoon and Outline.* — All that has been said regarding the importance of a well-prepared cartoon for wax-painting is equally applicable to fresco. When the picture is so small that it can be painted in a single day, it may be transferred directly from the cartoon to the *intonaco*, or finishing coat. If the picture be large, it is better to transfer the whole cartoon by pouncing to the *arriccio*, before any of the *intonaco* is laid. Sometimes it is difficult to handle a large cartoon in awkward places; then the picture may be drawn on the *arriccio* with charcoal, being enlarged by the squaring process from the sketch, just as the cartoon would be. It is not absolutely necessary to transfer the whole picture to the *arriccio*, for one can work piecemeal on the *intonaco;* but it is obviously a safer method. The stereopticon might be used for the transfer of the sketch to the *arriccio*, were the conditions favorable to its use, but not for the subsequent outlining on the *intonaco*. The portion to be painted in one day having been indicated by the painter, the mason prepares it with the *intonaco*, as previously described. The corresponding portion of the cartoon is cut off (or a tracing is made of it, if it be desirable to keep the cartoon), and transferred to the wet *intonaco*, either by pouncing or by passing over the outlines with a style which leaves a corresponding depression in the plaster. For delicate works pouncing is preferable. Wilson, who closely inspected the frescos of the Sistine vault on a movable scaffold, says that Michael Angelo used the pounce-bag, but frequently accentuated the less delicate lines with some sharp instrument, after the cartoon had been removed.

(*d*) *Brushes.*—These should be of bristle, rather long and supple. If short and unyielding, they rub up the plaster. Those used at Siena were round, and very ordinary compared with the best French or English brushes. Marten or sable brushes were avoided chiefly on the ground of expense, though the work was beautifully finished. Marten's hair or otter's is said to resist the action of lime better than sable's.

(*e*) *Palette.*—This should be of tin, with a rim round it, to prevent the colors from running off, and a cup in the middle for pure water which is the medium for fresco. At Sienna the palette was a large wooden slab, so propped as to be stable and handy.

(*f*) *Colors.*—Those that are fit for fresco have been fully catalogued at various times and by various authors. The different nomenclatures are somewhat confusing. As a general rule it may be said that all the earth and a few mineral colors can be used, but neither animal nor vegetable colors. Here is a simple palette:—

Lime white (*bianco Sangiovanni.*)

Yellow ochre, Naples yellow.

Earth reds: Venetian red, light red, burnt Sienna and the like.

Terre verte, chrome green.

Raw and burnt umber.

Earth black is the best. Ivory black is too oily for fresco.

Cobalt blue, indigo, and pure or imitated ultramarine.

Burnt vitriol (purple).[2]

Vermilion may be rendered fit for fresco by placing it in a glazed earthenware vase and pouring lime-water on it. Afterwards the water should be poured off, and the operation repeated several times.

The white may be prepared in many ways. Cennini's method is elaborate but reliable. "Take very white slacked lime [from the pit] and put it into a little tub for the space of eight days, changing the water every day, and mixing the lime and water well together, in order to extract from it all unctuous properties. Then make it into small cakes, put them upon the roof of the house in the sun, and the older the cakes are, the whiter they become. If you wish to hasten the process and have the white very good, when the cakes are dry, grind them on your slab with water, and then make them again into cakes and dry them as before. Do this twice, and you will see how perfectly white they will become. This white must be ground thoroughly with water." Pozzo curtails this process considerably. The idea is to get rid of the caustic qualities of the lime; for this being a pigment with which all the others are more or less mixed, it would increase the already sufficient causticity of the *intonaco*.

It will be noticed that the palette for fresco is a quiet one, which, in a measure, accounts for its harmonious tones. The colors, when dry, appear lighter and warmer than when first applied to the cool, gray plaster, that ultimately dries white. To judge of their final effect the painter tries the colors on a piece of dry umber, which immediately absorbs their moisture.[3] It is well to prepare the whole of a needed tone at once. It is difficult to match tones in fresco. Warm colors are said to be more durable than cool, which is almost tantamount to saying that the earth colors are the safest.

(*g*) *Painting.* — It would be as vain and misleading to give a receipt for fresco as for oil or water-color painting. For amateurs such receipts are not without value. Every professional painter has his idiosyncracies and a handling that harmonizes with them. There are before me five receipts for painting a head in fresco, differing widely in details, but corresponding in essentials — which are worth signalizing. Fresco has not the depth of varnished oils, but a blonde, dead quality, that is the desideratum in mural painting. It is a cross

---

[2] Some authors recommend the addition of size to colors that do not mix freely with water.

[3] Dry, white absorbent wood is also recommended.

between distemper and water-color—semi-transparent and semi-opaque —not so clear as water-color, nor so heavy and lifeless as distemper. Consequently, the execution savors of both media—here a wash and there *impasto*. There are two schools of fresco; the one characterized by its comparatively thin, transparent qualities, and the moderate use of *impasto,* the other by a more generous use of it. To the former school belong all the earlier painters, from Cimabue (1242–1302) to Raphael and Michael Angelo inclusive. Theirs are the methods recommended by Cennino Cennini. The other school came later, and is championed by Adrea Pozzo, Jesuit father, painter, architect, and author (1642–1709.) The modern Siennese still prefer the delicate, refined manner of Cennino, while many others adopt the vigorous handling of Pozzo. The latter is more in harmony with our modern oil methods.

The following notes, many of which were jotted down on the staging, may be of service. (1) To avoid injury (from plastering) on the parts already painted, begin at the top of the picture and paint downwards. (2) Keep at hand a plentiful supply of pure water. (3) Draw in the subject with a dark tone and indicate the shadows. (4) Begin with light, transparent washes, applied with a broad brush, and finish with impasto. (5) Better warm washes over cool, and strong over weak. (6) The first washes appear very faint, but the painting acquires strength and consistence as it advances. Just before completion the water is rapidly absorbed from the brush as soon as it touches the wall, which means that the work must cease. Were it continued no crust would be formed, and chalky spots would make their appearance on the painting when dry.[1] (7) The setting of the plaster may be retarded in hot weather by sprinkling it with water. If there be danger of freezing, wait till milder weather. (8) Colors may be partially removed by washing, but it is better to avoid the necessity. (9) Those who so wish, may apply a final glaze over the damp colors, but it must be done rapidly and lightly. (10) During the work it may be necessary to pause at intervals to allow the moisture to be absorbed. (11) When the day's task is completed the masons cut away the unpainted plaster with a sharp

---

[1] The Munich artists invented a contrivance for retarding the drying of the work, which enabled them to leave it for several hours and then take it up again. "They have a board of sufficient surface to cover that part of their work, and this is padded on one side, this cushion being then covered with waxed cloth ; a wet piece of fine linen is then spread over the fresh plaster and painting, and then pressed to the surface of the wall by the cushioned side of the boar t, while the outer side is buttressed firmly by a pole from the ground." — *W. B. Sarsfield Taylor.* (Reference is made to Cornelius, Kaulbach and others.)

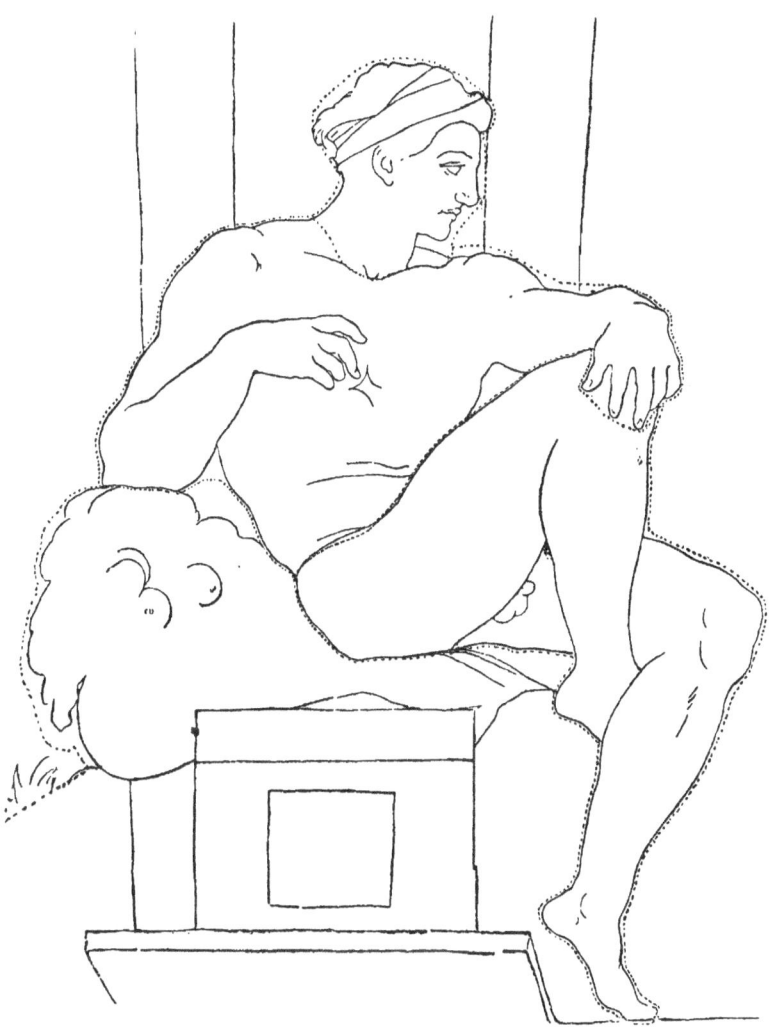

instrument and bevels the edge. It is needless to observe that the mason must be an adept. When painting a figure, it is well to paint a portion of the background at the same time, to avoid hardness of contour and preserve the integrity of the outline. On the following day the mason joins the fresh *intonaco* to that of the preceding day, and so on till the picture is completed. Heads should be finished at a sitting, and nude figures joined at a convenient line suggested by the anatomy. Wilson says that Michael Angelo painted his figures

on the Sistine Vault in about three days each,[1] and indicates with a
dotted line on tracings from two of them, the successive divisions.
One of these figures is the Adam — about ten feet in height. I give
here a similar tracing from Braun's photograph of one of the young
men on the cornice. The dotted lines are suppositious in one or two
places, but elsewhere the photograph indicates the divisions very
clearly, notably about the head. (12) All retouches must be made
with color, tempered with size, that is, "*a secco*" (dry), or when
the plaster is no longer wet. A good size may be made of two parts
water to one part yolk-of-egg, mixed with a little vinegar to preserve it. This size is too yellow for the blues. Caseine mixed with
water and quicklime is said to be an insoluble size. Parchment or
fish glue is also used. "Secco" is perishable, and the less of it the
better. Notwithstanding the example of some of the best frescoers, it
is almost universally condemned, except for slight retouches.[2] When
a considerable part of the work is unsatisfactory it must be destroyed
and repainted.

Andrea Pozzo, the representative of the impasto school recommends a rough ground. But if the painting, he observes, be near the
eye and should appear too rough, a sheet of paper must be placed
over it, and the protuberances gently rubbed down with a trowel.
Here is a quotation from him that reminds one strongly of modern
ways : " For uniting tones, soft brushes must be used, though of hog's
bristles, and not very moist ; and occasionally, too, *the fingers* give
good effects in the heads, hands, and other small things, particularly
when the lime begins to set."

---

[1] Later, in the Last Judgment, he painted more rapidly, generally finishing a
colossal figure in two days, "though," says Wilson, "he could execute an entire
figure in one day."

[2] "He who can finish 'a *buon fresco*' will always be the best painter, and his
work far more lasting ; but seeing that lime always undergoes some change,
especially in the shadows, one can, and ought, to retouch either with delicate
strokes of pastel prepared from egg-shell, or with brushes half dry and charged
with the requisite color. If such retouches are made in uncovered places, they
are made in vain, for the first rain will carry them off." (Andrea Pozzo, Prospet-
tiva de' Pittori, etc. P.II. S. XI. Roma, 1758.

CHAPTER VII.

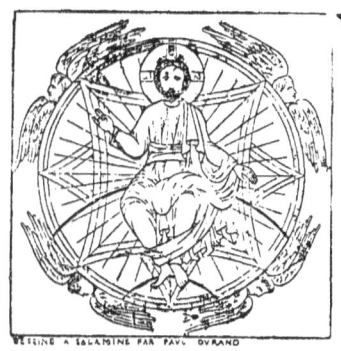

WHEN Christianity crawled out of the catacombs she was indigent and ill-clad. Raised suddenly from the dust — rather from the bowels of the earth — by the imperial fiat she must needs be clad with official splendor. Rich basilicas supplant the gloomy crypts, and lustrous, majestic mosaics the rude and hieroglyphic paintings of the catacombs. Previously mosaics had been used with profusion chiefly for pavements, but now they glisten on either wall of the temple, that they who know not their letters may thus learn "the noble actions of those who have served God faithfully." Byzantium is the capital of the Empire. If she is not always beautiful she is at least resplendent. An Eastern love of sumptuousness is ousting the sculpturesque feeling for form. Mosaicists are exempted from taxation to give a fillip to their art. When mosaics are too costly, paintings are substituted.

So it came to pass that painting posed in the garb of mosaic, and not the reverse, as in the days of Titian, and later still, in those of Cavaliere Arpino (1560–1640). There is something awfully grand in those simple creations of solemn, impassive aspect, and colossal size, towering o'er mortals below—actually and ethically. This was a great age for mural decoration, which, with varying excellence, has lived uninterruptedly to the present day. The compositions were more symmetrical then than in the days of the Italian Renaissance, more stately, and, if I may be allowed the term, more processional. They were deficient in varied action, and dramatic force and life; but they gained thereby in grandeur and dignity. Religious impressiveness was the desideratum; whereas the Italian artists of the sixteenth century strove far less impersonally for pure beauty, under the pretext of religion, though the patronage of the church gave them a tremendous impulse and that opportunity for expression without which art cannot exist. Gross ignorance often characterized the anatomy of the Byzantine figures — for Christianity was clothed — but "the draperies still showed traces of the grand style," and the heads were life-like and expressive. These were evil days for monumental sculpture. For a long time the traditions of the art survived, and the old influence was felt, but it was never in odor of sanctity with the church. The goldsmith was the sculptor's legitimate successor. The iconoclasts of the eighth and ninth centuries gave the *coup de grace* to sculpture. Religious figure-painting was not exempted, but it was treated more leniently. It took refuge in foreign lands and in the monasteries where zealous monks could paint and illuminate without fear of detection, or in spite of it. But the iconoclasts though fanatics, were not barbarians. On the contrary, they encouraged the arts in their civic character. Magnificent buildings were constructed and adorned with splendid mosaic figure-compositions. Painting gained rather than lost, for it became less hieratic. Byzantium was at the zenith of her power under the Macedonian dynasty (867–1057), and the arts flourished with the exception of sculpture, which was never rehabilitated by the triumphant antagonists of iconoclasm. Bas-reliefs were tolerated as less real than statues and more akin to painting. Byzantine stuffs, ivories, bronzes and *objets d'art* were pre-eminent. Then came the ghastly sack of the town by the Crusaders (1204), in comparison to which the pillage by the Turks (1453) was as sounding brass. The wholesale looting and burning of all that was choicest and best in both literature and art by those vandal enthusiasts, left but little of value for the much abused victorious Moslems. Priceless treasures perished in the sickening devastation. Contemporary descriptions of the city on the eve of its calamities read like tales of fairyland. Even when its glory had departed, some two hundred years later, it contained not less than 3,000 churches. In 1261 the Greeks again wrested the remnants of the city from the Latins, and there appeared the adumbration of a Renaissance. But the palmy days of the Eastern Empire were past, and mural decoration, notwithstanding certain restorative efforts that bore some fruit, was on the decline when Mahomet II obliterated it with whitewash. Mosaics were then giving place to less costly paintings. Just what this painting was in its best days we do not know. We must judge it inferentially from the mosaics and miniatures that war and fanaticism have spared. At this time the types were already fixed and it was relegated to the monasteries.

Of all the monasteries those of Mt. Athos were, and still are, deservedly the most celebrated. The Holy Mountain, as it is called by the Orthodox Greeks, rises from the southern extremity of the most easterly of the three Macedonian peninsulas. Its monasteries have long maintained a semi-independence, even under Turkish rule. They form a monastic republic. Their early history is at times ob-

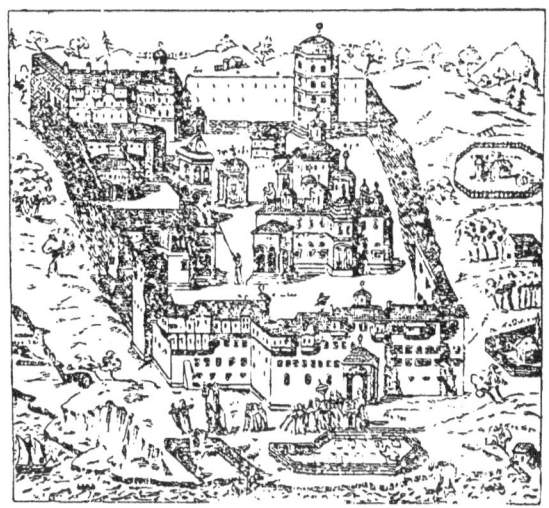

A Monastery on Mt. Athos, after a Byzantine Engraving.

scure; but however miraculous may have been their origin, they attained no importance till the tenth and eleventh centuries. The republic was organized by zealots of high birth. Slaves, Bulgarians, Armenians, in fact all nationalities of the Greek faith, hastened to found convents on the Mount. The emperors multiplied the privileges of the Athonites, and freed them from the patriarch's authority. During the short-lived Latin Supremacy (1204–1261), they were sorely vexed; but they were amply indemnified on the return of the Greeks to Byzantium. Even Mahomet II granted them the maintenance of their privileges. "Thus by a remarkable combination of circumstances, everything seems to have conspired to preserve this monastic state from those depredations that in so many other places have overthrown from roof to foundation the Greek churches and convents." [1]

---

[1] "*L'art Byzantin*" par Ch. Bayet. A. Quantin, Paris.

Though there are still some interesting mosaic fragments of the twelfth or thirteenth century, the paintings in these monasteries, both by their number and importance, first claim the attention. Unfortunately the Athonite painters have shown but little veneration for

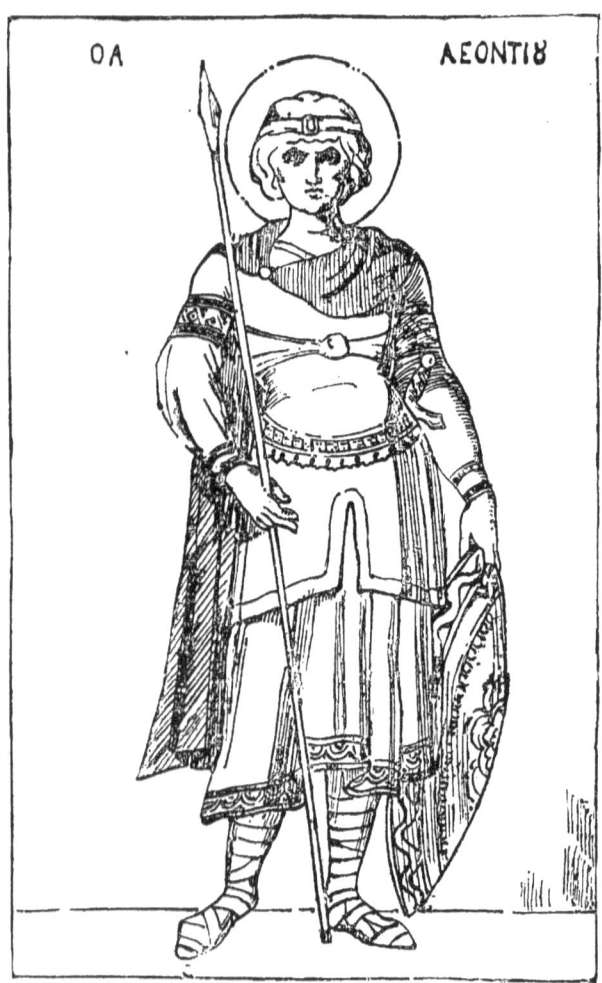

Fig. I. Mural Painting from Mt. Athos.

the works of their predecessors. They have kept their paintings in a chronic state of restoration, or have entirely repainted them. Many of the convents have their own painters who require but little time and money for their labor; so that it is difficult to find frescos antedating the sixteenth century. But inasmuch as the personal inspiration allowed the painter is comparatively slight, and seeing that the types, color, and composition were fixed by almost immutable laws at a very early date, it is fair to assume that the paintings of to-day, though doubtless inferior in execution, very strongly resemble those of the best epoch.

An interesting and important discovery was made by Didron on Mt. Athos in 1839, bearing directly on the Byzantine technique and iconography. As this chapter is but little else than a compilation — though not devoid of interest, I trust, owing to popular unfamiliarity with Byzantine mural painting—I shall freely utilize Didron's investigations, sometimes translating them literally, sometimes paraphrasing them.[1] After visiting many churches in Greece, he was greatly impressed by the large number of figures, colossal and diminutive, that swarmed on every available wall-space — narthex, nave, apsis, dome, archivolts — everywhere, in fact; and also by the concordance of the same figures in different churches. In that of Salamis (not large, I should infer, though he makes no direct statement as to its size) he counted over 3,000 figures, all executed by one master-painter, aided by his three pupils, according to an inscription borne by an angel:

"1735. *This holy and venerable temple has been painted by the hand of Georgios Marcos, from the town of Argos, with the assistance of his pupils, Nicolaos Benigelos, Georgakis, and Antonis.*"

"If in France to-day," writes Didron, "where our painters are well enough informed, a single artist should be commissioned to represent in some monumental edifice — in the Cathedral of Paris, I will suppose — the universal history of a religion as illustrated by its heroes, and the events of that history, it is doubtful if he could execute so vast a composition without long and profound research. I will go further and say that we have not a single painter capable of bringing such a work to a successful termination. There is not one of them learned or strong enough to carry such a burden. But at Salamis the painter has not only represented scenes and characters, but he has particularized them by means of explanatory inscriptions and quotations, and these quotations are drawn from the Bible, and from a vast number of religious works. . . . The difficulty is thereby greatly increased, and surely no French artist could be found with the knowledge that such an enterprise exacts. What a man this painter of Salamis must have been to accomplish such a task. Neither my companions nor myself could cease to marvel. I questioned the monks of the convent, especially the most learned, but

---

[1] "*Manuel d'Iconographie Chrétienne*" par M. Didron, Paris, 1845.

could get nothing out of them. . . . Yet I was at Salamis, in the
very church where he must have passed his life, and I was address-
ing monks whose immediate predecessors must have been contemporaries of the painter."

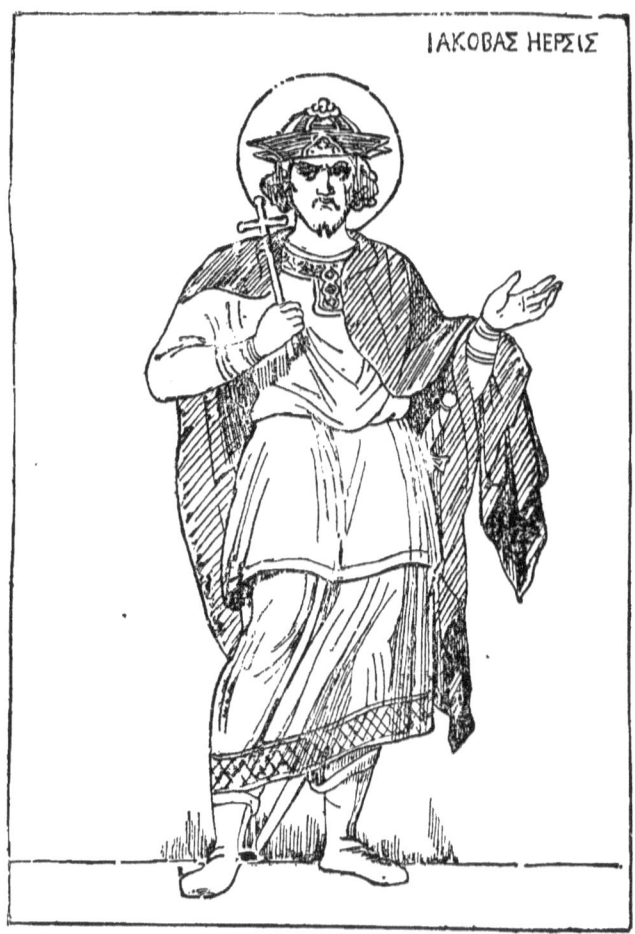

IΑΚΟΒΑΣ ΗΕΡΣΙΣ

Fig. 2.   Mural Painting from Mt. Athos.

Didron had not yet seen Mt. Athos, the great formative school of
Byzantine painters, the Italy of the Eastern church.   There were
in it in his days nine hundred and thirty-five churches, chapels and
oratories, almost entirely covered with frescos, and filled with pictures
on wood ; not to mention the paintings on the refectory walls and
elsewhere.   Arriving at the Mount, it so happened that the first
church he entered was new, and from which the staging had not yet

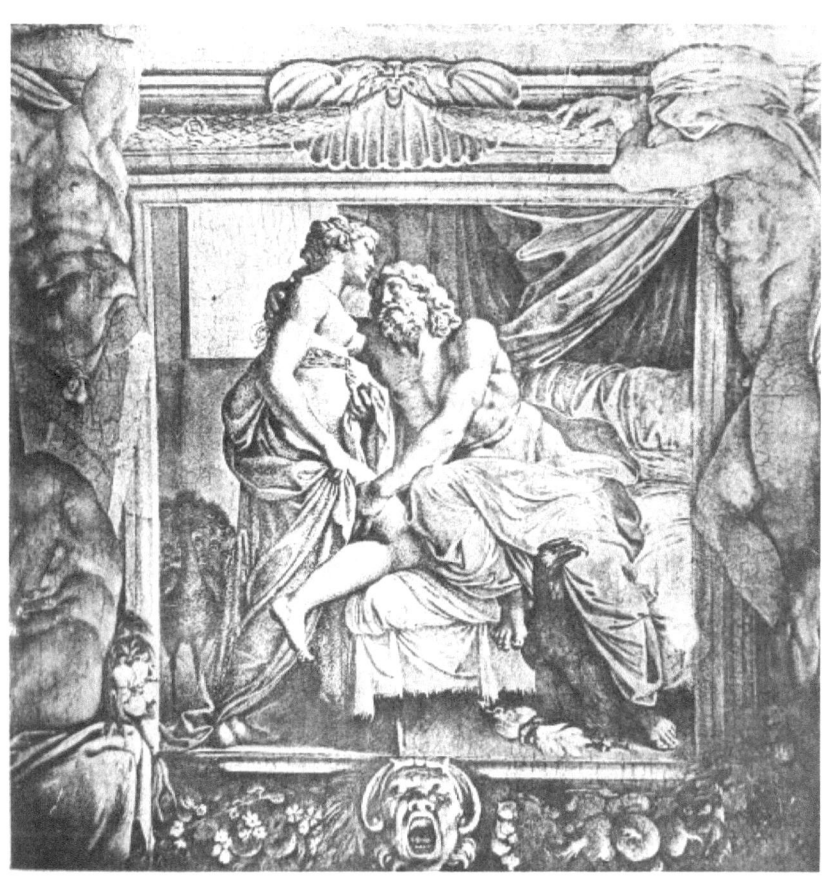

'Jupiter and Juno' (Fresco) by Annibale Carracci (1569 - 1609).
Farnese Palace, Rome.

been removed. " A painter from Karès (the capital of Athos), assisted by his brother, by two pupils, and two young apprentices, were frescoing the whole of the interior porch that precedes the nave. The first of the pupils — the eldest and a deacon — was destined to take charge of the atelier at the master's death. I rejoiced greatly at the happy chance that would probably reveal to me the secrets of these paintings and painters, and which would doubtless answer the questions that I had vainly asked at Salamis and Athens. I mounted the staging and saw the master painter, surrounded by his pupils, decorating the narthex of the church with frescos. The young brother spread the mortar on the wall; the master sketched the picture; the first pupil filled in the outlines drawn by his chief, on those parts of the picture which the latter had not time to finish ; a young pupil gilded the *nimbi*, painted the inscriptions and ornaments, while two others, younger still, ground and diluted the colors. In the mean time the master-painter 'drew in ' his picture, either from memory or from inspiration. In an hour, under our very eyes, he traced on the wall a picture representing Jesus Christ charging his apostles to evangelize and baptize the world. The Christ, and the eleven other personages, were about the size of life. He drew them from memory without cartoon, sketch or model. On examining the other pictures that he had finished I asked him if he had executed them in the same way; he answered in the affirmative, and added that 'he very rarely effaced a line.' "

" We were dumbfounded, for these paintings were incontestably superior to those of our second-rate artists who paint religious pictures. By some persons — and I am of the number — the painter of Mt. Athos would be classified with the best living artists, especially if executing religious paintings."

Of course, due allowance must be made for Didron's very natural enthusiasm which has its licenses as well as poetry, so that we can graciously pardon any exaggeration. M. Bayet, in his recent handbook of Byzantine art says of these Athonite paintings, that " One must not expect as a rule to find in them either careful drawing or a scholarly study of color, but merely the traditions of a great decorative school." He bears testimony, however, to their impressiveness.

Having passed a month in making the tour of the Mount, Didron again returned to his decorator, whose work in the mean time had advanced apace. He had many questions to propound concerning certain artists, living and dead, whose names he had read on their signed works. With but one exception, Father Joasaph — for such

was the painter's name — had never heard of them, and that exception was the celebrated Panselinos, the patriarch of the school.
During their conversation Joasaph worked continuously, " and I,"
says Didron, " continued ecstatic before his prodigious facility and

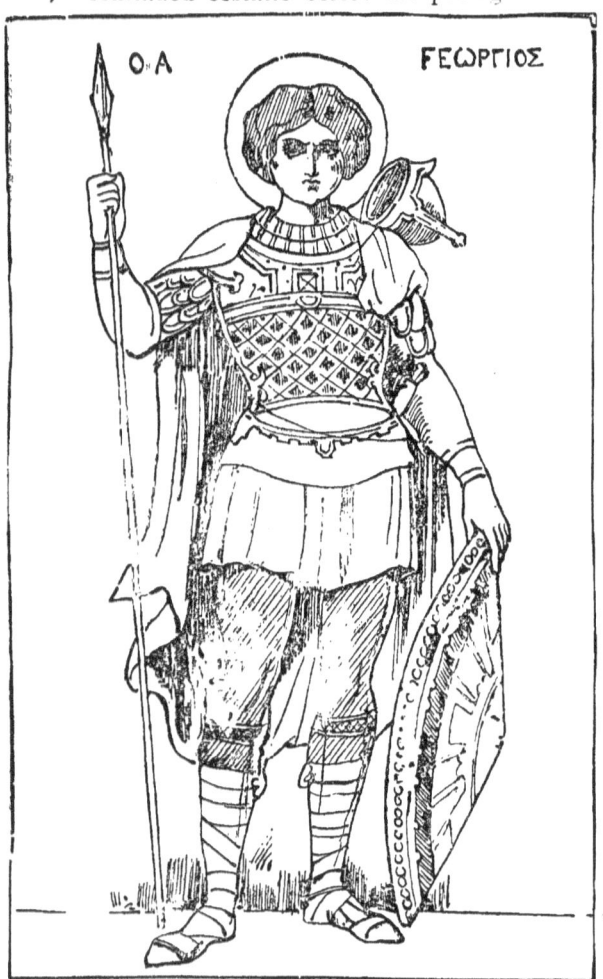

Fig. 3. Mural Painting from Mt. Athos.

astonishing memory." " But, sir," he said to me at length, " all this
is very much less extraordinary than you suppose, and I marvel at
your surprise that increases rather than diminishes. Look, here is
a manuscript that teaches everything we have to do. In this place
it tells us how to prepare our plaster, our brushes, our colors, how to
compose and where to place our pictures ; in that place are written

the words and inscriptions we have to paint, and which you have just now heard me dictate to these young people, my pupils."

"I seized," continues Didron, "with eagerness, with avidity, the manuscript that Joasaph showed me, and I read in the table of contents that the work was divided into four parts. The first part, entirely technical, was devoted to an exposition of the methods of painting employed by the Greeks, their manner of preparing brushes and colors, of laying the grounds for frescos and pictures, and of painting on these grounds. In the second part were described in detail, and with remarkable precision, those symbolical, and especially historical subjects that painting may represent. The third part determined the place in a church, porch, refectory, or fountain, where such and such a subject, or figure, should be placed, in preference to any other. Finally, in an appendix, the types of Christ and the Virgin are fixed, and some of the inscriptions given that abound in Byzantine paintings. This manuscript was entitled : Ἑρμηνεία τῆς ζωγραφικῆς, *Manual of Painting.*"

"Then the immutability and identity of the types figured in every part of Greece, and from Syra to . . . Constantinople, were explained. The form of the hair and beard, the age, physiognomy, costume and attitude are recorded in this book. Thus, with a fair memory and average intelligence, assisted, on the one hand, by this *codex*, and on the other by the continual view or study of the old paintings, and especially by the constant practice of art, almost any painter could easily be a Joasaph. Seeing him execute such works, I had, in fact, a certain admiration for the man, who had nothing to recommend him in expression, word, or bearing, and who was commonplace, rather than distinguished. So the fine series of paintings at Salamis was accounted for, and the complete oblivion of Georgios Marcos. What was then happening at Mt. Athos must have happened in France and all Christian Europe in the Middle Ages. The composition and distribution of the sculptures that decorate the portals of Amiens, Reims, and especially Chartres cathedrals, would bear witness to a great genius, if any Picard, Champenois, or Beauceron artist had invented them ; but they only call for an ordinary man, aided by a manuscript similar to that of Mt. Athos. It is just the same for glass-painting."

The particular copy of the *codex* that Didron saw was not more than 300 years old, and had been freely annotated both by Joasaph and his master — annotations that would be incorporated with the text when re-copied. Thus the later *codices* are somewhat more voluminous than their prototype. The "*Manual of Painting*" was composed by a painter who signed himself Denys, monk of Fourna d'Agrapha. He "flourished" probably about the middle of the fifteenth century, and was, therefore, a contemporary of the oft-

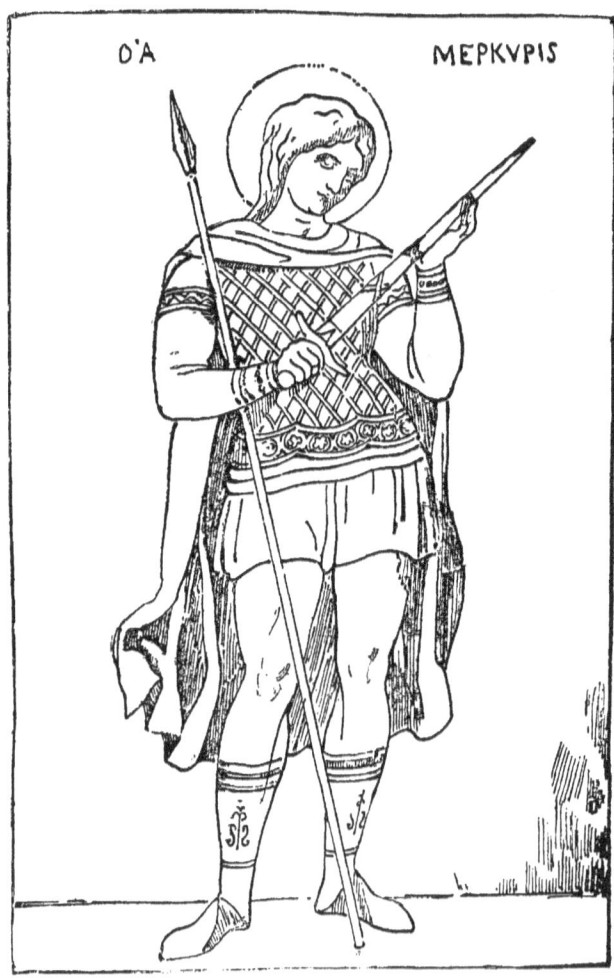

Fig. 4. Mural Painting **from** Mt. Athos.

quoted Cennino Cennini. Strange that these two painters, of no great artistic fame, mutually alien in school as well as country, yet so like· in their innocent faith and veneration, should each have composed a manual of his art, and that both should have been published for the first time in the present century, and within less than thirty years of each other (Cennino's in 1821; Denys's in 1845). Denys belonged to the famous school of Saloniki, whose recognized chief was Panselinos, the Giotto — or, as some style him, the Raphael — of the Byzantine school. Though not the immediate master of Denys, the latter stood in the same attitude of veneration towards him, as the protagonist of his school, that Cennini did towards Giotto, though both were dead. Cennini writes: "This plan was adopted by Giotto, the great master, who had Taddeo Gaddi, his godson, for his disciple for twenty-four years; his disciple was Agnolo, his son; I was Agnolo's disciple for twelve years, and he showed me this method," etc. Denys writes: . . . "The little art that I know I have studied and acquired with difficulty, since childhood, striving to imitate, as well as I could, the celebrated and illustrious master Panselinos of Thessalonica. After having worked in the admirable churches on the Holy Mount of Athos, which he adorned with magnificent paintings, this painter, by the mastery n his art, shone with such dazzling brilliance that he was compared to the moon in all her splendor." (Πᾶσα Σελήνη = Πανσέληνος = full-moon). It is fair to assume that Panselinos was a contemporary of Giotto — an assumption that is supported by historical evidence and the style of his work. Though the acknowledged head of the Byzantine school, it must be remembered that he found the types already fixed, some dating back to the fourth century. Doubtless he played with these types, as all men of genius must ever play with restrictive conventionalities, though probably much less than the leaders of the Latin schools, who were allowed far greater latitude in their interpretation of sacred themes. The Greek artists never emancipated themselves from the decrees of Nice,[1] though, doubtless, every now and then able men, like Panselinos, took certain venial liberties. The fact that all the Athonite painters were monks, and some of them both monks and priests, must still further have tended to cramp their inspirations, and to keep them within prescribed conventional bounds, grateful to ascetics, but baneful to art. As I remarked, in a previous chapter, an excess of superstitious zeal would hamper a creative artist; and for this reason it is better for art, that the functions of painter and monk should be divorced, even though the latter be merely nominal. The Manual does not state whether Panselinos was a monk; it merely refers to him as "the celebrated and illustrious master."

[1] "Non est imaginum structura pictorum inventio, sed Ecclesiæ Catholicæ probata legislatio et traditio. . . . . Itqui consilium et traditio ista non est pictoris (ejus enim sola ars est), rerum ordinatio et dispositio patrum nostrorum, qua ædificaverunt. (Synodus Nicæna II.") 787 A. D.

But few of his works are still extant. Those at Saloniki — the seat of the school — are but mere fragments, peering here and there through their shroud of Turkish whitewash. The monks of Mt. Athos are very ready to show the visitor a goodly number of his paintings; but their statements are contradictory and fabulous. Some of these paintings, however, appear to be very old and of a good style; among others — those of the Prôtaton at Karès. M. Bayet says that, "a Nativity of Christ and a Presentation of the

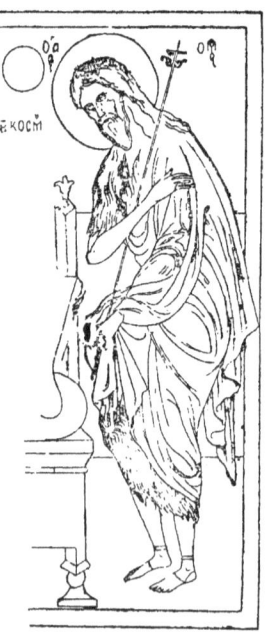

Virgin in the Temple are very remarkable and much superior to the ordinary paintings of Athos : they are natural, and of an exceedingly pure taste. The forms of the women are slender and elegant, their movements full of life; their proportions are correct, and a refined beauty illumines their regular features; other compositions show the same qualities. Unfortunately, all these paintings are threatened with impending ruin; the lines are becoming effaced, the colors are growing pale, the plaster is cracking and falling. One cannot but feel sad in seeing the almost unknown *chefs d'œuvre* of an art, in itself so little known, thus miserably disappear."[1]

To see such a manuscript as the Manual of Denys, is to desire to possess it. Didron made Joasaph an offer for his copy, but the latter naïvely replied that he could do absolutely nothing without it; in losing his Manual he would lose his art — his very hands and eyes. "Besides," he added, "you can find other copies of this manuscript

Fig. 5.

---

[1] Figures 1, 2, 3, 4. These figures are traced from chromo-lithographs in "*Les Arts Sumptuaires*," Haugard-Maugé : Paris, 1858. Ch. Louandre, in the accompanying text, states that they were drawn by D. Papety, in the convent of Agluá Labra, on Mt. Athos, and at the time of his writing were in the Louvre. The originals formed part of a vast fresco attributed by tradition to a monk named Pantelinos. [He surely means Panselinos.] They represent Saints Leontius, James-the-Persian, George, and Mercury. Whether by Panselinos or not, they evidently belong to the best period of Byzantine art, if one may judge from these copies. They are heroic, solemn, impressive creations, quietly harmonious in both line and color. Vitet says that they "are of the grandest character, proudly and simply posed, truly Christian, yet conserving withal a certain family likeness to the gods of the Parthenon."

Figure 5 is hereby given as a foil to the others. It is from a drawing by Paul Durand, published in Bayet's *Byzantine Art*. The date of this mural painting is not given.

at Karès; every atelier has a transcript of it, and, notwithstanding the decadence into which painting has fallen on our holy mountain, there are still at Karès four complete ateliers." And so Didron hastily betook himself to Karès, and straightway went to the atelier of one Father Agapios, an aged man, who painted chiefly for his amusement. Inasmuch as he received no more orders, and needed some ready money, he was on the point of selling his copy, but on reflection changed his mind, thinking that death might not be so very near, and hoping that he might receive other commissions; in which case he feared that his *confrères* would not allow a copy to be made from their manuscripts to replace a sold copy. He might, perhaps, wish to leave his Manual at his death to one of his assistants. " In vain I pressed him; he refused. To soften this refusal . . . he sold to M. Durand, for a very small sum, a beautiful little original drawing, in red crayon, of the Virgin with the child Jesus in her arms." Finally one of the painter-fathers offered to have a copy made from his manuscript for the zealous Didron. This after a time was made, and after still further time arrived in Paris, where it was translated by Paul Durand, Didron's fellow-traveler and most industrious draughtsman. To him we are indebted for many of the drawings made from Byzantine frescos with which we are familiar. The Manual, as before observed, was published in 1845. Its technical part seemed, at first, to be the most valuable. It proved to be the least so. " The recipes given were either imperfectly understood, or not understood at all; the substances mentioned apparently had no analogies with us, either on account of some real difference, or because no synonym could be found. One could neither be sure of the measures, nor of the proportions, nor of the terminology. I begged M. Mialle, Professor of Pharmacy to the Faculty of Medicine of Paris, kindly to study this part of the manuscript. . . . M. Mialle was soon obliged to give up the work, and he wrote to me as follows: ' I send you a few notes that I could conscientiously make; I could have easily augmented their number, had I not feared to pervert the truth; besides, this Manual seems to me very incomplete and difficult to consult.'" Though the first, or technical part, has but little value, the three remaining parts that treat of the Byzantine iconography are of "capital importance;" throwing considerable light even on the Latin and Gothic.

Coupled with Didron's personal observations on the staging — the technical part of the Manual has great interest for those who are concerned with mural painting. It is another phase of fresco, which will be developed in the next chapter.

Notwithstanding the rigidity of its traditions, several attempts have been made to Italianize Byzantine art. Bayet cites as an example the works of an artist named Nicephorus, who executed, in 1795, at Ivirôn, scenes from the Apocalypse. Without doubt, he had visited Venice. "The Byzantine painters of Athos used harsh tones for the face and flesh; at least, they made no effort to blend them. . . . It is by means of vigorous and dark lines that they indicate the contours, and their drawing is sharp and hard." Nicephorus, on the contrary, used delicate lines and graded his tones, introducing freely the Italian chiaro-oscuro. Another painting, dated 1814, was inspired by Rubens's "Descent from the Cross.' "For the last few years, however, the Russians, established in the great monasteries of Rossicon and Saint Anna, have been affecting a clumsy imitation of western works. Even in the Greek convents I have found in the painters' hands specimens of German engravings, from which they copy the compositions. These plagiarisms will kill Byzantine art. The artists who remain faithful to the ancient traditions lament this decadence; but, notwithstanding their good intents, they have no longer vigor enough to resurrect an art, long since on the wane. Some of them are still very skilful, but their personality is gone." Father Macarios, the strongest painter on the Mount, after Joasaph, regretfully said to Didron that "formerly the brushes were better, the quality of the colors excellent, hands were deft and hearts ardent; men painted slowly and thoughtfully, that they might produce beautiful works and gain paradise."

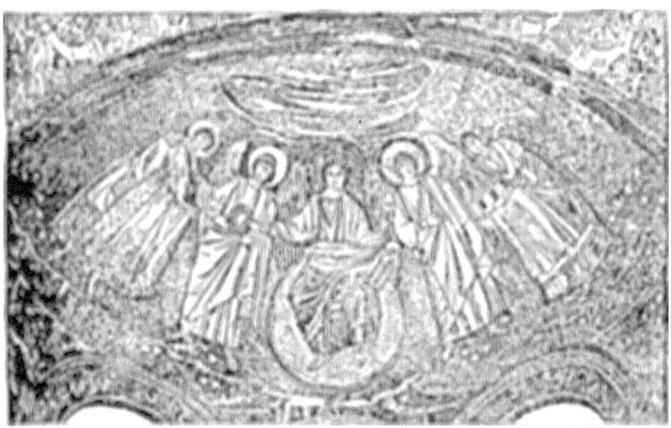

CHAPTER VIII.

BYZANTINE FRESCO.

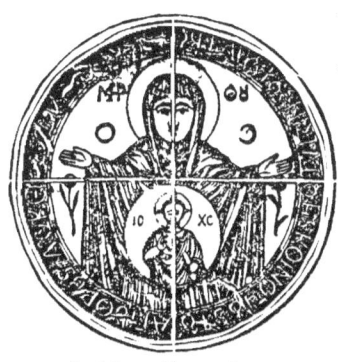

Seal from Mount Atnos.

EVERYTHING that throws light on the evolution of mural paintings of bygone days is important. To know what were the agencies that caused one form of artistic expression rather than another, has a didactic value; and as the time-test is the only true test of the stability of pictorial processes, it is necessary that we should know just what these processes were, in order that we may be practically edified. On such grounds several lengthy extracts from the Manual of Denys will be justified. The discovery of this manuscript was fully chronicled in the last chapter. Denys's Exordium is a beautiful and innocent orison to the Virgin:

"TO MARY,"

"MOTHER OF GOD AND FOREVER VIRGIN." [1]

"O thou, who art as resplendent as the sun, much-beloved and all-gracious Mother of God, Mary! Saint Luke, source of eloquence. most learned physician, perfect master, and thoroughly versed in all the sciences and all knowledge, having been sanctified by the precepts of the Gospel—which he wrote and preached aloud—wished to declare to the whole world the very holy love he bore thy gracious and divine Majesty. He judged, and rightly, too, that from his stores of science and spiritual riches he could make thee no worthier offering than the representation of thy admirable beauty, so full of charm, which he had contemplated with his very eyes. That holy and learned personage employed all the resources of color and golden mosaic to paint and faithfully limn thy image in

---

[1] Translated from Paul Durand's French version.

his pictures, according to the rules of his art.   I, too, in my turn — feeble imitator — desired to follow in the footsteps of that holy man, and devoted myself to religious painting, hoping that my powers would be in no wise inferior to my good will, in order to fulfil my duty to thy sacred person, thy venerable majesty, and thy wonderful magnificence.   But I confess that I deceived myself in this bold project, for neither my capacity nor my talents responded to my desires; nevertheless, I did not wish to abandon completely this fine scheme, nor to lose all the fruit of my labor; therefore I have dared to offer and place in thy hands, the explanation and interpretation of that art which I have acquired with the greatest care and most conscientious exactness, in order to form the very best method. For I am not unaware, O Virgin! that thou and the Creator of all things deign to accept everything that man can do; therefore I offer thee this work, which I have devoted to painters gifted by nature, to aid them in the beginnings of their art, and especially to indicate to them a good system. . . . Especially do I desire that thy dazzling and gracious image may be unceasingly reflected in the image of their souls, and may keep them pure to the end of all time; that it may raise the lowly, and encourage those who look upon and imitate that eternal model of beauty.   May I, too, by the help of thy blessed virtues, obtain the happiness of beholding thee face to face!"

Then follows an exhortation to the profession, beginning thus:

"TO ALL PAINTERS,"

"AND TO THOSE WHO, FOR THE LOVE OF KNOWLEDGE, MAY STUDY THIS BOOK."

" Knowing, O all ye disciples of laborious painters, that the Lord in his holy Gospel cursed him who buried his talent, saying unto him: 'Wicked and slothful servant, thou oughtest to have put my money to the exchangers, in order that at my coming I should have received mine own with usury.'   I myself feared to incur this malediction."

And thus the exhortation concludes:

" I laboriously and carefully collected all this material, assisted by my pupil, Master Cyrillus of Chio, who revised it most scrupulously. Pray, then, for us, all of you, that the Lord may deliver us from the fear of being condemned as wicked servants.

" The most unworthy of painters,   DENYS,
Monk of Fourna d'Agrapha."

"SEVERAL PRELIMINARY EXERCISES AND INSTRUCTIONS"

"FOR HIM WHO WISHES TO LEARN THE ART OF PAINTING."

"Whoever wishes to learn the science of painting, should begin by approaching it gradually, and by preparing himself for some time beforehand, drawing simply and without intermission, using no measure till he has acquired some experience and given proof of capacity. Then let him address to Jesus Christ the following prayer and supplication before an image of the Mother of God, the virgin Conductress, whilst a priest blesses him: 'King of Heaven, etc.' . . . Then, having traced on his head the sign of the cross, let him say with a loud voice: 'We pray the Lord — Lord Jesus Christ, our God! Thou who art endowed with a nature divine and limitless, . . . who hast illumined with thy Holy Spirit thy divine Apostle and Evangelist Luke, to the end that he might represent the beauty of thy most pure Mother, . . . thou, Divine Master of all that exists, enlighten and guide the soul, heart and mind of thy servant; so direct his hands that he may worthily and perfectly represent thy image, that of thy most blessed Mother, and those of all the Saints; for the glory, joy and adornment of thy most Holy Church. Pardon the sins of those who may venerate these images. . . . Amen!"

"INVITATORY AND CONCLUSION."

"After the prayer, the pupil must learn with exactness the proportions and types of figures; he must draw much; he must work unremittingly, and, with God's help, he will become skilful at the end of some time, as experience has demonstrated in the case of my own pupils. I have toiled with pleasure over this work, to the end that painters, my brothers in Jesus Christ, and all those who shall adopt this book, may labor for the glory of God. Let them pray to God for me. [Here is a note of warning to malevolent critics.] But if any wicked or envious one, should blame, in any way whatsoever, my disinterested enterprise, let him know that he will only wrong himself; for, as a certain author has said, envy is an evil thing but at least it has one advantage, that it devours the eyes and the heart of its possessor. God knows that I composed this work only to be useful, so far as lay in my power, to whoever intends to consecrate himself to this art, and to give himself up to it with the love of a zealous disciple, and eager above all things to possess the precepts of this book. It is to him that I address, in all friendship, the following counsel: Know well, O studious pupil, that if you wish to devote yourself to this science of painting, you must find an able master, who will teach you in a short time, provided he directs you according to our instructions. But if you only meet with a master whose teaching and art are imperfect, try to do as we did, that is, seek some originals by the celebrated Manuel Panselinos. Work from them a long while, exerting yourself till you have mastered the proportions and types of this painter's figures. . . . It is not only Saint Luke who is blessed, but all those who represent and try to show forth the miracles, the holy portraits of the Lord, of the Mother of God and of the other Saints; for this art of painting is agreeable to God, and is well-viewed by him. Thus all who work with care and piety receive from heaven grace and benedictions. But let all those who only strive for the love of money, and who are neither painstaking nor pious, reflect well before they die : they should remember with fear the chastisement of him whom they imitate — of Judas, expiating his crime in the torments of hell-fire, from which we hope to be redeemed by the merits of the Mother of God, of Saint Luke the Apostle, and of all the Saints. Amen."

It is interesting to compare the Italian Cennino's [1437] exordium with that of Denys. The former is instinct with piety, but of a less slavish kind. There is in it a recognition of personal inspiration, and an artistic freedom unknown to the Byzantine. The quotations that follow are from Mrs. Merrifield's translation.

"Chapter 1. Here begins the book on the art, made and composed by Cennino da Colle, in the reverence of God, and of the Virgin Mary, and of St. Eustachius, and of St. Francis, and of St. John the Baptist, and of St. Anthony of Padua, and generally of all the Saints of God, and in the reverence of Giotto, of Taddeo and of Agnolo, the master of Cennino, and for the utility, and good, and advantage of those who would obtain perfection in the arts."

" In the beginning the omnipotent God created the heaven and the earth, and, above all, animals and food; he created man and woman after his own image, endowing them with all the virtues. But Adam was tempted, and fell through the envy of Lucifer, who, with malice and subtlety, induced him to sin against the commandment of God (first Eve sinned, and then Adam); . . . Then Adam, knowing the sin he had committed, and being nobly endowed by God as the root and father of us all, discovered, by his wisdom and his necessi ties, how to live by his own manual exertions. And thus he began by digging, and Eve by spinning. Then followed many necessary arts, different each from the other, and each more scientific than the other; for they could not all be equally so. Now, the most worthy is Science; after which comes an art derived from Science, and dependent on the operations of the hand, and this is called Painting, for which we must be endowed with imagination and skill, to discover things (concealed under the shade of nature), and form with the hand, and present to the sight, that which did not before appear to exist. And well does it deserve to be placed in the rank next to Science, and to be crowned by Poetry, and for this reason, that the poet, by the help of science, becomes worthy, and free, and able to compose and bind together or not at pleasure. So to the painter liberty is given to compose a figure, either upright or sitting, or half-man, half-horse, as he pleases, according to his fancy. I have therefore undertaken to adorn this principal science with some jewels, for the benefit of all those persons who feel inclined to learn the various methods, and who worthily and without bashfulness set themselves about it; devoting to the before-mentioned science what little knowledge God has given me, as an unworthy member and servant of the art of painting." . . .

"It is the stimulus of a noble mind which induces persons to study these arts, made pleasing to them by the love of nature. The intellect delights in invention, and it is nature alone, and the impulse of a great mind which attracts them, without the guidance of a master. The delight they take in these studies induces them to seek a master, and they gladly dispose themselves to obey him, being in servitude, that they may carry their art to perfection. There are some who follow the arts from poverty and necessity; but those who pursue them from love of the art and true nobleness of mind are to be commended above all others."[1]

THE PROCESS.

As the difference between the recipes of Denys and those of the modern Athonite painters is but slight and unimportant, and inas-

---

[1] It would be interesting for further comparison, did space permit, to quote from the book of the Latin monk Theophilus, written probably in the early part of the eleventh century: "I, Theophilus, an humble priest, servant of the servants of God, unworthy of the name and profession of a monk," etc. He tells us that Greece was the painter of the world in his day, and France the glass-worker. He makes but one slight and questionable reference to fresco. Speaking of a pigment called prasinus, he says: "Its use is rather advantageous as a green color on a *fresh* wall." [Schedula Diversarum Artium.]

much as the former are at times somewhat obscure, and would be still more so were they not elucidated by the modern methods, I shall give Didron's account of what he saw on the staging in the Monastery of Esphigménou, supplementing it by a few excerpts from the manual.

"This, then, is the manner in which I saw a fresco painted . . . by Father Joasaph, his brother, a first pupil who was a deacon and prospective inheritor of the atelier, [a second pupil] and by two children from twelve to fifteen years."

"The porch of the church, or narthex, which was being painted at the time of our sojourn, had just been built. It was scaffolded to receive the frescos in the upper part of the vaults. Workmen, under the painter's direction, were preparing in the court-yard the lime for plastering the walls. As it is applied in two coats, there are two kinds of lime; the first, a sort of mortar, rather fine, is mixed with straw, chopped small, which gives it a yellowish color; cotton or flax is mixed with the second, which is less coarse in quality. The first coat is laid with the yellowish lime; it sticks to the wall better than the second. The second is white and fine, and, owing to the cotton, makes a pretty stiff paste; it is this coat that receives the painting."

"The workmen then bring the yellow lime, and lay a coat of it on the wall about one-fifth of an inch thick. Over this coat, several hours afterwards, a pellicle of fine white lime is spread. This second operation requires greater care than the first, and I saw Joasaph's brother, himself a painter, apply this second coat of lime. Three days are allowed for the evaporation of the humidity. If one should paint before the expiration of this time, the lime would soil the colors;[1] if after, the painting would not be solid, and would not penetrate the lime, which would be too hard, too dry to absorb the colors.[2] It is hardly necessary to state that the thermometric state of the atmosphere may curtail or protract the interval that must be allowed for the drying of the lime before beginning to paint."

"Before drawing, the master-painter smoothes the lime with a spatula; then by means of a string he determines the dimensions of his picture. In the field of this figure composition he measures with a compass the size of the different objects he wishes to represent. The compass that Father Joasaph used was merely a reed, bent double, split in the middle and controlled by a bit of wood that joined the legs and opened or shut them at will. One of the legs was pointed,

---

[1] The materials with which the lime is mixed might soil the colors. There is no reason why the lime should. Didron inexactly uses the same word, *chaux*, both for the lime itself and for the lime mixed with the straw or tow.

[2] In other words, the crust of carbonate of lime would have been formed.

the other was provided with a brush. It would be impossible to fashion a more simple, convenient and economical compass.

" The brush with which one of the legs is furnished is dipped in red ; with this color the picture is delicately outlined. The compass is chiefly used for the nimbi, the heads, and the circular parts ; the rest is drawn by the hand, provided only with a brush." In a little less than an hour Father Joasaph outlined a life-sized picture, representing Christ in the midst of his apostles, entirely from his head, and without a single alteration, as related in the preceding chapter. He began with the figure of Christ. " First he did the head, then the rest of the body. always descending. Afterwards he drew the first apostle to the right, then the first to the left, then the second to the right, then the second to the left, and so on symmetrically for the rest. The painter sketched with his hand raised, so to speak, and without a mahl-stick ; this instrument used by our painters, would indent the moist lime. But the hand, when it trembles or is fatigued, is rested on the wall itself."

The outlines of the figures are filled-in with black, relieved here and there with blue, but always in flat tints. This is done by an inferior painter who draws the draperies and ornaments on this ground. The nude parts are reserved for the master.[1] All the draperies are completed, and the nimbus is outlined, before the head, hands and feet are painted. The master then takes up the work and completes the head. He prepares the face with a blackish tint, and strengthens the outline with a still darker color. He paints two figures at a time, going ceaselessly from one to the other : a change that permits the absorption of the washes without loss of time. A preliminary wash modifies the black undertone, and other washes follow quickly, the last having more body. Now the painter takes advantage of the undertone for his shadows ; now he puts on his high lights ; now he colors the hair ; here he reddens the lips, there the cheeks ; then he colors the eyes, and so on to the end. The nimbus serves for a color-test. [It is not always easy to follow Didron in his details of the process. Being a layman he is at times obscure, but not in the essentials.] The two heads were finished in a trifle less than an hour. The same painter completed a " Conversion of St. Paul," a fresco 3 x 4 metres, containing twelve figures and three horses, in five days. " This painting was not a *chef d'œuvre* assuredly, but it was better than those that cost our painters of the second class, six or eight months' labor. I doubt even if our great painters charged

---

[1] Hence the many inequalities of execution in large works.

with a religious composition could do more uniformly well; there would
be higher qualities, but greater faults in their work than in the fresco
of Mount Athos." Prof. Franchi, of Siena, with all his Italian facility,
devoted nearly three hours to a delićately-moulded head in fresco.
Wilson says that Michael Angelo allowed an entire day for the heads
in the Sistine Chapel, which were very carefully finished.[1] Much less
time means much less modelling. Didron does not state how much the
Athonite painters modelled their figures; but from his notes and from
sundry implications in the manual, I should infer that the colors were
not merely laid on in flat tints — which were doubtless used at times
with great effect — but that the lights were broadly blended into the
shadows, and the features, hair and contours emphasized by a bold
and obvious use of the line. Elaborate modelling was suppressed, as
the short time required for painting two heads clearly proves.

The gold and silver for the nimbi and costumes are applied when
the plaster is thoroughly dry. The picture is then enriched with
the finest colors, "particularly with Venetian azure," and the ornaments that decorate the halos, stuffs, etc., are painted. The coarser
colors which were used for the figures must be thoroughly dry, so
as not to injure the more precious colors, nor the gold and silver.
This last paragraph is a paraphrase of Didron's longer one. In it the
secco process, so grudgingly used by the Italians, is recognizable;
only Didron has omitted one important element, the size, which is
always mixed with the colors for secco retouches. The Manual of
Denys, however, supplies the omission, for it gives explicit directions
for the use of azure "a secco." "Take bran, wash and rinse it.
Then let the water that has served for this purpose stand; afterwards boil it, and when it is cooked, you can mix it with the azure,
and paint the grounds. Others maintain that to make a water sufficiently glutinous, the bran must be boiled for a very long time and
then filtered. In either case, before using the azure, be sure that
the wall is very dry." A special artist, whose sole business it is to
letter, writes the name of the personage on the field of the nimbus,
or around it; and he traces on the scroll held by the figure the
consecrated legend recommended by the Manual. When this is
done "all is finished." Having summarily described the modern
Athonite or Byzantine process of fresco, I shall conclude with a few
supplementary extracts from the Manual, which will now be more
readily comprehended, and with several observations, deductions,
and comparisons suggested by Didron's researches.

---

[1] He probably means one long sitting; the balance of the day being spent in
the preparation of his cartoons, etc., perhaps.

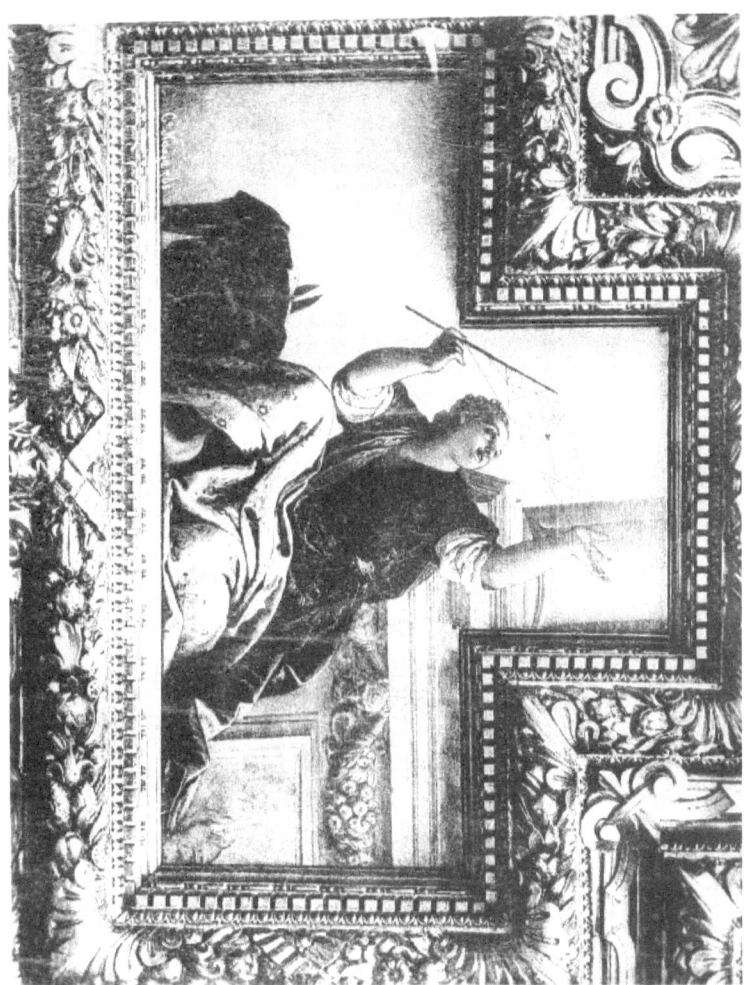

'Recompense' (Oil Painting) by Paolo Veronese, (1528 - 1588), Ceiling

1. " *How to purify lime.* When you wish to paint on walls, choose good lime ; let it be as fat as lard, and see that it contains no uncalcined stones. If it is poor and filled with such stones, make a trough of wood. Dig a pit of the necessary size, put the lime in the trough, and add water which must be stirred with a hoe till the lime appears to be thoroughly diluted. Pour this into a basket placed over the pit, which will arrest the stones. Then the milk of lime thus obtained must be let alone till it has coagulated and can be taken up with a shovel." [Further than this the Manual does not state how long the slaked lime should be kept].

2. " *How to mix lime with straw.* Take some of the purified lime and put it in a large trough. Choose fine straw without dust, mix it with the lime, stirring it with a mattock. If the lime is too thick, add water till it can be worked easily. Let it ferment two or three days, and you may then apply it."

3. " *How to mix lime with tow.* Choose the best lime you have prepared, put it in a small trough. Take tow well cleansed from all bark and well crushed; twist it as if to make a rope, and by means of a hatchet, chop it up as fine as you can; shake it well to allow the dirt to fall, and throw it into the trough, where you must mix it carefully with a shovel or mattock. You must take care to try and try again, till the lime does not crack on the wall. Let it ferment as you did the other, and you will thus have lime prepared with tow, to form the superficial coat " [on which the picture is painted].

It will be observed that Father Joasaph and his coadjutors substituted cotton or flax for tow.

4. " *How to plaster walls.* When you wish to paint a church you must begin with the highest and end with the lowest parts. . . . Then take water in a large vase, and throw it with a spoon against the wall to moisten it. . . . If the wall is brick, wet it five or six times, and give it a coat of lime, two fingers and more thick, that it may retain its humidity, and that you may profit by it. If the wall is stone, wet it only once or twice, and lay on much less lime, for the stone readily absorbs moisture, and does not dry. During the winter apply one coat in the evening, and a superficial one the following morning. In the fine season do whatever may be the most convenient, and having applied the last coat, level it well, let it acquire some consistence, then work."

5. *How to paint on walls.* The picture having been outlined, " polish the drapery [the plaster on which it is to be painted], and lay on an undertone. Try to finish very quickly what you have polished,

for, should you delay, there would be formed on the surface a crust that would not absorb the colors. Work the face in the same way; draw the outline with a pointed bone, and put on the flesh-color as promptly as possible before the formation of a crust, as we have said before."

6. " *How to prepare the white for wall-painting.*[1] Take some very old lime, try it on your tongue ; if it be neither bitter nor astringent, but insipid, like earth, then it is good. It is with this lime, well-selected and well-ground, that the white is prepared. If you cannot find such lime, take old plaster that has been painted, scrape off the colors entirely, and grind it on a marble slab ; throw it into a vase full of water, allow it to precipitate, and strain it. You will obtain white by this method. If you cannot find such plaster, you must cook lime, spread, dry, and finally grind it. Always take care to try if it be bitter or astringent; for such must be rejected, as in that case the crust would be formed too quickly, which would greatly impede the work ; if it is not bitter you can work without fear."

7. Though the *Manual* recommends a sort of palette, the modern Athonite painters use none. Each color is diluted in a cup or vase, and taken from it when needed with the same brush that has served for the other colors, having first been rinsed in water. The tints are tested on the field of the halos that are subsequently gilded. I have seen Japanese artists work in this way, without a palette ; and, like the painters of Mt. Athos, they designed from imagination with great rapidity — and at times upside down — without auxiliary sketches or models.

8. From the foregoing description it will be seen that the Byzantine resembles the old Roman method in one important respect, wherein both differ from the Italian. According to Vitruvius the ancient plaster was laid over a dry rough-cast in six succeeding coats — the first three lime and sand, the last three lime and marble-dust — and well beaten while all were wet. Thus a compact mass was formed that would retain its moisture for several days and permit the painter to work leisurely. The average thickness of this plaster was about 2.7 inches. While the Byzantine plaster was very much thinner — the modern about one-quarter of an inch, the mediæval somewhat thicker — the moisture was retained by mixing straw with the first coat of lime, and, while this was still wet, by applying a second coat of lime and tow (or cotton or flax). Three days elapsed before the painting was begun. Both Roman and Byzantine surfaces

---

[1] White lead is not suitable for frescos.

were polished, an operation that retarded the setting of the plaster by presenting a greater obstacle to the penetration of the carbonic acid. The Italians allowed the rough-cast to dry thoroughly before the *intonaco* was applied. This was about one-tenth of an inch thick and applied in two coats of lime and sand. Sand accelerates the setting and hurries the painter, who must finish before the crust is formed. But this disadvantage of sand as compared with straw, or tow, is more than offset by its superior binding qualities. The Italians retarded the setting of the plaster as much as they could by washing the lime in water containing carbonic acid, thus ridding it of some of its causticity, but not enough to compromise the final induration of the plaster. They were obliged to work surely and promptly, but not hurridly. The Byzantines could work more leisurely; but from certain observations recorded by Bayet, I should judge that their paintings were less durable. The Roman method *seems* the best from all points of view, but we must content ourselves with this doubt-implying word.

I reluctantly close this chapter without further quoting from the *Manual* — there is so much of interest in it. The poor monk who, for seventy francs copied the manuscript, concludes his work with this prayer : —

"GLORY TO GOD."

" Having finished, I said : Glory to thee, O Lord ! And I said again : Glory to thee, O my Lord ! And yet a third time I said : Glory to the God of the whole Universe ! "

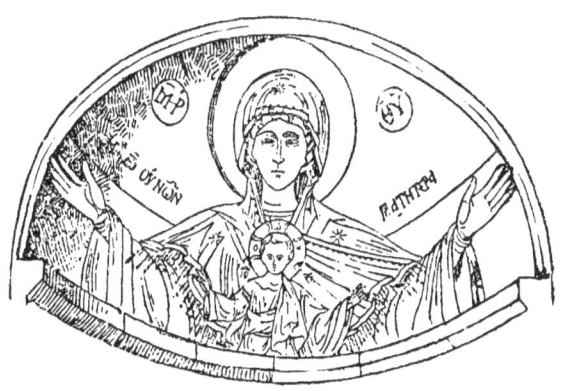

From Mt. Athos.

CHAPTER IX.

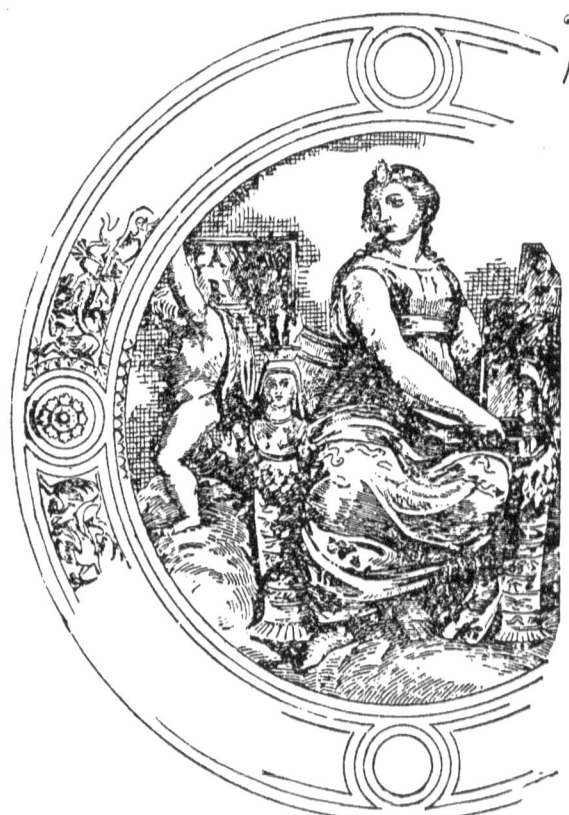

'Philosophy' by Raphael (Vatican), fresco.

A COMPARATIVE study of the various fresco methods would be utterly barren had it no practical import. Were it not pregnant with fruitful lessons, it would be well to leave such an examination to archæologists, and men of letters. I have been obliged now and then most unwillingly to trespass on their preserves. The history and criticism of art as understood to-day have too wide a range for a single mind. Its different epochs and various applications call for specialists. When the doctors have disagreed on subjects pertaining to my craft, I have merely applied a painter's instinct and experience to form a personal opinion. A great deal has been written about the Pompeian frescos, but none have written more convincingly than Donner and Cros, both painters.

Though, as I have before remarked, there is something positively marvelous about the preservation of these paintings, yet we are forced to
accept the conclusions of such practical men—at least for the present
—that they are frescos. Pompeii was buried to the depth of a little
more than sixteen feet by the eruption of Vesuvius (A. D., 79), the lower
thirteen feet being composed of pumice, the remainder of fine ashes.
Subsequent eruptions added their quota of volcanic matter, which
was finally covered by about two feet of vegetable mould, in all from
twenty to twenty-four feet. Though the water might quickly percolate through the ashes and sand, yet the paintings must have been
thoroughly drenched after every heavy rain, and we cannot attribute
their preservation to the nature of the soil; for any such hypothesis
would be shattered by the equally wonderful preservation of the Far-
nesina frescos (as I am told by a competent eye-witness) discovered
in 1879, that have lain imbedded for centuries in the deposits of the
"yellow" Tiber. The much older fragments of painted plaster recently found in the pre-historic palace of Tiryns have not fared so
well. Those on the walls which were most exposed to the action of
water filtering through the superjacent soil are the least well preserved. Other detached fragments found among the débris on the
floors are less injured, and of these the bits that were found face
downwards, and consequently more efficiently protected from the
effects of water, are the freshest of all. It is to be regretted that
Schliemann and Dörpfeld do not develop their reasons for believing
these paintings to be frescos — the one reason given being somewhat
insufficient—but accepting them to be such, we can readily account
for their comparative decay, when we are told that the walls were
first covered with clay, and then plastered [no analysis of the plastering, which was evidently rude, is given].[1] Light tends to fade
fresco colors, and the absence of it has undoubtedly contributed to
the preservation of ancient pictures. The paintings left *in situ* at
Pompeii, though many of them are protected from the rain by pro-
jections, are rapidly disappearing; but this is not a fair test, as

---

[1] At the Boston Museum of Fine Arts there are some fragments of colored wall-
plaster from Assos. The largest piece is about two inches thick, but does not
represent the entire thickness of the plaster. It is composed of three clearly-
defined coats. So much of the first has been detached that its original thickness
cannot be determined. Curiously enough it is made of lime and chopped straw,
as was recommended hundreds of years later by the monk Denys, and as practised to-day by the Athonite frescoers. The second coat is a mixture of coarse
sand and lime, grayish in tone. It is six-tenths of an inch thick. The third, or
superficial coat, two-tenths of an inch thick, is composed of lime and a finer
quality of sand, and is much whiter than the preceding coat. On this third coat
is spread a color resembling vermilion, pale and dirty when dry, but brilliant
and fresh when wet. It is applied *a buon-fresco*. The plaster is rather friable.

it is well known that fresco can neither withstand the attacks of sun nor atmospheric corrosion. Those that were removed to the Museum at Naples have not deteriorated. The durability of the ancient frescos must be chiefly ascribed to the excellence of the plastering; and their relative degree of soundness is apparently in direct ratio to its solidity. This is further corroborated by the relative condition of the Italian Renaissance frescos. Though these may be superior artistically to extant ancient frescos, they have deteriorated more rapidly. Neither Donner nor Cros find any signs of pouncing or point-tracing in the mural figure work of the ancients, a fact that accounts for the many faulty proportions. The Pompeian painters worked freely and drew carelessly, notwithstanding the mechanical excellence of their methods. In this respect they resembled the Byzantine artists who also drew from inspiration without preparatory cartoons. But the latter carefully established the proportions of their figures with the compass, attempted much less, and were thoroughly versed in conventional expression. There is a great difference in the present condition of the Italian frescos. Their decay is not proportional to their years. Some of the earliest by Giotto [1276–1337] and his school are much sounder than others painted several centuries later. It must not be supposed that all old plaster is good. Croaking fanatics too frequently fall into such errors. As a matter of fact the Italians were careless plasterers. They took care that the lime was thoroughly slaked—an example we might follow with profit—but they often applied it to the wall in the rudest fashion, as uneven and broken surfaces testify. The Venetians were notably negligent in this respect, much more so than the Tuscans, who were not always over-careful. There are instances where the former applied the *intonaco*, or painting-coat, directly to the wall, without the interposition of a preparatory rough coat (*arriccio*) : of course such plaster and the paintings thereon were short-lived. The ancients did not economize the plasterer's labor, and as a result their paintings have stood admirably. If we may judge from the tone of Cennini's book, Giotto and his followers were painstaking and lavish of labor. The relative soundness of their work corroborates this view. Moreover the thinly-painted frescos have generally outlived those painted with more body. In some instances frescos have perished because they were not entirely *buon-fresco*, but a compound of fresco and distemper. In the Loggie of the Vatican, Giovanni da Udine (1494–1564), pretended to imitate the plastering of the ancients, as revealed by the frescos in the recently-discovered Baths of Titus; but his failure to comply with all their laborious conditions compromised his paintings. Many instances of sound Renaissance fresco may be found at Siena : among others those in the library of the cathedral by Pinturicchio (1454–1513), which according to my note-book are "wonderfully well-preserved." With us, apparently, all the ingredients of plaster are equal, perhaps superior, to those of bygone times, but undue haste curtails the length of time necessary for slaking the lime, and economizes the care and labor requisite for a stanch wall surface. The more one consults the authorities on plaster and cements, the more one is bewildered. They are plethoric with sound advice and sound combinations, which are anything but sound in practice, why, I am not prepared to say. But the unpleasant fact remains that our plaster, which is the only possible ground for fresco, is wretched. It seems to me as though the fresco process might be improved, were some competent chemist to devote himself to the problem. I have lately made a few insufficient experiments, in the hopes of elucidating much that is mysterious, but without any trustworthy results. It was impossible among other difficulties to find lime that had been slaked a year. There is a great deal to be explained about the nature and formation of the crust, the causticity of the lime, the changes it undergoes by keeping, etc., that can only be explained by a chemist.

I can hardly forgive a well-known and usually sympathetic English writer on art for his depressing and unappreciative estimate of fresco, and for his inadequate review of mural painting in general. "Fresco," he says, "ought to be looked upon as a slight and cheap art, to be done without much effort, and without any attempt at elaborate finish." [1] The impressive, beautiful and *highly-finished* frescos of Raphael and Michael Angelo, not to mention others, deemed by many the grandest works of art ever produced, though this is a matter of opinion, sufficiently refute such an unfortunate statement, which, if made by a less reputable personage, would be suffered to pass unnoticed.[2] Many of my readers are doubtless aware of the

---

[1] The term "finish" should not be confounded with elaboration. The best Italian frescos were thoroughly finished, though not elaborate. Elaboration is possible in fresco, but it is not wanted.

[2] To illustrate the impressiveness of Michael Angelo's frescos, injured as they are by time and more particularly by man, I quote a few red-hot notes, jotted down in 1878, after one of my periodical visits to the Sistine Chapel. It is scarcely necessary to apologize for their informality. "Capital place to compare the genius of Michael Angelo with that of his immediate predecessors. His vault completely kills all below it; and the longer one looks the more the killing process goes on. Indeed I found it very difficult to pay any attention to the Pre-Raphaelites. Often as I go to the chapel, I am always captivated by some new beauty. To-day by the delightful tone of the vault. It is infinitely more decorative than the frescos on the walls by the precursors, notwithstand-

efforts made to revive mural painting in England about 1841. The attempts at *buon-fresco* were failures.[1] The English (delightful poets!) have always been singularly deficient in those masterly technical powers—the birthright of the Latin races—which are essential to the execution of imposing mural compositions; though here and there a foreign-trained painter may have proved himself an exception to the rule. Fresco is no medium for the feeble, or for those who cultivate a certain dilettanteism of execution. It exacts a virile and spontaneous handling, and experience allied with consummate skill. It is not a tentative or hap-hazard art, if the cartoons are properly prepared, and provided the painter knows his business. Its very limitations are in a way advantageous, and lend strength and fire, just as the limitations imposed by time and weather stimulate the sketcher; with this difference in favor of the mural painter, that his drawing and color have been prepared beforehand. He may paint much or little at a sitting, only that much or little must be completed. It is of course a disadvantage to paint piece-meal, but then all mural painting has to be conducted on a piece-meal basis, though less than in *buon-fresco.* Because there may be a lack of practitioners, it would be unjust and ill-advised to condemn and discard a noble art, and that not a lost one; for I have seen charming frescos in Italy executed by contemporaries, less grand in conception than those of the Renaissance, but apparently as well painted. A great deal was said and written at the time about the unsuitability of fresco to "British

---

ing their profuse use of gold. To-day, too, I was overcome by the grand 'Creation of the Sun and Moon,' massive, eternal figures moving like the whirlwind. I noted also a fine, pensive, seated female figure in the 'History of the Virgin.' The Signorellis, Botticellis, etc., seem like pigmies as compared with Buonarroti. Yet they are interesting. The serried ranks of Ghirlandajo; the stiff and clumsy attempts of Botticelli to express action, the glimmerings of the antique in Signorelli, the importance of space recognized by Perugino," and so on.

Symonds in his *Renaissance* (1879), most sympathetically apprehends and describes the beauty, nobility and poetry of this inspired vault. "There is no luxury of decorative art, no gold, no paint-box of vermilion or emerald green, has been lavished here. Sombre and aerial, like shapes condensed from vapor, or dreams begotten by Ixion upon mists of eve or dawn, the phantoms evoked by the sculptor throng that space. . . . The grace of coloring, realized in some of those youthful and athletic forms is such as no copy can represent. Every posture of beauty and of strength, simple or strained, that it is possible for men to assume has been depicted here. Yet the whole is governed by a strict sense of sobriety. The restlessness of Correggio, the violent attitudinizing of Tintoretto, belong alike to another and less noble spirit. To speak adequately of these form-poems would be quite impossible."

[1] One of the artists who "had nearly been driven mad by the trouble and annoyance which the old system of fresco caused him," and who abandoned it for another process, in a letter addressed to Lord Elcho, says that "Fresco may do admirably well where a slight bravura sort of art is required, but this should be the *passe-temps* for those whose aim is very moderate and whose employers are easily satisfied. Fresco has had a fair trial here, and is to give way before something a thousand times better in every way." [!!!]

genius," and to British climate. The truth is that British genius was
unsuited to *buon-fresco*. Several foreigners have since executed
successful, and thus far, durable frescos in London. The esteem in
which fresco was held by the painters of the fifteenth century may

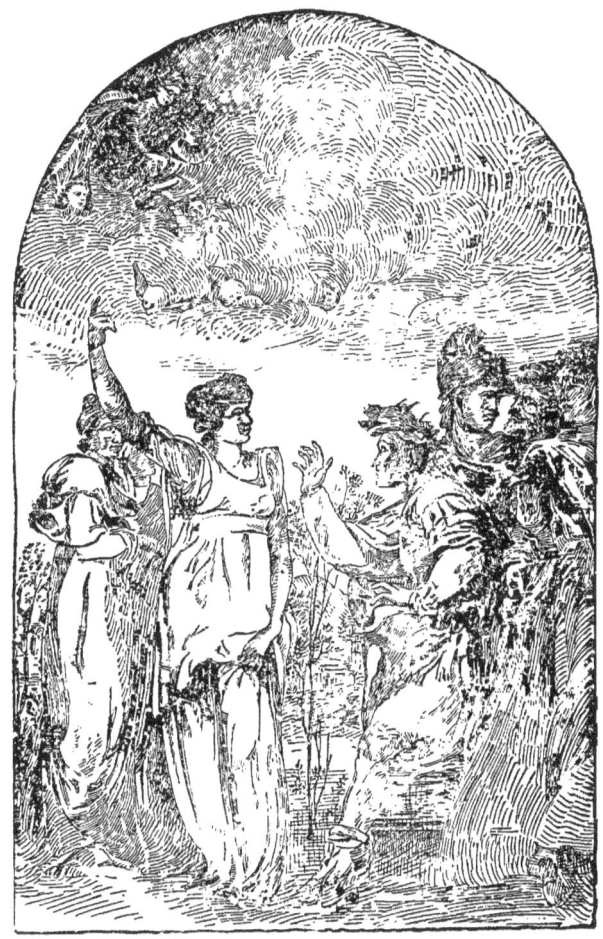

'Augustus and the Sibyl,' by Baldassare Peruzzi [1481-1536]. Ch. of Fonte Giusta,
Siena, (fresco).

be gathered from the recently-published letter of Francesco della
Cossa to Francesco Gonzaga.

"Much honored prince; very noble lord. . . . It seemed to me
strange that my work should be paid at the same rate as that of the
others, who have neither spent the time nor the money that I have.
I tell you this, my lord, because I have always painted in fresco,

which, as every master of art knows, *is one of the most advantageous
and best methods of working.* . . .

> "Your noble lordship's most humble servant,"
>
> "FRANCESCO DELLA COSSA."[1]

The somewhat restricted palette imposed by fresco is very much
in its favor, and yet it is far from meagre, as has been already shown.
Its light, simple, quiet tones are eminently adapted to mural decoration, which ought not to affect realistic relief. It gives a dead surface, which is the *sine qua non* of wall pictures. All dark, dead-
colors are less deep, or black, than the same colors when varnished.
But as gloss and depth of tone are just what it is necessary to avoid
in mural painting, it is an advantage to be deprived of them.[2]
Though both are void of gloss, there is a difference of tone between
fresco and distemper. The former seems lively and transparent
when compared with the deadness and opacity of the latter, though
by no means thin. On a bit of plaster before me there is some yellow ochre applied when the plaster was wet, in the fresco manner.
By the side of it is more of the same pigment applied to the same
plaster when dry. The difference of tone between the two is considerable, the former being yellower and brighter than the latter. Moreover, "*alla prima*" methods — final methods without retouchings —
naturally yield fresher and franker tones than more laborious methods,
unless the painter applies the latter with great precision, and as
nearly "*alla prima*" as possible.

Fresco may be employed for humbler purposes than figure compositions. There is probably no more perishable and common medium
than distemper ("kalsomine" is the high-sounding name now in
vogue). Distemper, as used by the ancient and mediæval painters
for their wall and easel pictures, frequently protected by a coat of
wax, varnish or oil, was a very different thing from the unprotected
distemper used to-day for tinting walls or ceilings, and too frequently
for decorating them. As the colors are soluble in water, it is ruined
by contact with moisture, either on its face or from behind. It is
liable to peel if applied in more than one coat, or with too much
size, and is easily defaced by friction. A slight abrasion exposes the
underlying plaster. Altogether it is "poor stuff." A plain tone,
ornamented, if desired, with a simple pattern that would not require
more than a day for its transference to the side of a room or space to

---

[1] "FERRARA, 25 March, 1470." From the French translation in the *Gazette des
Beaux Arts*, December, 18·5.

[2] An exception to this rule will be noted in chapter X.

be decorated, might be applied to the wet plaster without the necessity of the troublesome joinings demanded by elaborate ornament. What could be simpler? Water is the only medium. The colors must be suitable to fresco, and these are the cheapest and best. While for important works it is essential to keep the lime for at least a year, as no risk should be incurred, it is probable that a month, or even less, would suffice for inexpensive flat tones, though of course the longer the better. Walls tinted in this way would be more pleasing and durable than with the lifeless "kalsomine." They would not, perhaps, bear the friction of oil-painted walls, but would be less likely to change color, and would, moreover, be far cheaper. That the required tone must be determined before the plastering is finished might be deemed an objection; though to some people any imaginative brain-work is irksome. A more serious difficulty would be to protect the frescoed walls from the subsequent operations of careless workmen. The best of all plans for tinting plaster walls is to mix the pigments with the plaster before its application, which guarantees the colors from disfigurements caused by blows or abrasions. Very deep lines cannot be obtained in this way, for the plaster with which the pigments are to be mixed must be regarded as a white. The pattern, of any color, could be added while the plaster is still wet. It is not possible to spread a perfectly flat tone over large surfaces in this way, for the differences in handling of the several workmen cause differences in tone, though all use the same plaster. As walls are rarely void of ornament, either fixed or movable, such inequalities would not be objectionable. But it is almost impossible to make the average house-painter understand that the very qualities he is working for with might and main are precisely those that are most offensive to the artist, and one of these is a dreary, dead, and even flatness.

When the relative merits of fresco and wax-painting are compared, the present state of things must be taken into consideration. In the choice of a medium the painter is guided by actualities rather than by potentialities. If for very cogent reasons he is forced rather than persuaded into the use of the wax medium, let us not on that account slight a noble and beautiful method. Without experience fresco is a most difficult process; but as to that, all processes are difficult. though fresco is a little more so than the others at first. A demand for frescos would certainly create the supply. Any painter gifted with the decorative qualities and trained to mural work could master the perplexities of fresco in a few months. What

these decorative qualities are will be indicated in the final paper.
However skilful a painter may be in other departments, unless he is
gifted with them by nature, and has developed them by training, he
should never touch the wall. It is to be hoped that architects — for,
owing to its nature, the initiative must be taken by the architects —
may some day be pleased to utilize a process so thoroughly architectural as fresco.

There are obviously many places, especially in completed buildings, where the nature of the ground would preclude the use of
"*buon fresco*," unplastered stone, for example, cement, wood, or any
surface where the use of plaster might not be desirable. Ordinary
lath and plaster, unless specially prepared, would be a poor recipient
for fresco. It was shown in Chaptor IV, that, with proper precautions,
wax-painting might be applied to any surface: to stone, by first
treating it to a hydrofuge; to plaster, by saturating it with the
medium. Even when the plaster has cracked, or is disposed to crack,
wax-painting is perfectly safe, if canvas be applied to the wall in the
manner already described. This will bridge over the existing cracks
and prevent their future development — always provided the space
to be decorated is not very large, since expense might otherwise preclude its use. But where the conditions are favorable, and expense is
not an object, the application of canvas is recommended as the best
and safest ground. It would be wearisome to recapitulate the durable qualities of wax-painting. They have been fully developed
elsewhere. Its simplicity, too, has been proved. In certain respects
it is more simple than fresco, in others, less so; it is quite as simple
as oil, and a good deal simpler than "spirit-fresco." Simplicity is of
the greatest importance to the painter, whose means of expression
should be facile if he ever hopes to be eloquent. In common with
fresco, wax-painting has light, airy tones, and a dead surface. It
may be applied semi-transparently, or with the impasto of oil-painting, which it resembles in technique, though free from its decorative
defects. If has none of the lifelessness or opacity of distemper.
As any color may be mixed with the wax medium its palette is very
extended. It has this advantage over fresco, that the first painting
is not necessarily a final operation. While it may be used *alla prima*
— and the more so the better, seeing that *alla prima* handling has
great merits, and that repaintings are liable to engender slovenliness
— it may also be retouched indefinitely, without injury to its quality
or durability, as in *buon fresco*, or without fear of cracks, as in oil.
Apparently, wax-painting is the most durable of all pictorial mural
processes.

FRESCO—SECCO.

The following garbled extract from Sarsfield Taylor will adequately describe this offshoot from *buon fresco :* " After the general plastering of the wall intended for this process has been finished, and a superior coat of pure lime and sand has been laid over the surface, the whole is then allowed to dry thoroughly. When this wall is found to be in a perfectly dry state, the surface, so far as may be required, is rubbed with pumice-stone, and late on the day previous to that on which the painting is to be commenced the plaster must be carefully washed with water into which a small portion of lime has been infused ; next morning the wall must again be washed. After this is completed the cartoon is fastened up, and the outline being pounced, the artist commences his work. The colors used in this method are similar to those employed in true fresco ; they are mixed in the same way with water, and the white pigment is lime."

" If, as the operation goes on, the wall should become too dry, a syringe, pierced with many fine holes, is used to moisten it. Painting done in this way will bear washing as well as real fresco, and is equally durable. As regards mere matters of ornament, it is a more certain and ready mode of working than solid fresco ; for, owing to the complicated forms of ornaments, it is impossible, in the latter art, to make the joinings at the proper outlines ; therefore, merely decorated walls in fresco never are satisfactory to the eye of taste, and this defect is very evident in the Loggia of the Vatican. Another great advantage *fresco-secco* has over *fresco-buono* is, that the former may be quitted and taken up again at any point. We have now shown all its advantages. On the other hand we are bound to say that, except where merely ornamental painting is concerned, it is in every other respect a very inferior art to real fresco ; for paintings in secco are always opaque and heavy in their character, differing quite in this essential point from true fresco, which is lightsome, and has much clearness of tone, often a fine transparency. *Fresco-secco,* therefore, cannot be placed in the same elevated ranks as *fresco-buono;* indeed, with few exceptions, it has always been in the hands of inferior masters of the later Italian schools, and none of the works of these men in this style have any high reputation. There appears, however, to be an important difference in the durability of the German *fresco-secco* and the Italian of the present day ; the former will bear washing, the Italian *fresco-secco* of the present time will wash out. both of which useful facts Professor Wilson ascertained at Munich and Genoa."

Having had no personal experience with *fresco-secco*, I give the above for what it is worth, though much of it is incomprehensible.

It seems too good to be true. I have made several experiments in my studio with *fresco-secco*, following the above directions, but without the given results. In every case the color thus applied was washed off by rubbing it with a bristle brush filled with water, though it adhered far more tenaciously than the same color dissolved in pure water and applied to dry plaster. It seems impossible that *fresco-secco* should resist water as effectively as *buon fresco*. The latter is protected by a thin but strong crust of carbonate of lime, the product of the wet plaster (sand and hydrate of lime) and the air, while the former would only be protected by the very feeble crust of carbonate of lime formed by the air and the weak infusion of lime-water with which the dry plaster (sand and carbonate of lime) has been soaked. The color might be more deeply imbibed by plaster that has been saturated with water than by dry plaster, but its surface would be none the less soluble in water. As to the " impossibility " of adapting *buon fresco* to the " complicated forms of ornament " I can merely say that I have seen very elaborate ornament executed in this manner. Though *fresco-secco* is in every way inferior to real fresco, it might profitably be used for ornament instead of tempera, especially on ceilings and in places that are not exposed to friction. No process could be simpler or cheaper.

CHAPTER X.

OIL-PAINTING.

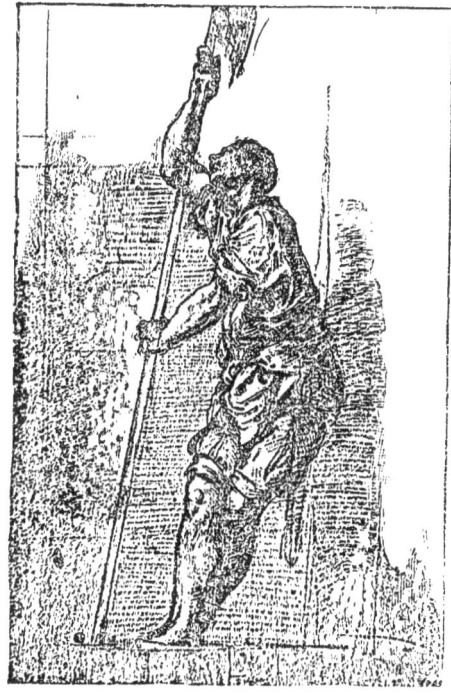

From a Drawing by Titian.

OIL painting is too well known and widely practised to call for any technical description. The object of these chapters has been to consider the adaptability of the different processes to mural painting, rather than to describe their technics. If unfamiliarity with some of them has necessitated a detailed technical exposition, it has been made with a view to estimate their decorative capabilities. From divers allusions dropped here and there in the preceding papers it must have been inferred that oil is not a suitable vehicle for mural paintings. In order to understand why not, it will be necessary to make a few trite chemical statements.

Oil is composed of an oil acid linked with glycerine ether; from it both glycerine and soap can be made.

Soap is a compound of an oil acid linked with alkalies or oxides, as potash, soda, lead, zinc, iron, lime, etc. In making, the glycerine ether of the oil, with which the alkali or oxide is mixed, is set free. Some soaps, such as toilet soaps, are soluble in water — castile soap, for instance, which is made from olive oil and soda. Other soaps are insolu

ble, such as lead, zinc, or iron soaps, which include the pigments
made by the chemical union of white lead, zinc, or iron oxides with
linseed oil. Pigments are said to be more or less durable according to
their soap-making powers in combination with linseed oil. Both red
lead and white lead are strong soap-makers; zinc white, iron-ore
paint, umber, yellow ochre and others are less so; while such colors
as ivory black, vermilion, madder lake, Prussian blue, etc., do not
combine chemically at all with linseed oil, or, in other words, they
are not soap-makers.

Those pigments that have the strongest chemical affinity for linseed oil — the strongest soap-makers — dry and harden the most rapidly; those that have but a feeble affinity for it, or none at all, must
be mixed with a drier — such as manganese or litharge — which has
a strong affinity for it. While it seems to be certain that soap-making,
either by the pigment itself with linseed oil, or by means of a drier,
improves the solidity and durability of paint — unless it be rendered
brittle by an excess of the drier — it is equally certain that all soap-
making has a tendency to redden or yellow. Condit says of white
lead that "it is a paint and not a whitewash only, because about one-
fourth of the lead unites with the oil to form a soap . . . but it has
such a tendency to redden that white lead made by a process (one of
Gruneburg's processes) producing a large quantity of this part of white
lead which unites with the oil would turn yellow in an hour after mixture as a paint." In another place he says: "Strong soaps have
more tendency to redden than weak soaps, when simply exposed to
the air. . . . It is plain why lead changes color more than zinc—it contains more soap. Again, it is plain that boiled oil [with driers], which
contains much oxy-linseed-oil-acid and much soap, will darken sooner
and more completely than raw oil. To avoid change of color we
must avoid that which most quickly dries and hardens the paint
— soap. Even manganese driers with zinc white will yellow the
paint. It is important, therefore, for all these reasons, to use as
little oil as possible in interior house-painting with white colors." It
is also important to use zinc white rather than white lead for inside
work. The cure for this change of color is sunlight.

It has already been shown, in the chapter on *buon fresco*, that
caustic lime forbids the use of many colors that are frequently used
in oil painting. Caustic lime, moreover, combines with oil to make a
soap. For these reasons oil painting cannot be used on fresh plaster. But even when the plaster is thoroughly dry, the walls should
first be protected with several coats of oil paint, if they are to re-

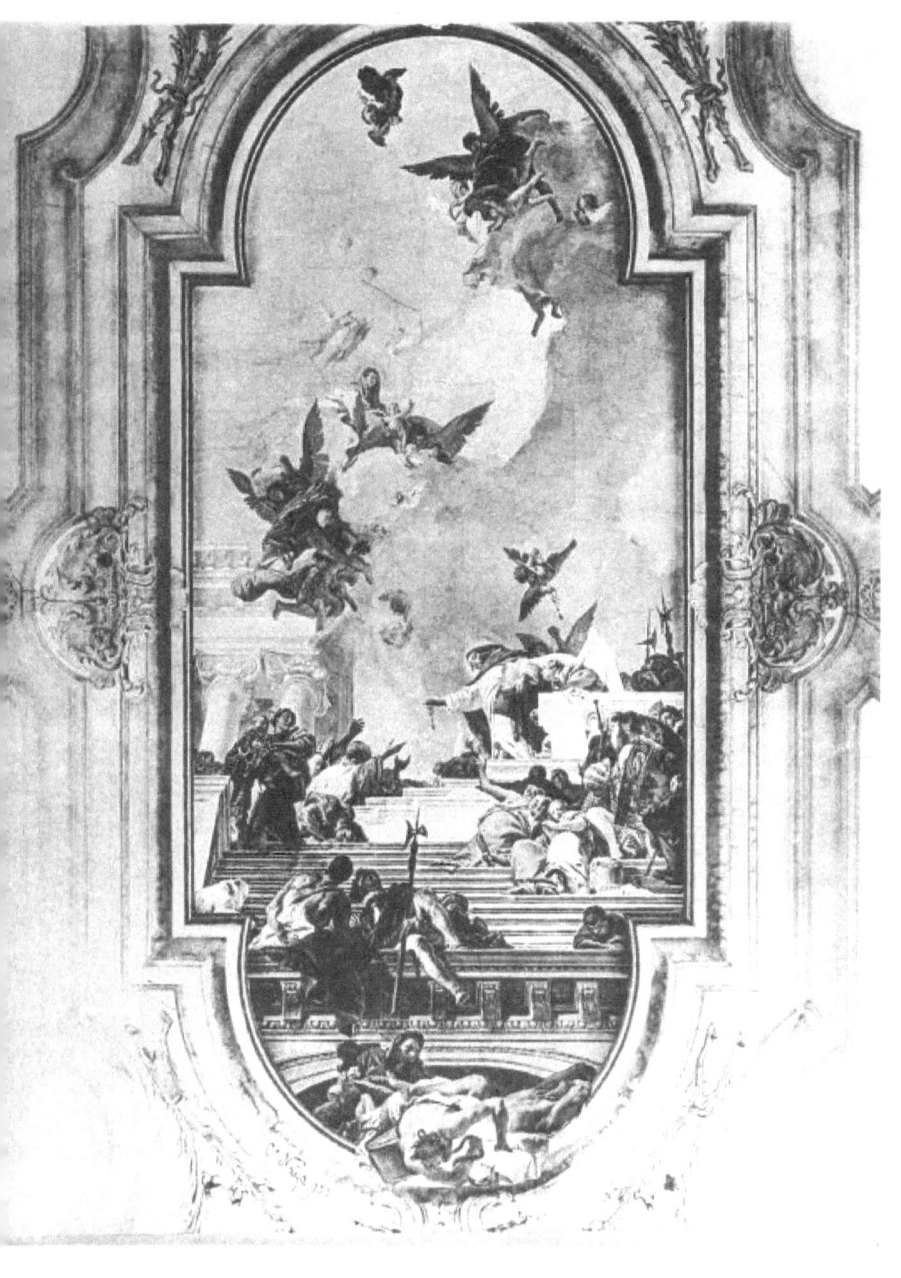

Ceiling in Church of S. Maria del Rosario, Venice (Fresco) by Tiepolo.
(Giovanni Battista, 1697-1770)

ceive oil pictures; for even dry plaster (carbonate of lime, or chalk, and sand) changes some pigments, especially if the latter are exposed to dampness, which is almost inevitable. "All organic colors may be affected. Chalk in white lead or zinc white easily produces a yellowish white when mixed with oil. In addition to these changes, oil is saponified by wet chalk, which quickly becomes yellowish in the absence of sunlight. All oil-painted walls change color, and picture-frames hung on wet walls leave their photographs in reddish-yellow."[1] It is very obvious, then, that mural paintings in oil must never come in contact with plastered walls, but should either rest on several intervening coats of oil paint, or, better still, on a canvas ground fastened to the wall by the white lead process.

The yellowing of oil is not caused by soap-making alone; it is also caused by want of sunlight. The less light there is, the yellower and darker oil-mixed pigments grow with time. Every artist must have noticed how oil sketches yellow or darken in a portfolio. As usual the cure is sunlight. Here are one or two corroborative extracts by Condit. Dr. Liebreich says that "the oil should in all colors be reduced to a minimum, and under no form should more of it be introduced into a picture than absolutely necessary." "The changes in white lead and linseed oil are rapid and inevitable. A foul, tawny yellow quickly overspreads the work, utterly destructive of delicacy and freshness." (*Quarterly Review*.)

Certain pigments common in oil-painting, such as white lead, chrome and Naples yellow, etc., are liable to be blackened by sulphuretted-hydrogen gas, white lead in particular. As many inaccurate ideas are apparently entertained as to the influence of sulphur gases on pigments, it will be well to state the case accurately. Sulphuretted hydrogen is the product of sewage, or of animal and vegetable decomposition. A stream of this gas turned on dry white-lead paint will change it to a deep umber.[2] Professor Norton says that the "white lead blackened by sulphuretted hydrogen will bleach by the action of sunlight easily, until the oil has become perfectly hard, a process which takes several weeks. After the hardening this bleaching action is slow, but it is probable that it always continues to a greater or less extent. It is thought to be due to the ozone in the air." Fresh paint blackened by sulphuretted hydrogen bleaches rapidly, even in diffused daylight.

---

[1] *Painting and Painters' Materials*. Charles L. Condit and Jacob Scheller: New York, 1883. An excellent, practical book, which treats at length of varnishes, oils and pigments, and their reciprocal relations.
[2] It was shown in chapter V, that the same stream turned on oil-white lead mixed with the wax medium had no blackening influence.

One naturally asks, " How much danger from blackening by this gas do paintings undergo?" Perhaps less than pessimists imagine. The white-lead paint of whole neighborhoods has been blackened by sewage gas. It has also been blackened to a considerable extent in cer-

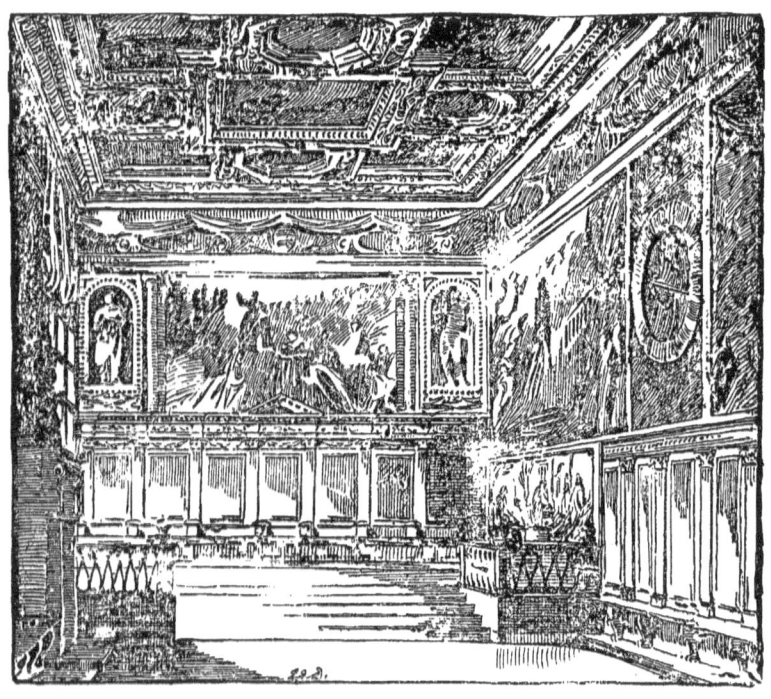

Sala del Collegio, Ducal Palace, Venice.

tain manufacturing districts. Bath-rooms, too, have suffered in this respect. There would, however, be no great danger from it in well-drained houses. It must be present in very appreciable quantities to blacken paint. Much that is erroneous has been written about the discoloration of pigments by the chemical action of certain gases, the product of burning illuminating-gas. These are sulphurous and sulphuric acid gases — the latter containing more oxygen. But neither blackens lead, though they both attack bronze.[1] Sulphuretted hydrogen in very small quantities escapes combustion, but hardly enough of

---

[1] In answer to a question, Prof. Norton writes that "Gold would not be affected by the acids. I have heard it said that it tarnishes after a term of years in such a position [over a gas-light]. The side of the State-House [Boston] dome next the chimney is tarnished, as probably you are aware. Exactly why gold tarnishes in such a position I am unable to say. Probably from some sulphuretted hydrogen present in the gas which escapes the combustion."

With regard to the moisture generated by the combustion of illuminating

it to blacken the pigments. What does very sensibly blacken pigments over a gas-jet is the carbon of the smoke, as every one must have observed. If the colors are thoroughly dry, the carbon can easily be removed : if not, it adheres tenaciously. Probably the heat of the gas often softens pigments mixed with oils or resins, thus affording the carbon a secure lodgment. There is also sulphurous acid and sulphuric acid in all chimney-smoke, and very probably a little un-consumed sulphuretted hydrogen. But it is the latter that blackens. The paintings by Baudry, in the *foyer* of the Opera at Paris were covered with a layer of carbon a few months after the opening of the building. It was feared that they were seriously compromised. Recently the gas has been replaced by electricity, the pictures have been cleaned, and, if we may credit the rather unscientific accounts, they are as fresh as when first painted. The discoloration of lead pigments by sulphuretted hydrogen can, to a certain extent, be re-moved by the action of oxidizing agents, such as hydrogen peroxide, which, acting on the lead sulphide (black), converts it into (white) lead sulphate. It is therefore evident that white lead should be replaced whenever it is possible — and certainly for the finishing coats — by zinc white, which "is the only perfect white color," not being affected by sulphuretted hydrogen, nor yellowing, to any great ex-tent, the oil with which it is mixed.

I have endeavored to show, as concisely as possible, why it is that oil paintings darken with age. Any one, probably, by a slight effort of the memory can corroborate this fact. I never remember to have seen an old oil picture that had not grown dark. Under cer-tain circumstances, of an exceptional nature, which will be noted later, a slight darkening, or rather mellowing, may not be objection-able; on the contrary, it may even be advantageous; but where a light, decorative effect is intended, and especially when the surround-ing tones are white or delicate in color, and have not proportionately mellowed, the effect is very discordant. Not unfrequently oil paint-ings are inserted in the panels of a room — a salon or boudoir, for instance, treated in white and gold. Within a very short time, per-haps at the outset, they will seem dark and heavy, as compared with the gleaming white (usually zinc white, turpentine, and just enough oil to bind it) of the woodwork. Sometimes this is repainted after a lapse of years, while the pictures, of course, remain untouched, and

gas, and its possible injury to mural paintings, he says: "When gas is burned, all the hydrogen in the gas, both free and combined with carbon, is turned to water. A very considerable amount of water would thus be formed. If the room were suddenly cooled, moisture might gather on the walls to a slight extent. On the other hand, the burning of gas always raises the temperature."

this operation may be repeated, till the pictures look like black spots in comparison. In rooms of this description either the same mellowing ingredients should be used for the woodwork that are used in the oil pictures — which would annul the desired effect — or the paintings

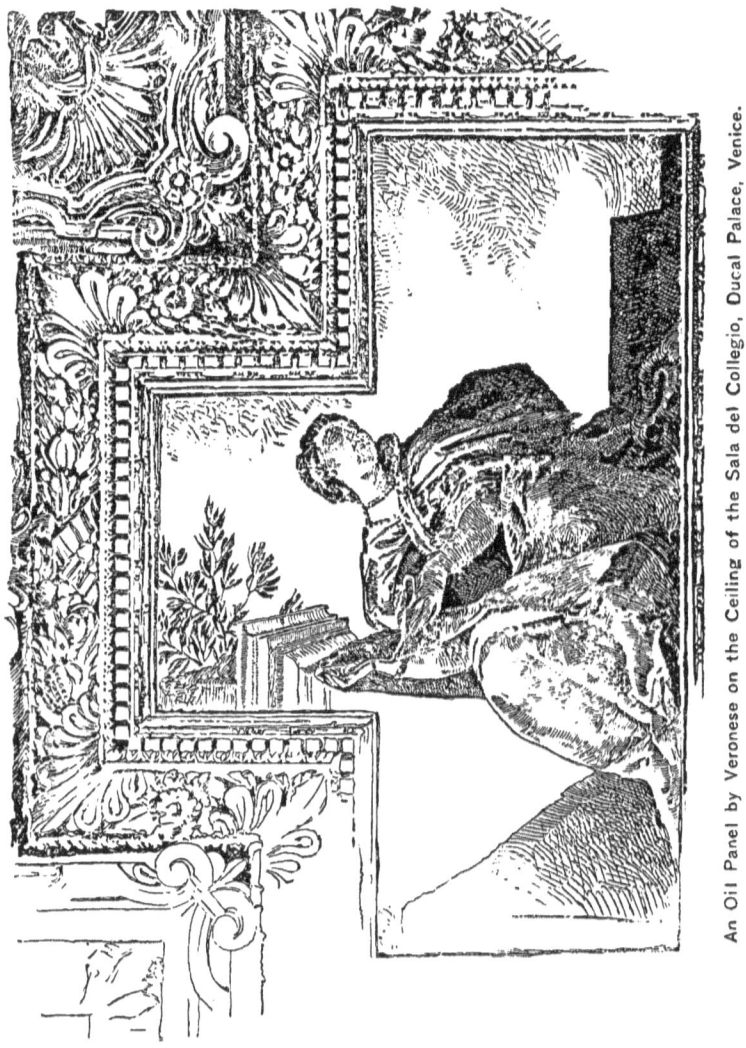

An Oil Panel by Veronese on the Ceiling of the Sala del Collegio, Ducal Palace, Venice.

should be pitched in a whiter key than is possible in oils as usually prepared, *i. e.* the oil should be largely replaced by turpentine or another medium used. But whatever may be thought about the darkening of decorative canvases or panels painted in oils, there can be no doubt

about the darkening of oil pictures painted on plaster; it is both swift
and sure. There is great doubt, in my opinion, whether even a heavy
priming of the plaster with several coats of oil-paint would eventually
protect the pictures from the action of the lime, not to mention other
darkening influences. To cite a deplorable example of a prematurely
and utterly ruined oil painting on a plaster-wall, I have only to name
the 'Last Supper' (1498), by Leonardo da Vinci. "Ignoring the old
method of fresco-painting," says J. P. Richter, "Leonardo mixed his
colors with oil — a fatal innovation, as it proved. Donato Montorfano's fresco of the 'Crucifixion,' painted in 1495, which faces the
'Last Supper' in the same refectory, is to this day in an excellent
state of preservation, while Leonardo's production in its shattered
condition is a melancholy proof of the falsity of his theory. Already
his pupil Lomazzo, in his ' Trattato della Pittura,' says of it, 'La pittura
è rovinata tutta [the painting is entirely ruined]. In the course of
a few centuries it has been repainted no less than three times."
Murray, in his Northern Italy, gives some interesting information
concerning the causes that led to the decay of this celebrated painting. As all the conditions attending the production of a decayed
mural painting are of great import to the decorator — for they are
his warning beacon-lights — and as this particular painting is world-
renowned, it will be well to make one or two pregnant quotations :
" Leonardo employed sixteen years upon the work ; but he used a
new process, which proved its ruin. The ground is plaster impregnated with mastic or pitch, melted in by means of a hot iron.
This ground he covered with a species of priming, composed of a
mixture of white lead and some earthy colors, which took a fine
polish, but from which the oil-color flaked off. The materials with
which the wall was built are of a very bad quality, rendering it sus-
ceptible of injury from damp. As early as 1500 the refectory seems
to have been flooded, owing to its low situation. The vicinity of the
kitchen smoked the painting, which exhibited early symptoms of
decay. . . . Scanelli, who saw it in 1642, speaking hyperbolically,
observed that it was then difficult to discover the subject. . . . In
1800, owing to the drain being blocked up, and the rain falling for
fifteen days, the refectory was flooded to a considerable depth. The
late Professor Phillips, R. A., in 1825, examined its condition with
careful and minute attention, and could with difficulty find a portion
of its original surface. . . . Till this time all paintings on walls
had been wrought in fresco; but oil painting, which had become
known and practised in smaller works, better suited da Vinci's mode

of proceeding, as it admits of retouching.[1] . . . It would appear that
the vehicle which he employed, whatever it was, had no union with
the ground, and, therefore, the surface cracked. At the opposite
end of the refectory is a very large and well-preserved fresco of
the 'Crucifixion,' by Montorfano. . . . The good condition of this
painting causes one the more to regret that Leonardo did not employ
fresco. His error is very curiously exemplified on this same wall.
You see two white spaces in the corners. Here Leonardo painted in
oil the portraits of the donors of the Cenacolo, but only a trace of
the figures can be discerned." Scaling is the disease to which the
disappearance of all these paintings by Leonardo in the refectory
must, in the main, be attributed.

Every student of the Vatican *Stanze* knows that two of the
allegorical figures in the Hall of Constantine — 'Justitia' and
'Mansuetudo' — were executed in oil by Giulio Romano and Francesco Penni, from the cartoons of Raphael, and under his supervision.
It would be difficult to say with authority why this experiment was
made: one can only surmise. Shortly after the death of Raphael,
the frescos in the stanza of Heliodorus had so deteriorated in places
that they were clumsily retouched by Sebastian del Piombo. (This
deterioration could not have continued, for to-day they are in a
fair state of preservation.) Possibly they exhibited symptoms of
decay in the life-time of Raphael, who may have wished to substitute for fresco an apparently more durable process. It is not
improbable that he was incited to the change by Sebastian del
Piombo, who seems to have been a gossip, mischief-maker, and — if I
may use so unclassical a word — a "blower." This Venetian artist
had established a reputation as a colorist in Rome, and his deficiencies in design were supplemented by Michael Angelo's pencil. He
had executed several mural paintings in oil, and, with his accustomed
brag, had doubtless vaunted their superior force and richness. (Lanzi
says of his 'Flagellation,' painted in oils on stone in the Church of
S. Pietro in Montorio, that it is "as much blackened by time, as the
frescos which he executed in the same church are well-preserved.")

---

[1] "He would often come to the convent at early dawn; and this I have seen
him do myself. Hastily mounting the scaffolding, he worked diligently until
the shades of evening compelled him to cease, never thinking to take food at
all, so absorbed was he in his work. At other times he would remain there
three or four days without touching his picture, only coming for a few hours to
remain before it, with folded arms, gazing at his figures as if to criticize them
himself. At mid-day, too, when the glare of a sun at its zenith has made barren all the streets of Milan, I have seen him hasten from the citadel, where he
was modelling his colossal horse, without seeking the shade, by the shortest
way to the convent, where he would add a touch or two and immediately
return." Bandello; from Richter's *Leonardo*.

That he was the champion of oil painting for walls, is evident from his letter to Michael Angelo concerning the decorations in the Hall of Constantine, undertaken by the pupils of Raphael just after his death. He writes (pretending to quote Cardinal Bibbiena) " that they had executed a specimen of a figure in oil on the wall, which was a beautiful work of art, so much so that no one would now look at the rooms painted [in fresco] by Raphael, that this hall would excel the others, and would be the finest work executed in painting since the time of the ancients." [1] The adoption of his favorite process by the disciples of Raphael makes "him, for the moment, fair to them, and he relates their success in glowing terms." If such talk temporarily influenced Raphael and his followers, it was but for a short time. Penni and Romano soon saw that what was gained in strength by the use of oil, was more than offset by the loss of decorative effect. The experiment was confined to the two figures before mentioned, which were suffered to remain. With this exception the hall was completed in *buon fresco.* It was not then known that mural oil paintings would blacken with time. These figures are now much darker than the others, and less sound. The lower part, in particular, of the ' Mansuetudo ' has badly cracked, and shows signs of scaling, while no such signs are evident on the companion figures executed in *buon fresco,* which are still fresh and far more decorative. Michael Angelo's exaggerated and explosive, though not improbable, retort to those who urged him to paint the ' Last Judgment' in oils, instead of in fresco, " that oil painting was an occupation fit only for women and idlers," undoubtedly meant that he did not deem oil a suitable medium for mural decoration — for he knew how to paint in oils. Didron says that the modern Byzantines almost never use oils for mural decoration, because they hold them to be less durable than colors applied *a fresco.* The use of oils has certainly been known to them as far back as the days of Panselinos, for Denys, his follower, gives a receipt for painting oil pictures on linen. Notwithstanding this knowledge, fresco has ever been their means of decorative expression on the wall.[2]

---

[1] Wilson, from the Buonarroti Archives.

[2] " Because," said Father Joasaph, " to paint in oils it would be necessary to wait till the plaster is dry, and, as the color would not [then] penetrate the plaster, it would be less solid." This explanation — as rendered by Didron — is not altogether satisfactory. Possibly the crust of carbonate of lime, that forms on plaster, might prevent the penetration of the colors. If this were removed by scraping, the ground would be too absorbent — unless it were thoroughly saturated with oil, or an equivalent, an operation, perhaps, requiring more time and money than the Athonites could afford — and the colors, deprived of the oil that binds them, flake off, or fall off in powder.

Modern mural painters are prone to work in oil — and by oil is meant linseed oil or a like substitute, not an essential or volatile oil, such as oil of spike-lavender or spirits of turpentine — because it is a familiar medium.   Mural painting is the exception; the easel picture the rule; therefore our painters are more "at home" with the technics of the latter, which, if large, is almost invariably painted in oil.   In the sixteenth century it was not so; every man of note painted on the wall, and, though there was no lack of oil-easel-pictures, these, in many respects, were mural paintings on a small scale, hav-

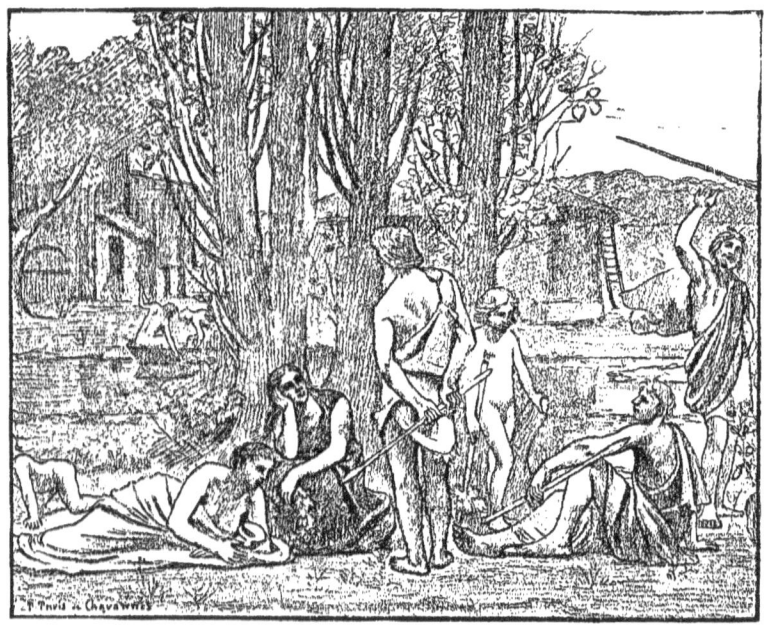

From a drawing by Puvis de Chavannes. 'Pro Patria Ludus.' (Mural Composition.)

ing all the grandeur of monumental compositions.   The 'Vision of Ezekiel,' by Raphael, to mention a well-known example, might be reproduced on a colossal scale, without necessitating any technical changes.   The stately Italians of that epoch could not, or would not be informal.   Their forms are chosen and simplified.   Literal nature, as we understand it, had no charm for them.   Selection, idealization, elimination (decorative necessities) were the canons of their art.   Our art, on the contrary, is more picturesque and intimate, and, at times, tends to be photographic.   When our painters are called upon to execute monumental works, though they may have

the good sense to modify their style to suit the exigencies of the
work in hand, they naturally find it difficult and irksome to emanci-
pate themselves from their every-day methods; and if, by a vigorous
effort, they do manage to change both style and method, they are
not unapt to run into an opposite extreme, by producing paintings
of an archaic rudeness and simplicity. So it happens that they generally find it more convenient to paint in oils, sometimes on the wall
itself, sometimes on a canvas, to be attached to the wall afterwards.
That it is better to paint directly on the wall itself, has already been
shown. At times one is inclined to think that the vanity of exhibiting
the work before it is placed *in situ*, has enough influence with the artist
to induce him to execute it in the studio. There is one thing to be
said in favor of executing studio-painted wall-decorations in oils, and
that is, oil is more elastic than the other media, and colors mixed
with it are less likely to crack and scale when the canvas is rolled
for transportation. The best contemporary mural painters, when
they use oil, reduce it to a minimum, and deaden it by an admixture
of spirits of turpentine, or wax, or by painting on an absorbent
ground. The mural paintings of Puvis de Chavannes (who, accord.
ing to Hamerton, paints in oil deadened by spirits of turpentine [1])
are certainly decorative and scholarly in tone and conception. But
why use oil at all? It is not a necessity, and the painting will surely
stand better without it.

It would be superfluous to preach light tones for walls and ceilings in these days, such a strong hold has the out-of-door feeling
taken on artists. Indeed, so little profit is drawn from the peculiar
qualities of oil, that one is tempted to question their use even for
easel pictures. A majority of the oil pictures in our current exhibitions might just as well have been painted in wax, distemper,
or water-colors. Artists are painting water-colors in oils, to put it
paradoxically ; but do their best they can never equal the whiteness
of water-colors (or the other media) in oils, because *oil is a yellow re-
hicle.* There was a time when the artist, if called upon to play the temporary rôle of decorator, was apt to pitch his work in the then mellow
key of the oil easel-picture. Now painters pitch their easel-pictures
in the light decorative key. So much the better for decoration.
Whether or not it is better for the easel-picture is quite another
thing, which it would be irrelevant to discuss here. Let it suffice to

[1] I have just received a letter from a former pupil, now profiting by the counsels of Puvis de Chavannes, which states that he [Puvis] "paints on canvas prepared with plaster [of Paris probably], which gives his work that dead surface,
and uses common oil-paints."

observe that in abandoning the glaze, and the rich transparent tones
so easily obtainable in oils, we abandon processes that immortalized
the Venetians.

We are now confronted by a decorative problem of an exceptional
nature, the solution of which permits the use of oils. The easiest
way to state it is to give a familiar illustration, which some
of my readers may have been holding *in petto* as a protest against
my condemnation of oil decorations. Almost every traveler has
been impressed with the actual splendor of the Ducal Palace at
Venice; but the imagination must be stimulated to picture its magnificence when the gilded carving on walls and ceilings, incasing
the sensuous tones of Paolo, Tintoret and Titian echoed the opu-
lence of sumptuously-clad senators. To-day all the pomp is above,
and the floors look starved. But in those days when Venice
was in truth Queen of the Seas, there was pomp above and pomp
below. Glistening frames and paintings harmonized with the sheen
of stuff. It must have resembled a vessel of burnished gold, with
precious stones therein, reflected and intensified by the polished
metal. Fresco would have been too cold, formal and spiritual
to sustain such magnificence. Its pale, dead surface would have
ill accorded with a gorgeousness that was Byzantine rather than Italian. A warm, shining medium, such as oil or varnish, was needed
to complete the harmony. Tintoret's ' Paradise ' has sadly blackened with time, but it is less noticeable here. The massive gold
frames counteract in a measure the darkening of years, and here we
have the rationale of the gold frame for oil pictures. When these
are not pitched in a water-color key, the slight yellowish tint induced
by the oil, varnish, or time, or by all three, improves rather than in-
jures them, provided of course, the yellowing be not carried too far.
The rich, yellow tones of the frame, with its countless réflections, not
only enhance the mellow tones of the picture, but they nullify the
dirty quality which the same picture would apparently have if framed
with pure white. It must be remembered that oil is a yellow medium,
while the vehicle for water-colors, fresco and wax-painting is colorless.
For the most part the Venetian paintings in the Ducal Palace are
really easel-pictures attached to the walls and ceilings, not because
they are painted on canvas, but because they have the qualities of
easel-pictures. So, too, has the series of paintings by Rubens for
Maria de' Medici, [See Illustrations.] which probably look just as
well on the walls of the Louvre as they did on the walls of the Lux-
embourg. We must bear in mind, however, that the easel-pictures of

these great masters, if not always decorative in tone and chiaro-oscuro, were almost invariably monumental in form and composition. The modern painters, on the contrary, are normally decorative in tone, but un-monumental in design.[1]

When effects, similar to those in the Ducal Palace are desired, the use of oil is legitimate. It is often advantageous to employ color transparently on metallic grounds, and then oil is a very convenient vehicle, though such a varnish as Siccative of Harlem diluted with spirits of turpentine might be substituted, perhaps advantageously. But whenever oil is used it should be with the greatest moderation.[2]

---

[1] All monumental painting is decorative; though all pictorial decoration is not monumental.

[2] I would have liked, both in this and other chapters, to institute several interesting comparisons between mural paintings — especially modern paintings — executed in different media, had I been sure of the processes. It was impossible to verify these processes except at a cost of time and labor that the result would not have justified. The only authorities that I could consult on this side of the Atlantic, either disagreed, or — from certain indications not worth noting here — did not command my confidence.

CHAPTER XI.

WATER-GLASS.

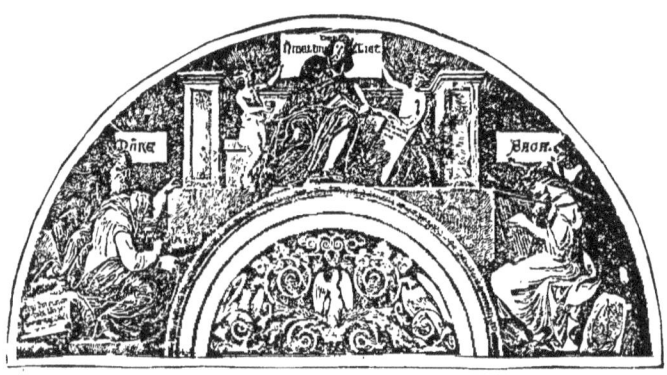

From the Frescos by Julius Schnorr, in the Royal Palace, Munich.

IT is with reluctance that I broach the water-glass method; for I have neither worked in it, nor seen the important water-glass pictures painted by Kaulbach and his school — not to mention others. The whole subject is amply treated in W. Cave Thomas's *Mural Decoration*. A translation is there given of the pamphlet by Dr. J. N. Von Fuchs,[1] the inventor of the process as well as an elaborate statement by Maclise of his personal experience with water-glass preparatory to painting his mural pictures in the Houses of Parliament. From these sources I shall draw just enough to give a general idea of the process, adding a few extracts from a paper that appeared in the *American Architect* (Vol XV., No. 429), descriptive of the later and improved Keim water-glass method; for no survey of the technics of mural painting would be complete without some reference to stereochromy, as its inventor calls this kind of painting (from στερεὸς, solid, firm, and χρῶμα, color).

---

[1] Dr. Fuchs published his first pamphlet on Water-Glass in 1825.

Water-glass, as its name implies, is a liquid glass. It is not mixed with the pigments — except occasionally, for retouching — but is applied to the finished picture, painted with colors dissolved in pure water by means of a sprinkler. In fact, it is a "fixative," and the process corresponds in principle to that of fixing a charcoal drawing. The colors, when dry, have but little consistence, and would speedily be brushed or washed away were they not firmly bound together by the hard, transparent, insoluble water-glass. Of this there are four kinds.

(a). *Potash Water-Glass.* A mixture of : —

  15 parts of pulverized quartz, or pure quartz sand,
  10   "   well-purified potash,
  1   "   powdered charcoal.

These ingredients are to be subjected to a strong heat till they are fused. As much heat is required as is necessary to melt common glass. When cool, it is pulverized and dissolved in about five parts of boiling water, by introducing it in small portions into an iron vessel and constantly stirring the liquid, replacing the water as it evaporates, by adding hot water from time to time, and by continuing to let it boil for three or four hours, until the whole is dissolved — a slimy deposit excepted — and until a pellicle begins to form on the surface of the liquid, which indicates that the solution is in a state of great concentration; it disappears, however, when the liquid is stirred, and the boiling may then be continued for a short time, in order to obtain the solution in the proper state of concentration — when it has a specific gravity of from 1.24 to 1.25. In some instances it will be necessary to dilute it with more or less water. When it has the consistence of syrup it can rarely be used.

The solution is allowed to cool, and left to clear in the well-closed iron vessel. The clear liquid is then decanted off from the deposit into stoppered bottles. For transportation it may be evaporated to a gelatinous mass by constantly stirring the liquid, and then packed into tinned iron vessels. Or it may be solidified by adding one-fourth its volume of alcohol to a concentrated solution, which is deposited after a few days in a solid mass at the bottom of the vessel.

(b). *Soda Water-Glass.* This is prepared in the same way as the potash water-glass; but alcohol does not precipitate it completely. There are two receipts for making it. This is the cheaper : —

  100 parts of quartz,
  60   "   anhydrous sulphate of soda,
  15-20   "   charcoal dust.

When completely saturated with silica it gives, with water, a some-what more opaque liquid than potash water-glass.

(c). *Double Water-Glass* : —

100 parts of quartz,
28   "   purified potash,
22   "   neutral anhydrous carbonate of soda,
6   "   powdered charcoal, or

a mixture of three measures of concentrated potash water-glass with two measures of concentrated soda water-glass will be found to answer for all practical purposes.

The first three kinds of water-glass, when completely saturated with silica, are more or less cloudy, owing to undissolved and very finely divided silica. To deprive them of this opacity, it is sufficient to add soluble silicate of soda and to allow them to stand for about a day, stirring them occasionally. The soluble silicate of soda is pre-pared by fusing together three parts pure anhydrous carbonate of soda and two parts powdered quartz.

A dust-like efflorescence, after some time, appears upon bodies impregnated with water-glass. It is not obnoxious, but proves rather that the process of hardening proceeds favorably, by which a little alkali is expelled, thus enabling the silica to act more freely ; it may easily be removed with a wet sponge. This efflorescence is not iden-tical with that which frequently makes its appearance on damp walls.

The applications of water-glass are various. Mixed with sand-like substances it makes an excellent cement. It imparts hardness to porous bodies, which absorb it, such as vessels of baked clay, plates, bricks, tiles, etc. Which kind of water-glass is best suited for a given purpose is a matter of experiment. Potash water-glass sets more rapidly than the soda with powdered substances, and may im-part greater solidity to them, though the difference cannot be con-siderable. Soda water-glass being more liquid, penetrates more readily into the pores of absorbent bodies. Soda does not combine so strongly as potash, and has a strong inclination to effloresce when combined with the carbonic acid of the air, and one of the advantages of the soda water-glass might be due, therefore, to its parting readily with the silica, and thus accelerating the silicatization of the mass. The double water-glass seems to unite the properties of the other two, and merits preference for the very reason that it contains two bases with which silica combines more powerfully. Water-glass, as applied to mural painting, is its only special applica-tion that here concerns us, and will now be briefly described.

The plaster that is applied directly to the wall is of the usual kind, the lime being thoroughly slaked, and sparingly used. Rich plaster does not readily absorb the water-glass, and will sometimes cause it to crack. When it is dry the water-glass is applied to con-solidate, and make it adhere to the wall. The application is repeated several times, allowing the surface to dry each time, and continued almost to the point of complete saturation. Soda and double water-glass treated with the soluble silicate of soda, are preferable to potash water-glass, because they are absorbed more easily. They should be diluted with equal parts of water. Owing to the uneven-ness of the wall the plaster will be thicker in some parts than in others, and it will be necessary to treat these thicker parts with more water-glass in order that the whole surface may be equally saturated. The composition of the second coat is similar to that of the first, though a fine sand may be used, if desired. If too fine, the water-glass is not readily imbibed. Kaulbach preferred a coarse-grained surface that felt to the touch like a rasp. When this second coat of plaster is dry it is sometimes rubbed with a sandstone or iron straight-edge, in order to remove the film of carbonate of lime that has formed during the process of drying, and which would prevent the absorption of the water-glass. A better method is to destroy the incrustation with dilute phosphoric acid (1 part concentrated acid to 6 parts water), brushed over the surface. Phosphate of lime is formed which binds well with the water-glass. When the plaster is thoroughly dry it is impregnated with double water-glass clarified with the soluble silicate of soda and diluted with its equal bulk of water. The operation should be repeated when the first impregna-tion is dry. Too much water-glass would close up the pores and inconvenience the painter. In that case time will effect a cure, or the pores of the ground may be re-opened by burning alcohol on it. The wall thus prepared may be painted on at once, if desirable. This is not a necessity ; delay increases the absorbing capacity of the ground.

Water-glass cement may be used as a substitute for the second coat of plaster. The water-glass is mixed with powdered marble or quartz sand, to which a little dry slaked lime has been added, in such pro-portions that the cement has the consistency of ordinary plaster. It has certain advantages over lime-mortar. The water-glass is equally spread through the whole mass, so as to ensure equal cementation and silicatization. During the repeated moistening of the picture, no lime will be drawn to the surface and disturb the colors, because no soluble lime is left in the mass ; moreover, no incrustation of carbon-

ate of lime will ever form. This cement becomes, when dry, as hard
as stone, and at first is non-absorbent. After a few days it acquires
the power of absorption, but loses in solidity; hence, the necessity of
one or two saturations with the diluted water-glass.

The colors are ground with pure water. The wall should be mois-
tened frequently, to displace the air from the pores and insure the
adherence of the colors, as well as to enable the painter to match the
tints uniformly. Care must be taken not to wet those parts too much
which have already been painted, because the colors are liable to lose
their freshness, the water bringing the finest particles up to the surface, which, however, may be brushed away, when dry, with a fine
brush. When finished, the picture is fixed, by means of a sprinkler
throwing a fine spray, with the fixing water-glass diluted with half
its volume of water. The alternate besprinkling and drying is continued till the colors adhere so firmly that they cannot be rubbed off
with the finger. If white pocket-handkerchiefs be smudged, it does
not prove that the colors are insufficiently fixed, or devoid of durability, for rubbing with force loosens grains of sand, the friction of
which detaches more or less color that indirectly stains the handker-
chief. The same is true of colors applied *a buon fresco*. Some of
the so-called meagre colors, such as black, require more water-glass,
which is applied by means of a soft brush. The water-glass is not
mixed with the colors on the palette, except for retouching pictures
that have been fixed; though it might with advantage be added to
the meagre colors. When so much water-glass has been applied
to the surface that it remains unabsorbed for a minute, it is better to
blot off the excess with blotting-paper, to avoid possible spots.

The painting is finished when the colors are fixed. It is well to
wash it after a few days with spirits of wine, to remove dust and the
little alkali that has been set free, and at the end of a few more days it
may be washed with pure water — not spring water. Paintings executed on the outside of buildings should not be exposed to the rain
before they are fixed, and ought to be carefully examined at the end
of a few months or a year, to ascertain whether they have acquired
any power of absorption. In that case, an after-fixing is recommended. Old plastered walls may be used for stereochromy, provided they be dry and sound and the plaster porous after it has been
rubbed with rough sand-stone.

Water-glass is more liquid when heated (from one hundred degrees
to one hundred and twenty degrees), and is more readily imbibed by
porous substances, and, therefore, better suited for fixing colors. The

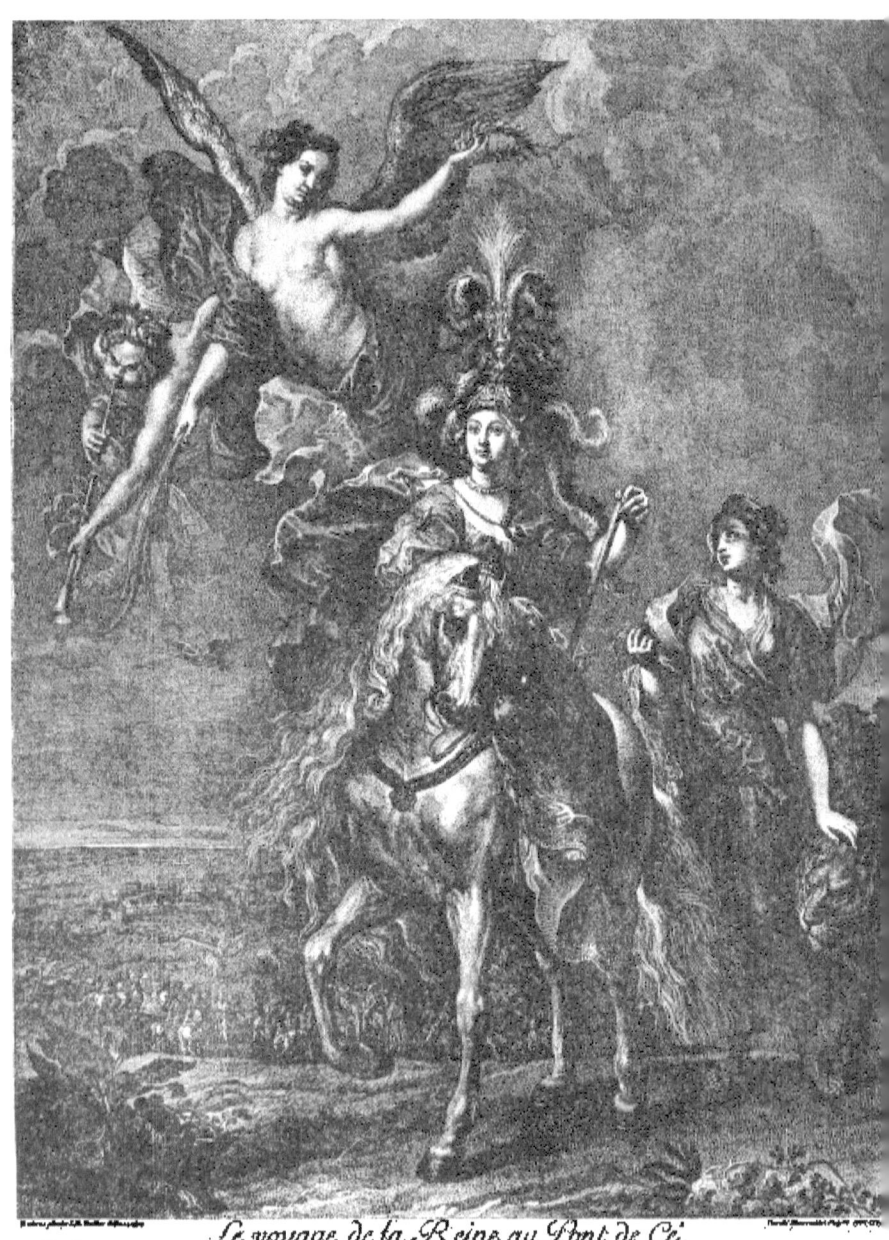

Le voyage de la Reine au Pont de Cé.

La Reine à cheval le casque en tête couverte d'une autre Bellone qui provoir une guerre qu'elle qu' se preparoit par les timides du Pont de Cé. Cette Princesse est accompagnée de la Victoire, et de la Renommée qui sont en l'air; et de la Terre qui la suit à pied avec son Lion. Au fond du Tableau est la ville du Pont de Cé, et au dessus de la ville on voit un aigle qui poursuit des oiseaux de rapine; Allegorie qui signifie l'intention qu'avoit la Reine à chasser les ennemis de l'État. — — — —

(After on Oil Painting by Peter Paul Rubens.)

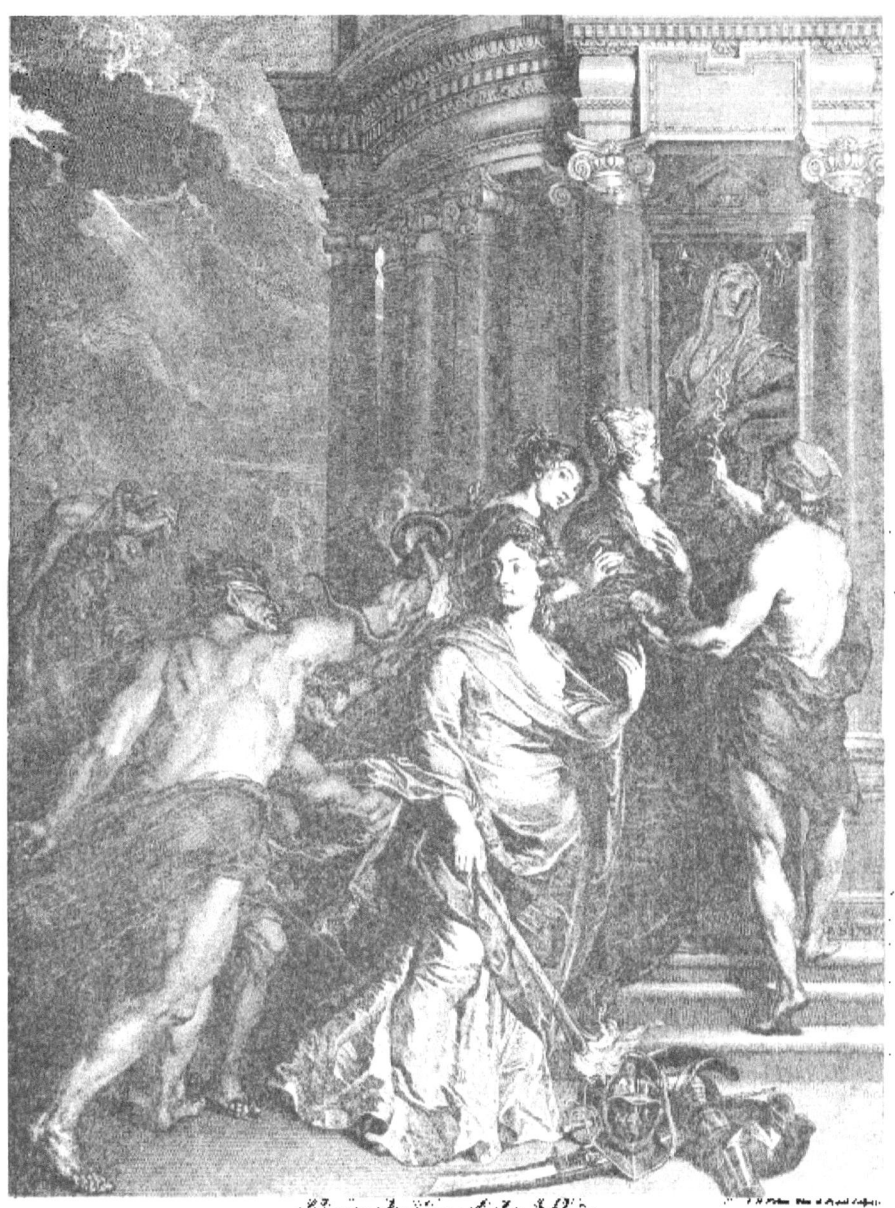

La conclusion de la Paix.

Le Baron ayant refusé la suite de s'accommoder avec le Roy, est conduite par Mercure au temple où les Dieux, l'Abondance & autres, et la Paix sous le devoir installent tous les insignes de la guerre pendant que le Temple, la Famille et divinité multiplient s'approchent pour leur donner de tout... et l'état de discorde s'oppose dans le transport de leur étonnant.

A Paris, chez le Sr Rubens peintre du Roy...

(After an Oil Painting by Peter Paul Rubens)

sprinkler may be heated by immersing it in warm water, and the wall-surface by burning alcohol on it, but only after the first fixation of the colors.

A word as to the pigments : No organic color, such as lake, is admissible. The white used is zinc white, which combines chemically with the water-glass. The colors should be ground as fine as possible. They undergo a slight change by fixing, but acquire their normal tone in time. Cobalt appears much brighter, and light ochre much darker, and are, therefore, not recommended. The colors when fixed do not shine.

Maclise, who made many experiments with water-glass both in England and Germany, and who gained much information from Kaulbach and other practitioners, says that the porosity of the plaster does not necessarily result from the coarseness of the sand, and was assured by the artists most conversant with stereochromy that any remarkable coarseness of the surface was by no means indispensable for insuring the absorption of the water-glass. The roughness or smoothness of the ground was entirely optional. They also stated, in disagreement with the recommendations of the discoverer, that it was not necessary to saturate the plaster with the water-glass previously to painting on it, but that a final fixation of the picture with the fluid sufficed. Such plaster as is used for *buon fresco* they deemed to be sound enough in itself ; and on a ground of this nature, Maclise saw the artists work in Berlin. But it should be smoothed with a wooden float, and not rubbed with an iron trowel, as in fresco, a process that brings the lime to the surface, rendering it non-absorbent, and, consequently, subjecting the colors to the risk of flaking.

The process being new, was at first necessarily tentative. Additional experiments revealed new facts or modified old ones. In a letter dated September 14, 1860, Pettenkofer thinks that the potash water-glass is quite safe, and less liable to effloresce than the soda water-glass. In another letter he recommends a ground of Portland cement. The first coat is composed of three parts of coarse sand and one part of cement. This surface, when still fresh, is covered with a thin coat of a finer mixture — three parts of fine sand to one of cement — from one to two-twelfths of an inch. When the upper layer has sufficiently sucked, sand is thrown against it. After a quarter of an hour the sand is removed with a sharp-edged iron ruler, together with the crust of the mortar. Then more sand is thrown against the surface, which, when dry, is sprinkled with a saturated solution of carbonate of ammonia in water. Kaulbach

painted a stereochromic picture on a ground of Portland cement and
sand in the Dominican Monastery at Nuremberg. Maclise tried it, but

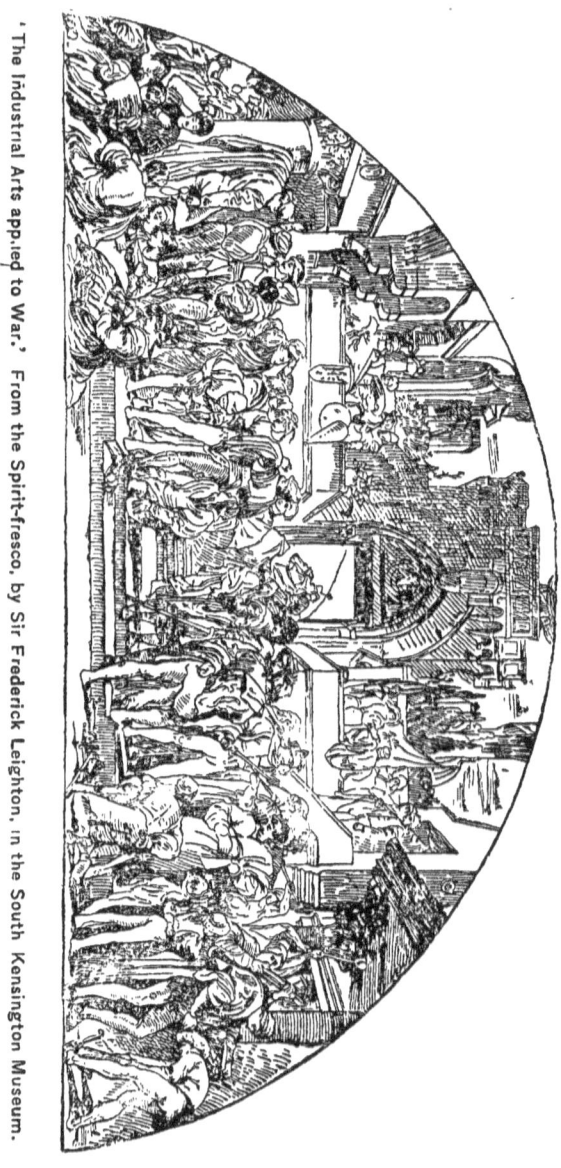

'The Industrial Arts applied to War.' From the Spirit-fresco, by Sir Frederick Leighton, in the South Kensington Museum.

apparently did not like it. It will be seen that the original process,
as invented by Fuchs, has been much modified in practice. It is not
impossible that to some of these modifications may be attributed the

partial failure of the water-glass process to fulfil its high promise. Maclise recommends several colors of the organic class prohibited by Fuchs; but I should think that the latter was in the right.

THE KEIM PROCESS.

This "is based on the stereochrome process of Schlotthauer and Fuchs, differing, however, from that in such important particulars as to constitute, practically, an entirely new process in itself. In the year 1818, Professor Schlotthauer, of the Munich Academy, who had for some time been engaged in experiments with a view to discovering some permanent process for mural paintings, turned his attention to the substance known as water-glass (silicate of sodium), the invention of the chemist Fuchs. The result was the adoption of the stereochrome process. In this process the surface to be painted on consisted of an ordinary mortar of lime and sand, impregnated with water-glass. Upon this surface the painting was executed in watercolor, and was then fixed by water-glass. . . . In practice, it soon became evident that a simple spraying of water-glass, applied to heterogeneous pigments, without reference to their peculiar properties as regards chemical composition, cohesive capability, etc., was not sufficient to insure their permanence; certain colors in particular, as ultramarine, umber, and black, were observed to be always the first to detach themselves, in the form of powder, or by scaling off from the painting, thus pointing to the fact that their destruction was not owing to any accidental defect in the manner of their application, but to some radical unsuitability arising from the chemical conditions of the process."

It would be unjust to the memory of Fuchs, not to state that the painters often neglected to follow his precepts. He particularly emphasized the necessity of saturating the plaster ground with waterglass; but neither Maclise nor the German artists whom he consulted deemed it necessary to follow this injunction. It is not impossible that their neglect may have had something to do with the ultimate decay of the pictures; unfortunately, there are no data on which to base an opinion. The exact nature of the grounds on which the pictures were painted, as well as their actual condition should be precisely known in order to come to an authoritative conclusion. Fuchs, moreover, attributing the failures, that were at first frequently made, to the upper layer of plaster, recommended as a substitute the *water-glass cement*, previously described. This he deemed more reliable than the plaster; yet it does not appear to have been used as a ground for mural paintings. Again : he insists that the meagre colors, such as black — the very colors that " were observed to be always the first to detach themselves " — require more water-glass, which should be added with a fine brush. He even thinks it would be well the mix the water-glass with such colors. Perhaps this injunction, too, was violated.[1]

Keim suggests several innovations in the preparation of the wall. If this be already covered with plaster, it will serve for the first coat, provided it be sound and dry. If not, the bricks must be laid bare, and the plaster between them picked out to a depth of about three-fourths of an inch. On this surface, a thin squirting is cast, composed as follows : —

> 4 parts of coarse quartz sand, infusorial earth and powdered marble, mixed in certain proportions (?) to
>
> 1 part of quick-lime, slaked with distilled water.

Upon this squirting-cast follows plaster of the ordinary consist-ence, and composed of the same ingredients. On this, again, a third or painting ground is laid, not exceeding from one-eighth to one-quarter of an inch in thickness. This last coat is composed of :

> 8 parts of the finest white quartz sand, marble-sand artificially prepared, and free from dust, marble meal and infusorial earth in the proper proportions (?) to 1 part quick-lime slaked with distilled water.

For works executed on the exterior of buildings, pumice-sand is recommended in addition to the other ingredients. A wall thus prepared " presents so hard a surface as to admit of sparks being struck from it with a steel." Only distilled or filtered rain-water should be used in this process ; for should the water contain lime it would affect the fixing-solution to the prejudice of the painting.

When the plaster is thoroughly dry, it is treated to a solution of hydro-fluo-silicic acid, to remove the thin crust of carbonate of lime. It is then saturated with two applications of potash water-glass diluted with distilled water, and when dry is ready for painting. The

---

[1] Mr. Otto Grundmann, Instructor in the School of Drawing and Painting. Boston Museum of Fine Arts, worked for some time in water-glass, with Godtfried Guffens and Jan Swerts of Antwerp, in the Church of St. Nicholas, Ypres, about nine years ago. They did not prepare the plaster ground with water-glass, nor did he think that these mural paintings had deteriorated. The same artists had executed other works in water-glass, and were well satisfied with the process. Mr. Grundmann says, that "blacks and blues are treated like other colors, and that a second coat of water-glass *may* be used [over the whole picture] if the first should not be enough." He saw the works of Kaulbach in water-glass at the National Gallery of Berlin. The 'History of the Reformation' was overspread with cracks, not long plaster cracks, but short cracks, such as are developed on oil paintings. It had not, however, grown dark. The exposed frescos on the outer walls had greatly suffered.

grain may be coarse or smooth according to the artists' taste; but the smoother the ground, the less absorbent it is, and the more difficult the fixing. If desired, the ground may be prepared in any tone, and all those colors may be used that are suitable for the stereochrome process. These are, for the most part, the natural earths and metallic oxides. Every color should remain chemically unaffected by the ground, by the other colors in contact with it, or by the fixing material. " To meet this end, the colors in this process are treated beforehand with alkaline solutions (of potash or ammonia), to anticipate any change of hue which might result from the use of the alkaline liquids which form the fixative. In addition to this, they are further prepared with certain other substances, such as oxide of zinc, carbonate of baryta, felspar, powdered glass, etc., as required by the peculiar properties of each, in order to obviate any other danger of chemical change taking place. . . . From the various nature of the properties possessed by some of the pigments, it was found that their capacity for absorbing the alkaline silicate with which they were fixed varied very greatly. There was also a marked difference in the degree of mechanical cohesive capacity, which they respectively possessed. To equalize them in these respects, without which the fixing would have been a work of great difficulty and uncertainty, alumina, magnesia and hydrate of silica were added as required. The result was that all the colors are equally acted upon by the fixing solution, and all attain an equal degree of durability after fixing, both as regards the mechanical and chemical action of this process upon them. In the year 1878, a large mural painting was executed by this process on the exterior of the parish church at Eichelberg, near Regensburg. Before its completion, and therefore before any of the fixing solution had been applied to it, it was drenched by a heavy storm of rain. Contrary to anticipation, it was found that the painting, so far from being in any degree washed away, had held perfectly firm, and even in some places seemed to be as hard as if already fixed. Mr. Keim's explanation of this unexpected result, which he subsequently confirmed by experiments, was that a chemical cohesion had already taken place by the action of the alkali, set free in the mortar, upon the silicates in the pigments."

The preparation of the colors and the fixing-glass is apparently a complicated process, and demands the services of an expert. But the artist would be freed from all such complications, and for him the process would be very simple. He can paint thinly or with impasto, and retouch *ad libitum*. It is to be observed, however, that pigments applied thinly can be more securely fixed than impasto, and are therefore likely to be more durable. (But impasto is also more liable to perish in the other processes, not to mention its tendency to collect dust. Yet at times it is too effective to be discarded, especially in combination with rich materials.) The palettes are constructed with small pans to hold the colors, of which the residue, at the end of the day's work, may either be replaced in the bottle or kept moist in the pan with distilled water.

"The last stage in the process is the work of fixing. In the stereochrome process the fixing medium employed was silicate of potash, thoroughly saturated with silica, in combination with sufficient sodic silicate to prevent it from opalescing. The chief defect of this lay in the fact that it was often apt to produce spots upon the painting. Mr. Keim has substituted silicate of potash, treated with caustic ammonia and caustic potash. The action of the carbonic acid in the atmosphere and in the water during the process leads to the formation of carbonated alkali, which makes its way to the surface, and would form, when dry, a whitish film over the painting. To obviate this danger, as well as to expedite the process of converting the silicate of potash, with the basic oxides existing in the substance of the painting, into silicate, the fixing solution is heated further with carbonate of ammonia. The effect of this upon silicate of potash is that silica is precipitated in a fine gelatinous form, and ammonia set free. This latter volatilizes, and carbonate of potash is formed, which is easily removed by washing, after the completion of the fixing. The fixing solution is employed hot, with the advantage of obtaining a quicker and more perfect formation of silicate than was possible in the stereochrome process, where the solution was applied cold. The effect of the fixative as it sinks into the ground, which has already absorbed the pigments, is to convert the painting into a veritable casting, uniting with colors and ground in one hard, homogeneous mass of artificial stone. The finished painting has proved itself impervious to all tests. It will admit of any acid, even in a concentrated form, being poured over it (save, of course, hydrofluoric acid)." It has other applications than that of mural painting. For house-painting it is claimed that it would last as long as the house itself, only needing an occasional scrubbing; it would also form an excellent protection against damp. Taking its durability into consideration, it is not more expensive than other systems.[1]

---

[1] Condit, referring as a house-painter to certain ready-mixed pigments, of which water-glass (silicate of soda) is one of the ingredients, says that he "has

There is much in the preceding paragraph, where comparisons are instituted between the Keim and Fuchs processes, to which exception may be taken. As we have seen, the latter did not recommend the potash water-glass for painting. This was an innovation introduced probably after the death of Fuchs (1856); for Prof. Pettenkofer recommends it as a substitute for the soda and double waterglass (in 1860) " which is apt to come up to the surface of the painting."

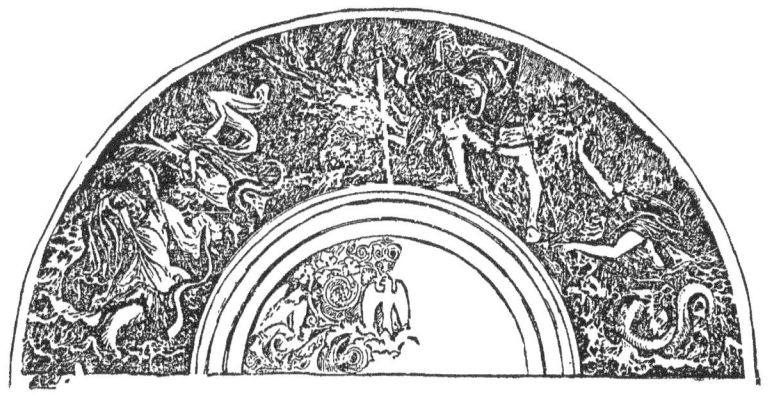

From the Frescos by Julius Schnorr, in the Royal Palace, Munich.

(An unobjectionable efflorescence, according to Fuchs, and easily removed.) Pettenkofer also counsels the use of caustic potash with the water-glass for fixing, in the proportion of one to fifteen, except for black, cobalt, and chrome red. The fixing solution *may* have been "applied cold in the stereochrome process," but contrary to the recommendation of Fuchs, who is very explicit with regard to the heating. Though the Keim is undoubtedly an improvement over the earlier processes, yet it evidently has not been compared with that of Fuchs, but with a less laborious one — and probably less secure —

seen such a paint in nearly perfect condition after ten years, a portion protected by a building being in an absolutely perfect condition, with a fino lustre. Some of the paint, however (probably too little oil), would crack and peel in the worst manner, the paint curling like a dried leaf. This, I am told by an old painter who has used these paints for ten years, it was specially and decidedly prone to do, if (1) any break, however small, occurred, the water seemingly shelling it off, either directly or by expanding the wood; (2) if placed over or under a lead and oil paint. We have, probably, here one of the best illustrations of the theory and fault of a good paint. It is hard and therefore durable, preventing even white lead from 'chalking' for nearly a dozen years. But as it contains too much hardening substance for its little amount of oil, it is too hard, has no elasticity, and cracks badly; moreover, the oil does not penetrate the wood (waterglass goes into this and the small elasticity, destruction is rapid and fatal, whenever it begins, as it *may* soon."

Such pigments and their application differ widely from the pure water-glass process; but even the behavior of these hybrids is not without its lesson.

substituted by impatient practitioners. This is worth noting, as indeed is everything bearing on the decay or preservation of mural paintings. It is to be deplored that there is no detailed, authoritative, and accessible statement of the actual condition of all the important water-glass paintings executed thirty or forty years ago. Very likely many of them are still sound.

Though the painter may, and probably must, take much of the above on faith, yet a presentation of the principle of water-glass has been necessary, in order that he (or the architect) may judge of its applicability as a decorative medium. In the second paper, I took occasion to doubt its durability when applied to the exterior of buildings, basing my doubts on the behavior of pigments exposed to sun and weather influences. Possibly these doubts are ill-founded. The principles on which the process is based seem logical, and the improved Keim method may prove far more durable in exposed situations than others that have been found wanting. Durability is but a relative term. No human product is everlasting. Buildings themselves are comparatively short-lived. A painting may fairly be called durable that co-exists with the wall it decorates.

There is much to recommend the process as a medium for interior decoration, if half that is claimed for it by men of repute be true. Given the materials, it is simple and direct; so simple that any mural painter could quickly master its technicalities. Like fresco, it is without gloss, though probably less luminous. It apparently possesses all the requisites for monumental painting on the wall.

CHAPTER XII.

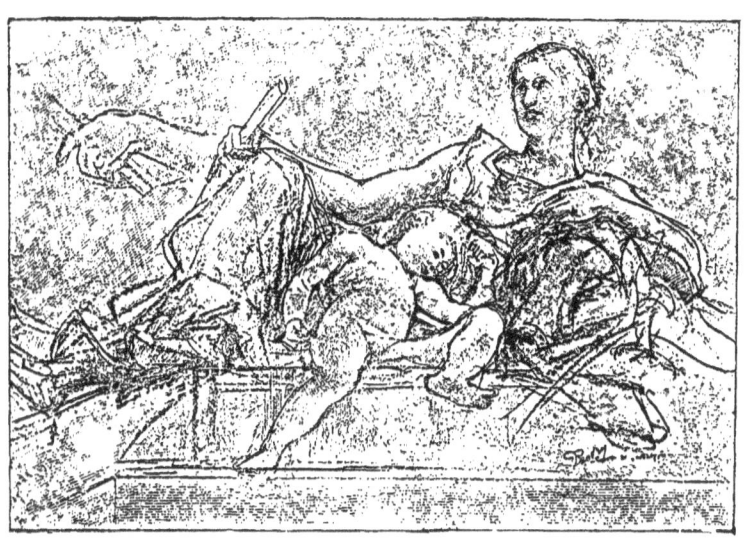

Study for Paul Baudry's Ceiling, 'The Glorification of the Law.'

HAVING briefly reviewed the technics of mural painting, it will now be relevant to consider the education of the painter and his essential qualifications. Perhaps there is no more fruitful method of procedure than to analyze the training of the Renaissance giants, and to institute a few salutary comparisons between their development and that of modern men — especially of our compat. riots. From what has already been expressed in these pages, the reader has doubtless drawn many pregnant deductions for himself; but, at the cost of repetition — for only by persistent re-iteration can we ever be heard — certain statements must be made. Much has been written, both tentatively and authoritatively, on the political, physical, and ethical conditions that are essential to the evolution of an artist. Some have maintained that art can thrive only within specified degrees of latitude and longitude. Some have defined the

political conditions most favorable to its growth. Of these a few
have stoutly affirmed that it must be fertilized by despotism — as if
despotism could nourish anything necessarily so free and spontaneous as art! Others have attributed its triumphs to religious zeal.
Doubtless race, climate, government, and religion enter, as ingredients, that subtle compound called art; but in just what proportions
it would be impossible to state with accuracy. While we know that
certain nationalities have shown a marvelous facility and disposition
for the arts, while it is self-evident that under certain physical influences the practice of art is out of the question, yet it would be very
unsafe to predicate what are the fittest environments for the artistic
growth of civilized nations, especially in these days when modern
inventions are rapidly levelling all the barriers that formerly isolated
them. Eugène Müntz writes,[1] "In order to prosper, the arts exact
a combination of circumstances the most complex, and no rigorous
correlation can be established between moral, religious, or political
development, and artistic production. The latter assuredly will
always bear the impress of its surroundings, but its intrinsic value
will result from very different causes. There are great nations, like
England, that have never been able to form an indigenous school,
and there are great epochs, like the French Revolution, that have
not witnessed the birth of a single chef-d'œuvre."

It is frequently said that America is yet too callow to evolve an
art. I do not believe it. If anything were to interfere with our
artistic growth it would be the acceptance of so baneful and fatal-
istic a theory. Nothing is more depressing to the artist than to be
told that his *entourage* precludes the realization of his dreams.
When man is pioneering in the primeval forests he has neither such
dreams nor the power to realize them. But the pioneering epoch was
passed more than two centuries ago in some of our communities, communities that were established by the offspring of an old civilization.
The Greek colonists of Magna Grecia produced artistic works of
almost equal merit with those of the mother country ; and at that
time things marched slowly. Ages were then required for the evolution
of a nation or an art; but recent inventions have unconscionably dis-
arranged the time-table of the sages. Our older communities have
begotten children that in a few decades have grown prodigiously.
As yet they are somewhat crude and undeveloped, but ambitious and
receptive. Far be it from me to nullify all that has just been said

---

[1] *Études sur l'Histoire de la Pienture*, etc., Paris, 1886.

about the inscrutability of the mysteries that generate an atmosphere congenial to art, by effusively predicting a brilliant artistic career for America; but I certainly wish to demolish the counter-proposition. If freedom, youth, energy, wealth, amalgamation of race, variety of climate, and a rare eagerness to learn from others, argue anything, it is surely the life, not the death of art. The commercial spirit may at times offend, but it supplies the sinews of war, as it were, those boundless opportunities so stimulating and necessary to the production of great works. Commerce did much for the arts both in Venice and Florence.

However widely opinions may differ as to the relative merits of the modern educational systems, they must be comparatively unanimous as to their inferiority to those of Mediæval or Renaissance times. Then the relations between master and pupil, as has been previously shown, were exceedingly intimate, the latter frequently living as well as working with the former, beginning at the foot of the ladder and working his way up to the topmost rung — if there was anything in him — passing through the successive mechanical and æsthetic stages, from the grinding of colors to collaboration with the master on an important easel or mural painting. The oft-quoted but precise words of Cennini — from which I have already drawn — give such a definite idea of the pupil's obligations that their insertion at length will be justified. "Know, that you cannot learn to paint in less time than that which I shall name to you. In the first place you must study drawing for at least one year; then you must remain with a master at the workshop for the space of six years, at least, that you may learn all the parts and members of the art — to grind colors, to boil down glues, to grind plaster, to acquire the practice of laying grounds on pictures, to work in relief, and to scrape the surface and to gild; afterwards to practice coloring, to adorn with mordants, paint cloths of gold, and paint on walls, for six more years — drawing without intermission on holydays and workdays. And by this means you will acquire great experience. If you do otherwise you will never attain perfection. There are many who say that you may learn the art without the assistance of a master. Do not believe them; let this work be an example to you, studying it day and night. And if you do not study under some master, you will never be fit for anything; nor will you be able to show your face among the masters." Again, he says, "Now then, you who, possessing noble minds, are lovers of this accomplishment, and who study the arts in general, adorn yourselves first with this vesture — namely,

love, reverence, obedience, and perseverence." Such was the normal
curriculum in Italy[1] and it will be seen that it strongly resembles
that of Byzantium as described in a previous chapter. It was an
admirable common-sense system of education, and one that is more
or less closely followed to-day by would-be lawyers, soldiers, architects, mechanics — by the students of every profession, except those
of art. The pupil left the atelier thoroughly equipped. He was well-
versed both in the material part of his art and in the science of pic-
ture-making according to the lights of his master. For some years
he painted in the latter's style. The idea of what we call originality
never entered his head — and there is really but very little scope for
originality without lawlessness. He was quite content could he slightly
improve on some *motif* of a predecessor. Raphael's *Sposalizio* was
inspired by Perugino's, but greatly surpassed it. After making several sketches for his *Entombment*, he finally adopted Mantegna's
scheme, impregnating it with his exquisite personality. Small won-
der is it that such works, the slow accretions of time and experience,
were very beautiful. (It was just so in the days of the Greeks. A
man died happy could he improve a moulding or a capital.) While
executing his maiden commissions, the young artist kept his eyes
open, drew from the paintings and sculptures of accredited masters,
and traveled when his circumstances permitted. If he were intelligent and receptive he gradually emancipated himself from his master's style, as will every artist of ability sooner or later. The man
who fears to be enslaved by his instructor, while following his
behests, must be made of poor stuff. His artistic parentage may be
revealed in the products of his brush or chisel, but why should he
be ashamed of it? Do not our very faces betray our origin? Are
we impeded in the race for life by our inherited experience? Do
we not rather deem it so much gain, well pleased if we may add
thereto our mite for the benefit of posterity? And if even this
cannot be accomplished we must bear in mind that the world has
need of qualified, non-creative subordinates. When art moves
in well-defined channels its course is smooth and prosperous. The
men of old had a definite purpose, knew whither they would go, and
went there by the most direct route. To them the Renaissance was
a tonic, not an irritant. The " Second Birth," the great "Awaken-
ing " meant liberty, not riot. The treasures of antiquity exalted,
but did not intoxicate them ; were used, not abused. The stream did
not overflow; for its banks were high and solid, the influx gradual
and controllable. But suppose the dikes had been less secure, and

---

[1] Slightly modified, but not essentially, in the latter half of the fifteenth century when men lived faster.

that tributaries from Egypt, Assyria, Persia, Japan, Greece, Byzan
tium, Arabia, Spain, France, Germany, etc., had suddenly poured thei
waters into the stream, what then? Would the artists have checkec
the torrent, or the torrent engulfed the artists? Something like this
is happening here to-day.

It was shown in chapter X. that the transition from the easel-picture
to the wall was an easy matter for the Renaissance artist. All their
works were in the "grand style," whether on paper, panel, canvas,
or plaster; so that as far as invention and design were concerned.
scarcely any change was necessitated by their passage from the
studio to the staging. Different technical conditions naturally
exacted variations of technique, but not of conception. The line was
occasionally and unobtrusively used — though much less than is com-
monly supposed — to define objects remote from the spectator, and to
detach them from their environments. It was rarely apparent, as a
line, in the best days. The figures and draperies were beautifully
modelled ("finished," the layman would say,) and broadly, withal.
Breadth does not mean, as some suppose, dash and coarseness; it
means simplicity, suppression of the meaningless, emphasis of the
broad and expressive masses at the expense of accidental, insignificant and belittling detail. The astonishing part of Giotto's, Raphael's, and Michael Angelo's mural work — and in fact that of all the
great frescoers — is that it looks well both near and far off. Every
painter knows how difficult it is to effect this result, or, in the slang
of the studio, to make a refined piece of work "hold" at a distance.
The execution of the nude on the Sistine Vault is perfection —
broad and careful, not in the least coarse or slovenly. The outlines,
without being hard, are firm and eloquent, so that there is absolutely
no doubt about the contour of a figure.[1] The same might be said of
a hundred or more frescos of that epoch. In later, decadent days
the work grew coarser, more summary and effective, and more scenic.
Bravura took the place of heroic delineation. Modern decorators
frequently paint too coarsely in the expectation that distance will

[1] Wilson, who had special facilities for examining the vault of the Sistine,
says that these frescos excite admiration "particularly when observed from a
distance of a few feet." "It might be thought that the vigorous draughtsman
with some tendency to exaggeration of form, might exhibit a similar dispo si-
tion in the use of the brush, but he painted in the soft Tuscan manner so much
in contrast with his forcible drawing." "The heads and faces were painted with
loving care and attention, the features being clearly outlined with dark, fine
lines to insure distinctness when seen from a distance." "It was frequently
Michael Angelo's practice to include portions of the background in his day's
work; he evidently did so to insure softness of outline." At an altitude of
sixty feet the "fine lines" were not noticeable, and the contours, though clearly
defined, were not harsh.

mitigate the effect. Certainly, distance softens asperities, but the choice of handling should be guided rather by the degree of light than by the degree of distance. A blaze of light will reveal any undue rudeness of execution at a very considerable distance. A coarse and vigorous treatment would be far more legitimate and agreeable on a neighboring obscure wall than on a strongly-lighted one, many times more distant. These facts are strikingly exemplified on the stage. Every frequenter of the theatre, not purblind, must have been alternately disgusted and amused by the injudicious and stupid, though generous, application of cosmetics to the features of the *corps de ballet*, choruses, and supernumeraries (not to mention the superior officers); disgusted, because the effect under the tell-tale glare of gas and electricity is positively loathsome; amused, because these poor receptacles of pigments fancy, like the ostrich, with his head in the sand, that "nobody sees." Could they but imitate that long and strong-legged bird in deed as well as thought! Buffoons and clowns, failing to recognize the revelations of light, revolt oftener than they amuse the discriminating portion of their audiences.

To return once more to the Renaissance artist. We have noticed the community of style between his mural and easel work. The difference in technique was conquered in the atelier. Wall-painting was not only practised, but practised under the eye of the master, and subsequent collaboration gave the necessary confidence. Thus the pupil thoroughly solved the material mysteries of the wall. Mural painting presupposes a certain decorative proficiency and knowledge of architectural forms. These, too, the tyro acquired in the atelier. And here is another bond of union between their easel and wall pictures. Both teem with architectural and decorative motives. The Renaissance painters revelled in the suggestions of antiquity, and evolved countless combinations of column, frieze, pilaster, arch, arabesque, and garland from their inexhaustible fecundity. There was but one style of architecture — that derived from Rome — and they played with it in the full exuberance of their Italian facility. The functions of painter and architect were frequently interchangeable, and, as a result, their paintings were strongly imbued with the architectural feeling for structural harmony, and their architecture with a pictorial feeling for ornament. Their field was limited by definite bounds, and they could easily cover it.

In contrasting the training of the modern artist with that of the Renaissance, it is not my purpose to follow his career step by step,

but merely to signalize certain significant variations.   No one for a
moment will suppose that any training however elaborate, can ever
supply the deficiencies of nature.   From childhood we have been
told that the artist is born.   This idea is so deeply rooted, that as a
corollary to it, many illogically believe in the *laisser aller* system of education, *i. e.*, no education at all.   It would be irrelevant to discuss
here whether such a system could produce an accomplished landscape, or still-life painter, but I strenuously hold that it can never
produce a figure, much less a mural painter.   Monumental work
must be grammatical.   The phenomenal success of men like Michael
Angelo, Raphael, Titian, or Rubens must be attributed in a great
measure to the exact equilibrium maintained between their invention
and execution.   The predominance of the former marks the amateur;
of the latter the professional hack.   The curriculum of the mural
painter is identical with that of the easel-picture painter, but must
be supplemented with other exercises.   Both should be thoroughly
versed in the chemistry of their craft (which they are not) ; but besides the normally prescribed studies, the mural painter should be
thoroughly conversant with architectural and decorative forms, as
well as with all the material conditions that concern his department.
In penning these lines, the American student is uppermost in my
thoughts, though much that is here written is equally applicable to
students across the seas.   There are, however, unpretending schools
in foreign lands, especially in Italy, that fulfil many of their technical duties to the would-be mural painter, as is evinced by the mechanical excellence of numerous monumental works.[1]

Very different with us are the relations between master and pupil,
than they were in Cennini's day.   Instead of an authority almost paternal on the one hand, filial obedience on the other, and an intimacy
quite equal to that of kinship on both, there are ill-defined connec-
tions of the loosest description.   Too frequently self-assertion and
distrust on the part of the pupil are met by the master's indifference.
This is a logical result of the temporariness of their contract.   Pupils
run after a teacher till fashion ousts him, and then follow the fashion.
Constant change of master is exceedingly detrimental, especially in

---

[1] I can personally attest the excellent mechanical results of the instruction
at the little school of Siena, which has doubtless its counterparts in other towns.
I saw several of the advanced pupils practising on the wall of a little chapel in
the Campo Santo, where their professor was frescoing.   Owing to his courtesy,
as already stated, I was permitted to experiment with them.   Maccari, a grad-
uate of the school, painted some first-rate frescos in the *Sud rio* at Rome,
though less transparent, perhaps, than the old work.   I refer purely to technique.   We know that Italian art is not what it was, though by no means so con-
temptible as many would have us believe.

the earlier stages of development. Every new pedagogue has always something new to preach, and were the novelty that comes with every change the desideratum, the pupil would remain a pupil till death intervened. The master should be chosen in the first place with judgment and under advice; then his beneficent counsels should be allowed full time to bear fruit. When the foundation of his education has been solidly laid, the tyro will be less distracted by seeing and hearing strange things. The superstructure may be greatly embellished by precious fragments culled here and there. How the assimilative Raphael profited by the examples of Leonardo, Michael Angelo, Fra Bartolommeo and others in his first free years! Yet such influences might have only distracted him, and proved anything but beneficial when under the tutelage of Perugino. A young pupil is not capable of judging for himself, and, if a free agent, will change instructors with the seasons. There is little analogy between the discipline of our methodical professional schools and colleges, which turn out excellent material, and the elastic regulations of our anomalous art schools, which may be entered without preliminary requirements, and for a brief or protracted period. Few of the latter have any real hold on their pupils. The private ateliers are scarcely worth mentioning; they are chiefly recruited from the amateurs, and their whole tenor is unprofessional. It is the misfortune of many able artists that they are driven by necessity to take pupils without discrimination. The public or quasi-public schools have an irresistible attraction to the serious pupil in this, as in other countries; for centralization is the tendency of the day, and the greater the pity, since the fierce rivalry of the private ateliers is a wholesome stimulant to pupil and art, saving both from a dreary, official monotony. But while it is true that there is a general tendency to uniformity of method, to the foundation of large central schools moulded on a common model, and to the unintentional suppression of the private atelier, within those establishments there is anything but unity. Art schools differ so radically from other schools that there can be but little analogy between their respective polities. Discipline in both is essential, in order to inculcate the means of artistic or literary expression. But here the analogy ceases. The range of studies in the latter is so varied, that specialists are needed to interpret them, even did a limited number of pupils permit the supremacy of one instructor. From the very diversity of their specialties, these separate units work in harmony and form an homogeneous whole, either under the control of an individual, or body of men who give it the necessary stability. Though this

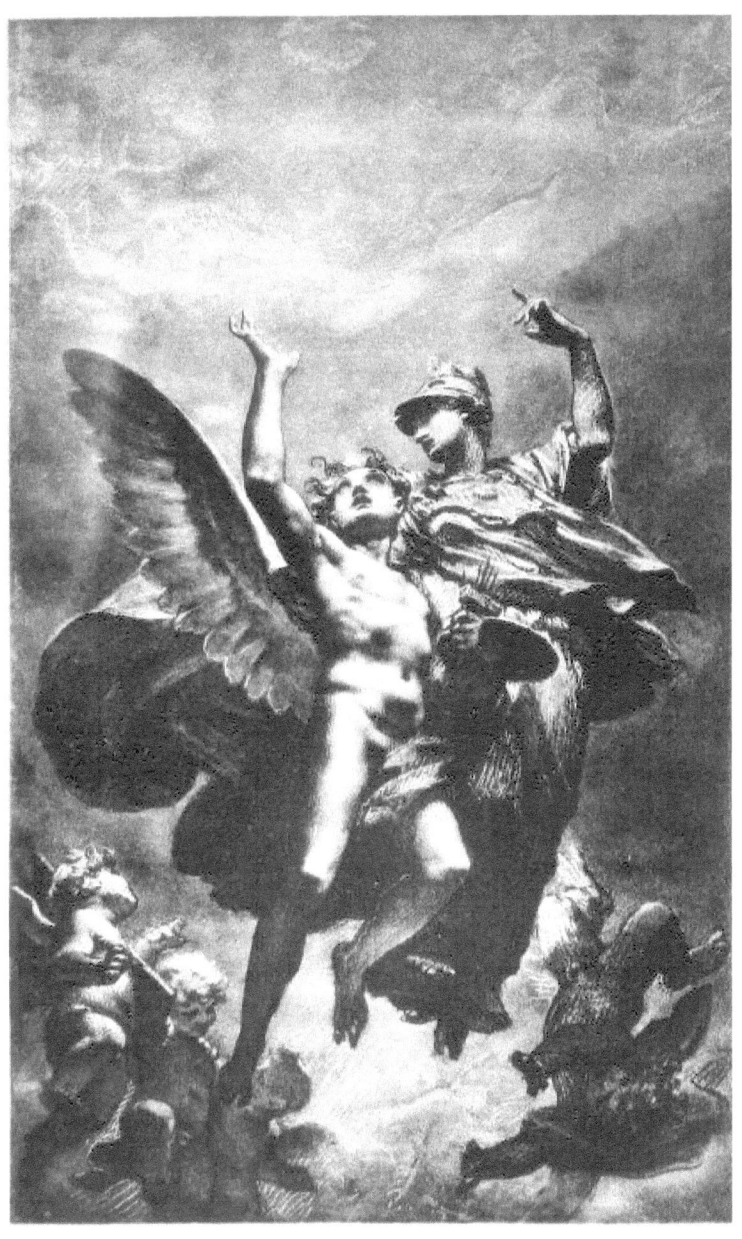

Minerve elevant le Génie vers l'Empyrée' (Drawing in black and white for a Ceiling) by Prud'hon (1760-1825)

polity obtains in a less degree in our art schools, nevertheless it obtains, with a strong tendency to develop in the same direction. But in no department of human culture is the need of a dominating personality so imperative as in æsthetics. There should be no such thing as unbelief for the pupil in the earlier stages of his evolution, faith and enthusiasm being as essential to him as to the catechumen; without them consistent progress would be impossible, for there would be nothing to build upon. Consequently in matters of taste, and especially of interpretation, there should be but one supreme authority for the beginner. Is this generally the case? By no means; for we have one master for the life, another for the portrait, a third for the antique — purely arbitrary divisions of one and the same thing. (Or, perhaps, the pupil to benefit, as he fancies, by the advice of many, and to extract the little good he may find in each, goes to one day-school and another night-school.) To work in unison the masters must be offshoots from the same parent stem; but too often they hold antagonistic doctrines, which, however interesting and sound they may be *per se*, when preached in concert craze the poor pupil, who has not always the power to discriminate between differences that are real, and those that are only apparent. Nothing but doubt and perplexity can result from such conflicting tenets. Certain auxiliary studies, involving neither taste nor interpretation, as anatomy, perspective and the like, may be advantageously pursued with specialists; but such studies only. To make matters still worse these conflicting elements are often under the control not of one strong, confident character, who might give unity to a body even so heterogeneous, but of a committee (what an innate love we have to govern by committees!) which is often made up of conflicting elements, and not infrequently recruited from laymen, who, however conscientious they may be, are generally without convictions, and hence timid. So that to the evil naturally resulting from such a government is added a general feeling of instability and temporariness that unsettles and cools both instructor and pupil.

Another, and perhaps the greatest objection to the public-school system (and I must denominate all schools public that are not absolutely under the control of the artist-instructor, even though a fee be exacted), is the perfunctory nature of the relations between teacher and taught. No man, much less an artist, can advantageously teach those who are not in sympathy with him. He is congealed at once. No pupil can profit by the counsels of a master whom he disapproves —and young America does not keep his disapprobation in the background. The very traits that have raised him high in some pursuits, have retarded him in the fine arts, where the discipline is lax, and the restraints insignificant. There is much in art that is the result of accumulated experience, and must be learned from the experienced, a fact very difficult for the scholar to comprehend. He is far too prone, owing to the lack of sympathy and confidence between himself and master, to be led by the few hectoring pupils that are found in every school-room, rather than by his preceptor. These conclusions may seem harsh and unflattering, but if true, why conceal them? The personal experience of many years as an instructor in a semi-public school, and of several in an atelier — not to mention the experience as a pupil—has forced me to them. Yet candor and affection compel me to state that I have met with a number of ardent and intelligent exceptions. The experience of others may not tally with my own; but these pages do not pretend to infallibility; and as knowledge is the result of all experience, I contribute my own, trusting that the complement may be forthcoming. This state of things is not peculiar to our own country. I should be very reluctant to disparage the French system of education, either on my own testimony, or on that of my compatriots; yet the following significant words from an eulogistic review [1] of Hippolyte Flandrin's mural paintings in Saint-Germain des Prés,[2] though published in 1862, certainly corroborate what I saw for myself a decade later, and what has very recently been reported to me by reliable students. "No more self-denial, no more modesty on the part of the pupils, no more devotion on the part of the masters; or rather there are no more masters and no more pupils. In vain I look for schools of painting; since we must be careful not to designate by such a name those school-rooms in which a greater or less number of young people are gathered about a sorry model, that they dare to call nature. There is no instruction worthy of a master in such places, no initiative, no action on the mind of the pupils, no community of work among them, no true affection, frequently, even, no sympathy in their way of seeing. There is a cold professor who passes among indifferent pupils doling out to them from time to time some common-place advice. Where are the great intellects about which other intellects, eager to learn, formerly clustered? Where is the benevolent guardianship of former

[1] A. Gruver, *Gazette des Beaux-Arts, Mars*, 1862. See also, a brochure by M. H. Lecoq de Boisbaudran, entitled, *Coup d'œil sur l'Enseignement des Beaux-Arts.* Paris, 1872.
[2] The medium used for these paintings was the *huile ciré* (oil and wax) invented by Baron Taubenheim.

days? Where is the docility, the devotion, the loyalty, of the pupils? Where is that communion of principles and ideas that created great works? The weak leave these pretended schools with
a routine that soon chokes them, and from which the strong emanci-
pate themselves with great difficulty. All await impatiently the hour
of deliverance, happy moment when they can shake off the academic
yoke, open an atelier, dub themselves masters in their turn, and
avenge the wrongs done them by their former instructors on their
future pupils. We forget too quickly that but a few chosen ones
can raise themselves unaided into the higher spheres; that the
taste and intelligence requisite to follow and comprehend the evo-
lutions of genius are already rare, and ought to satisfy the ambition
of men of talent, and that there is danger of being overwhelmed in
attempting the course of Phæthon. Yet never has the practice of art,
never has cleverness been wider spread; and all is dispersing in vain
smoke, all is at the discretion of caprice and fashion. Never was so
much spent for such small and poor returns."

"But if there are no more private schools where brains ferment,
where theories freely clash, and from which works are turned out
with passion to uphold sound or unsound ideas, at least we have official instruction. The palace of the School of Fine Arts is one of the
most splendid in our capitol; there the reproductions of the *chefs-
d'œuvre* of all ages are pompously displayed, and it is impossible
that with so many elements of instruction men of taste and scholarly
artists should not be formed. Besides is it not inadmissible that in
a country so completely administered, where the Government con-
trols celebrated schools, in which it fits its youth for all the liberal
professions, the law, engineering, the army, and medicine, there should
not also be a school wherein architects, sculptors and painters are
formed? That is inadmissible; nevertheless, it is true. Official instruction in the fine arts exists but nominally in France; the walls
of the school are admirably adorned, but within them the mind of
the pupils remains empty. The professors—for there are professors,
and very celebrated, too — . . . teach the scholars neither to sculpture nor to paint, still less to compose a group or a picture; all that
doubtless counts as a mere accessory, and is learned perhaps outside.
. . . There are, then, no more independent schools of painting in
France, that is to say, there are no longer doctrines rallying around an
illustrious master artists determined to work, fight, and give their lives
for the defence and propagation of their ideas; nor is there a public
school where the State makes good the loss of individual force. . . .

Assuredly, 'tis a sweeter task to adorn a boudoir than to contribute
to the majesty of a temple ; but as decorative painting has had its
being in all ages, as it is and always should be the true painting for
masters, it is evident that art cannot be too much encouraged in this
direction."

A propos of French instruction, I have heard competent authorities
bitterly complain that pupils too frequently denied their real master
— some nameless, unribboned, worthy man of the provinces, perhaps — and entered for a brief period the atelier of a Parisian nota-
bility, merely to profit by his name and fame. How many artists —
not from France alone — figure in dictionaries and catalogues as pupils of this or that celebrity, who would scarcely recognize them were
they to meet ! Yet these same artists are well aware that they owe
everything to masters more devoted, more efficient, but less widely
known ; whose names, forsooth, must be suppressed, because they
would make but dingy appendages to their own on the official list.
The tails to their kites must be flexible, long, and sufficiently weighty
to steer them upwards to success. Such denials render our catalogues practically useless for educational inferences.

Before dismissing this weighty question of the mutual attitude of
master and pupil, a modern tendency very pertinent to it should be
briefly noted, a tendency which Hamerton has emphasized in his
comparison of the actual paternal and filial relations with those of
the past, and that is the growing reluctance on the part of the parent
—and I will add, master — to issue the word of command, trusting
and preferring that the son—or pupil—may be prompted to the right
by his own free impulse, or if to the wrong, that time and salutary experience may mend and more than mend the error. This is partly
due to the reaction from the stern and disciplinary past, and is partly
the result of certain social and ethical revolutions that cannot be dis- ·
cussed here. That this unwillingness to control the minor exists is
very evident, and is not without its embarrassing consequences in the
training of art students.

In considering the qualifications of the modern artist for the wall,
we must not ignore his accomplishments—his fine and subtle feeling
for nature ; his marvellous faculty for rendering surfaces; his power
of synthesis, of summarily expressing in a few telling, loose, and
studiedly vague strokes, life, and earth and air; his power of analysis, that enables him to interpret almost photographically the minute
details of tangled reality ; his love for the effective picturesque ; his
delight in open air — all these faculties and feelings have made him

a great landscape-painter, not as was stately Claude, with his formal arrangement of temple, tree, plain and mountain ; or Poussin, or Salvator, but as a free and unconventional lover of rusticity. It may be questioned whether the out-of-door feeling — *la peinture de plein air* — is a great gain; whether the essence of it, all that could be assimilated by art, was not utilized long ago by the Italian frescoists and the dross rejected; whether many great men did not, and do not still, avowedly reject the whole of it on high artistic grounds ; yet whether these are facts or not, it may be safely averred that we are intimate with nature now as we never have been before, that our horizon is thereby vastly extended, and that our close and conscientious observation of man and his surroundings is a rectifying agent of inestimable value. The mischief is done when nature is made the end, not the means, an error we are too prone to commit; yet mistakes and excesses, much as we may deplore and endeavor to avoid them, are the almost inevitable concomitants of all great revolutions. For our consolation let us bear in mind that epochs of realism have usually preceded still greater epochs of—I will not say idealism, for that word, first-rate though it be, is just now in disrepute — but of art. Something great will surely be 'the result of our daily friction with nature. By a closer study of it, Giotto, the great reformer (1276–1337), shattered the hieratic conventionalism of Byzantium, and regenerated an effete art, which, now ebbing with his stolid imitators, now calmly manifesting itself in the beatific but exceptional inspiration of an Angelico (1387–1455), now rising again with artists who turned once more to Nature, such as Massaccio (1401–1428), Donatello (1386–1468), and the brothers Van Eyck in Germany (from 1366 to 1441), finally culminated in the glorious age of Leonardo, Michael Angelo, Raphael and Titian. Who cannot remember, on painted wall or panel, the sweet, pious, naïve, *every-day* faces of winged angels (those of Benozzo Gozzoli [1420–1497?] for instance), that lend them that ineffable, childlike charm; or the lifelike burghers, passive spectators of some great drama ; or the animated busts of heroes and scholars, characterized even to ugliness ; or again, the spare legs and spider-like arms of a David or a Precursor? Yet all this realism was tempered by an inherited aptitude and respect for design and composition, as well as by a passion for the antique. Following this modified realism came the generation of the demi-gods. Never was there a nicer adjustment between the real and the ideal; and how difficult this adjustment ! One step too far from the real — or rather the vulgar real — and there yawns the chasm of conventionalism, into which the successors of the demigods plunged. These god-like men give us the type rather than the individual, except in the portrait (and even this is monumentally simplified); chosen, not haphazard forms; nature, at her best, but always, always nature. However ideal the forms may be, they are founded on some suggestion, even though slight, from the real. One has only to look over the portfolio of a Raphael to be convinced. A little sketch from a fellow pupil will blossom as an exquisite angel; some bald-pated, ill-looking acquaintance, as a stately philosopher; yet neither saint nor philosopher would have that life-like ring had they been evolved purely from the imagination, and certain vital characteristics been ignored. This constant reference to nature saved these great painters from the cold, plastic academism of later days, while their idealism, which is nothing more at its best than rendering nature in her choicest garb, rescued them from the naïve, unselected, and sometimes amusing individualism (which had its charm) of their predecessors. At the same time it made them the monarchs of monumental painting, which despotically exacts, ennobled, purified and rhythmical forms.

And what does our unconventional rusticity, or our supreme faculty to immortalize the meanest thing in its meanest garb avail us for the wall? What our boasted neglect of balanced form and beauty of line for an art that especially calls for equilibrium of mass and harmony of contour? Of what advantage is picturesqueness to the artist whose chief aim is to avoid the accidental? Wherein does looseness of handling, or the broken line benefit the man who is ever striving to express himself with decision? For definition is as essential to mural painting as the omission of it is to the truthful rendering on canvas of variegated earth, mobile water, and glistening air. What does our photographic translation of nature's complexities bring to monumental interpretation, which enforces suppression of detail? Our out-of-door sympathies give us one thing — light; for though decorative painting must always conform to its surroundings, which often necessitate rich and low-toned harmonies, yet, as a rule, circumstances more frequently exact light and airy, than heavy and sombre tones. Nevertheless it is the stern duty of monumental painting, even in rendering out-of-door effects, to suppress the countless, incalculable, and often confusing eccentricities of direct, reflected or diffused light, and to give a strong — perhaps stronger— impression of *plein air*, by a discreet elimination.

Thus the studio practice of the modern artist aids him but little when he transfers his talents to the wall. He *may* have been thoroughly exercised in monumental composition, but the chances are against it; neither has his school nor subsequent practice acquainted him with architectural and decorative forms. His knowledge of the chemical and physical changes to which colors are liable, of the constructive details and necessities of walls and plaster is absolutely *nil*,

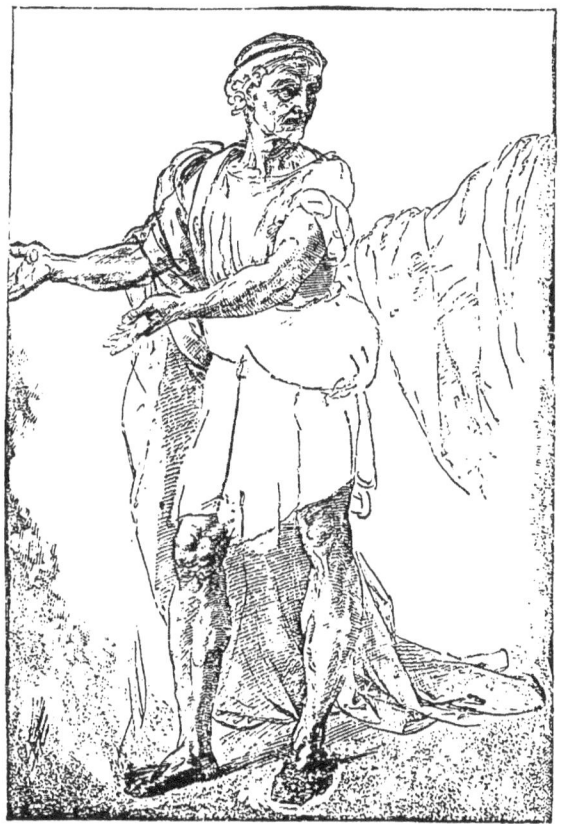

From a Drawing by Raphæl.

and his technique is diametrically opposed to that of mural painting. As a rule, his sporadic efforts on the wall have not been crowned with success; for they have either borne the stamp of vast easel-pictures, or, as previously observed, have overstepped the mark, and been characterized by an almost primitive rudeness.

I cannot refrain from quoting here some very pertinent lines by Eugène Müntz (*Études sur l'Histoire de la Peinture*, Paris, 1886): "It is to the *amateurs* that the modern painters address themselves:

it is by the refinements of drawing and coloring that they captivate us, rather than by the depth of their convictions. Individual fancy has replaced those emphatic rules that furnished to early Christian as well as to Mediæval art the motive of its being and its striking air of necessity." When it is remembered that the very best men in those days decorated church, palace, and public hall, while our best men paint for collectors, the sympathy between the former and their public, and the lack of it between the latter and our public can readily be comprehended.

It may be supposed that a special training, less long, less laborious, and more special, might with advantage be substituted for the ordinary routine of the art-student. Perhaps for the lower and more mechanical phases of decoration, yes; but not for the monumental painter, or for any decorator who hopes to stamp his work with his own personality, or to add one jot to pre-existent knowledge. The uninspired and shopworn decorative work—figure, floral or geometrical—that passes muster as art, is too well known to require elaborate condemnation. It is enough to say that such work is the result of a special, mechanical training, unsupported by those severe and laborious studies from life and nature which are the only true and possible source of fresh inspiration. There is no short cut; the decorator must be as conversant with vital form and color as the painter of the easel-picture, if he expects to create. That these studies, as usually conducted, can be amended and supplemented is true enough; for they are neither all-sufficient, nor at times rational; yet, as I have before observed, it is not my purpose, at least for the present, to examine seriatim the educational methods now in vogue. There is, however, one defect in them so apposite to the matter in hand that it cannot be blinked. We all know how much time and ingenuity are spent on elaborate life-drawings. Such exercises in moderation are not fruitless; yet many a clumsy hand can stump or scrub his way up to a highly-finished representation of the cast or life with a week's labor, who cannot possibly translate the same in a few suggestive, logical, and inerasable lines. In other words, such work, however useful it may be, is not enough, and unless fortified by other exercises, it would never teach a pupil to draw.

Now what the mural painter most needs is the power to delineate objects, at rest or in action, promptly, broadly, and intelligently. He must not only be able to portray what he sees, but he must *know* what he sees. His sketches must be rapid and to the point, his final drawing and brushing decisive and significant. His life is too short for tentative outline and modelling. Those wonderful drawings, the legacies of the old masters, tell the whole story far more eloquently than I can. Besides these things, they teach us that the faculty for representing objects, animate and inanimate, from the imagination should be cultivated. Not only is this faculty requisite in order to improvise,

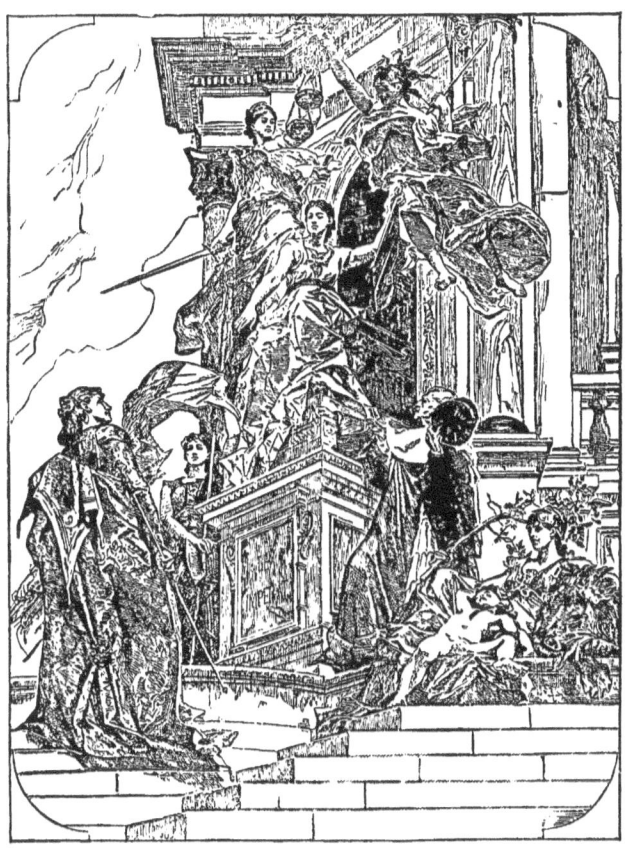

'The Glorification of the Law.' Ceiling by Paul Baudry.

to fix on paper or canvas the "first thought," untainted by models, but very frequently, also, to supply their deficiencies and limitations, both as to form and action. An artist who is dependent on his model for suggestions cannot hope to excel in an art whose corner-stone is fertility of invention and expression. The model is but the means — the precious means — that saves us from wearisome, stereotyped conventionalism. And what shall be said of the use of the photograph as an auxiliary? Assuredly, it has its purposes; but that will be a fatal day to artistic expression, when the photograph supplants skilful and inspired draughtsmanship, and becomes the symbol of our impotence.

Would it be an act of supererogation to say that the mural painter should assiduously glean fresh suggestions from nature? that he should stock his sketch-books with memoranda of artistic expression, as well as with the countless and unexpected revelations of the life about him? that his memory should be an encyclopædia of decorative motives? Would it be superfluous to state that he should be gifted with imagination, with the power of seeing clearly, simply and beautifully, heroic compositions, and that he should be born with a feeling for rhythm? Is there need to emphasize the necessity of familiarizing himself with the immortal works of the great decorators? For in truth there are no masters equal to those whose reputations have been consecrated by time. Without some knowledge of them no education is complete. Those who can, should travel intelligently and observantly, in the land of mural painting—in Italy. It is discouraging to think how many of our students halt in Paris, at the portals of that fair country, rich in artistic treasure; or if by chance they visit her, draw inspiration merely from her superficial picturesqueness. None better than the French themselves recognize the supreme importance of a careful study of the great Italian decorators. Did not Baudry live with them before girding himself for his life-work in the Opera? Did he not fortify his natural talents by their example, without in the least enslaving them? And, finally, it is but too evident that men who are suddenly called upon to suggest fitting themes for given places, widely differing in their purposes, should enrich their minds, if not with many — and the more the better — at least with a few, well-chosen, literary masterpieces. Good literature promotes good style.

In no department of the fine arts have professionals studied and practised more intelligently and successfully than in that of architecture. The very nature of their work has constrained our architects to pursue a methodical course of instruction. They have profited by the lessons of the past, without being trammelled by them, and have proved that a respect for tradition is not prejudicial to consistent development. They have distinctly added something to art, and to our honor be it noted that their efforts have just begun to attract the merited attention of their foreign *confrères*. Not that they are always guiltless of solecisms and eccentricities; not that they have yet adapted themselves satisfactorily to their bewildering environments; nevertheless they are working systematically in the right direction. Their brothers of the brush may well take a hint from their methods if they hope to keep pace with them. On the other hand the architects can do much to encourage the painters, and at the same time adorn their own art by giving them the opportunity that church and state gave in past times, and in other lands whose greatest pictorial triumphs have been on the wall. We may, for the nonce, be ill-provided with practitioners, but the occasion will surely raise them. If the training, aims and technique of our artists do not particularly fit them for monumental painting, these can readily be amended without antagonism to the spirit of the age. There is no reason why we should not greatly profit by our new-born aspirations and methods, if they be consistently controlled and developed; for the field of art itself and the means of expression have of late years been greatly enlarged. Our feeling for refined and delicate combinations of color, for instance, or, more succinctly, our tone perceptions (acquired, perhaps, from the Eastern nations, who have always been gifted with them), are infinitely more sensitive than they were in mediæval or Grecian days, and are a precious addition to our artistic repertory.

No one can have failed to note the great and increasing sympathy for decoration that obtains to-day; misguided and illiterate at times, imperatively exacting the new-fangled products of artist and artisan, morbidly craving startling combinations, yet withal genuine. This untutored demand and supply, this yearning to satisfy untrained desires, may account in part for the dangerous tendencies of our decorators, to glorify the material at the expense of art. The Greeks took care to make their Venuses beautiful; we should do well to follow their example. Barbaric splendor can never be a fit substitute for art. May we soon, too, throw off the malarious garb of "æstheticism" that we have borrowed from our cousins across the seas, who, in turn, borrowed it from a dead past; for however well it may become them, it is not for us. Strange that a young and vigorous people — a people that avowedly abhors the unreal, that professes a sincere cult for wholesome nature — should people their canvases with such sickly creations! Yet, notwithstanding these defects — and they are defects — I feel inclined to hazard the same remark about our decoration which I made with confidence on our architecture, that in certain departments of it, at least, we have added something new to art.

No effort has been made in these chapters to draw the line of
demarcation between monumental and the lower phases of decorative painting, since they fay into each other.   The latter, moreover,
are the almost constant auxiliaries of the former, and the same brain
must conceive, even though the same hand does not execute both.
If expense, perchance, should not always permit the gratification of
our taste for painted epic, we can at least indulge in less lofty, but
thoroughly artistic and grammatical prose.

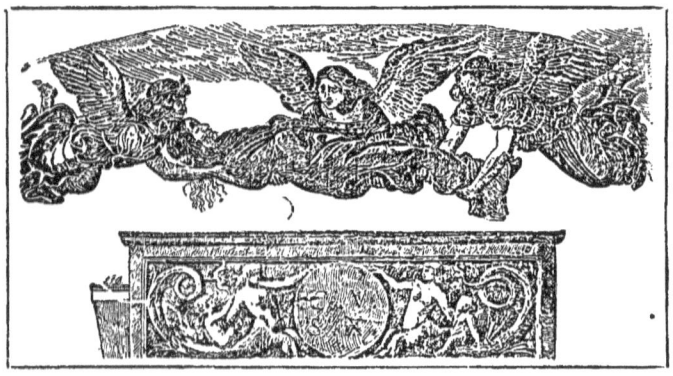

' Entombment of St. Catharine.'   Fresco by Bernardino Luini.   1460–1530.

NOTES.

"It came to pass that these Franks, whom the Italians continued to treat as barbarians, without having succeeded in arousing an artis tic culture comparable to that of Theodoric's time [455–526], at last eclipsed their ultramontane neighbors, thanks to the influence of Charlemagne [742–814]. We especially know that the great emperor of the Franks made it obligatory by law to paint the whole interior surface of churches. His emissaries were charged, while inspecting religious edifices, not only to examine the condition of the walls, pavements, and other essential features, but also that of the paintings (*volumus itaque ut missi nostri per singulos pagos prævidere studeant . . . primum de ecclesiis, quomodo structæ aut in tectis, in maceriis, sive in parietibus, sive in pavimentis, nec non in pictura, etiam et in luminariis, sive officiis*). Statutes, several times reënacted, settled the manner of contributing for their decoration. If for a royal church, the clergy and neighboring *abbés* were to provide the means; if for a beneficed church, the incumbent. When the emperor caused an oratory to be erected, even in the midst of the camps, the whole surface of the walls was covered with pictures. A church was not deemed completed till it had received this kind of ornamentation. According to the French doctors, the paintings had a two-fold object — to instruct the people, and to embellish the monument. Charlemagne meant that they should have a third : to obliterate from the Saxons' view, by an extreme magnificence, the richness of their ancient altars (*Eméric-David, Histoire de la Peinture an moyen âge*, éd. de 1863, p. 67, 68). Thanks to this enlightened protection, Franco-German painting soon surpassed the Italian."

"But the superiority of Franco-German art did not last. France, Switzerland, and Germany were in turn engulfed by the rising wave of barbarism; the artificial culture created by Charlemagne disap-

peared without leaving a trace; in the second half of the ninth, and
during the whole of the tenth, there were still, perhaps, artists, but
assuredly no art."   [Müntz, *Études sue l'Histoire de la Peinture.*]

CHAPTER I, PAGE 2.

To convey some idea of the esteem in which monumental painting
was held in Italy during the Renaissance (and still is•held), I give an
extract from the *"Aretin"* of Lodovico Dolce [1508–1568], who ranked
high among the literati of the age of Clement VII, both for his learning and taste.

"And who does not know how much painting contributes to the
beauty and elegance, to the enriching, embellishing, and ornamenting
palaces, and other noble edifices, though adorned with statues, busts,
basso-relievos, and other ornaments of architecture, cabinets, glass
mirrors, slabs, and tables of curious marble, porphyry, and other
precious stones, Persian carpets, and other rich and elegant furniture?
These appear as nothing without historical and other paintings and
pictures of the best masters.   And how easy is it to discover how
much superior, and how far more pleasing, the grand fronts or façades of palaces are, when painted by the ablest hands, than those in-
crusted with the richest marbles or porphyry, though variegated with
veins of gold.   The same may be said of churches and other public
edifices; for which reason the popes I have named as patrons of
Raphael, employed him in painting the hall and chambers of the palace above mentioned, and Michael Angelo, in decorating the Church
of St. Peter and St. Paul at Rome.   And for the same reason, the
best masters of the time had before been ordered to decorate the
Grand Council-Chamber (Venice) with their paintings, to which were
afterwards added two pictures by Titian; and it is much to be
wished he had executed the whole.   Had it happily been so, it would
now have been one of the most admirable and beautiful spectacles in
Italy.   The same reason also prevailed when George da Castelfranco
[Giorgione, 1477–1511] was employed in adorning the German office;
but that part which respects Mercury was painted by Titian when yet
a youth.   Of this I shall take occasion, before I conclude, to speak
further, and only observe here that the neighboring *barbarous* and
infidel nations are by their religion, the fountain of all their laws,
customs and manners, strictly forbid all representations of nature,
whether by painting or sculpture, or any other device whatever."
[English translation, London, 1770.]

The frescos on the exterior of the "German office" by Giorgione and Titian have almost entirely disappeared.

CHAPTER III.

There is no pretension in these pages to archæological lore. MM. Cros and Henry's solution of the encaustic enigma has been preferred and given, not only because it is the latest, but because, in the judgment of a practitioner, it is the most complete and plausible yet offered. Their erudition may, or may not, be on a par with their technical ingenuity ; but it must be remembered that the passages on which scholars rely for the true explanation of the mystery are provokingly insufficient, and until something more definite has been unearthed we must accept the interpretation that best accords with the technical revelations of authentic monuments and the spirit of extant texts. Recent, and experimental, applications of polychromy to statuary made in Berlin, have re-opened such knotty questions as how much or how little, and in what manner, did the ancients color their statues, questions that do not concern us here. It has sufficed to quote only that passage which is relevant to our subject — the very explicit statement of Vitruvius, that the ancients cauterized their marble statues, to protect them from atmospheric corrosion.

CHAPTER IX, PAGE 88. "THE ENGLISH DELIGHTFUL POETS."

"Some one has remarked," says Winkelmann, [1717–1768], "not without reason, that the poets on the other side of the mountain speak through images, but afford few pictures." [History of Ancient Art; B. I, Chapter III.]

The following extracts from the notes by the English translator [London, 1770] of Dolce's Aretin are appended as literary curiosities, certainly not for their critical acumen. The closing paragraphs — ludicrous as they now seem — augmented as they might be by an infinitude of cruel, perverted, and (in their day) honored judgments are eloquently and pathetically suggestive. Will our most solemn and authoritative verdicts be quoted for the merriment of posterity ? Does man ever see his contemporaries face to face ?

"And what is next to be lamented is (which from physical causes hath been endeavored to be accounted for), that true genius in the liberal arts (as well as the sciences and the art of government) hath hitherto been confined within very narrow bounds, and seems incapable of being extended much farther than that part of Europe and its confines which lies between thirty and forty-five degrees of North latitude, or fifty-two at the most, and between eight and fifty-seven degrees East longitude; that it hath never extended its influence farther to the North, nor nearer than twenty-five degrees **to** the Line. Painting and sculpture have been so far from making any progress towards the North, that they have been neglected and even despised in proportion as we advance northward, to the fifty-eighth degree of North latitude only; ' insomuch that the most valuable pieces of Correggio served only for blinds to the windows of the royal stables at Stockholm.'"

"'And tho' the English climate hath been warm enough to produce a number of eminent men in most sciences and professions; and notwithstanding the great munificence of Henry the Eighth, Queen Elizabeth, and Charles the First during the first fifteen years of his reign, and the great value they had for pictures, and the encouragement given by Queen Elizabeth to all sorts of arts, during a reign of near fifty years; and although it is acknowledged by foreigners that there are no workmen in the world that have greater beauty in the execution than the English, or know better how to manage their tools; and though England hath given to the world eminent poets, yet it hath not produced painters who have been able to attain to that taste in design which some foreign artists have brought over with them to England.'"

" The same hath been observed of France; that ' although Francis the First was one of the most zealous protectors that the arts and sciences could ever boast of, and notwithstanding the friendship and regard he shewed to Roux, to Andrea del Sarto, to Leonardo da Vinci (who died in his arms), and to every one that was illustrious for talent or merit, and the profusion with which he paid for the pictures he ordered to be painted for him by Raphael; and through his liberality and kind reception drew numbers of eminent men into France, and his bounties were bestowed continually on the possessors of this art during a reign of thirty-three years; yet they could never form an eminent painter among his own subjects.' Vide *Reflections on the Painting and Sculpture of the Greeks, translated from the German original, of the Abbé Winkelmann*, p. 1, 2, and *Du Bos's Réflexions Critiques Sur la Poésie et la Peinture*."[1]

" But notwithstanding the above observations upon the climates of

---

[1] " France, famed in all great arts, in none supreme."—*Matthew Arnold*.

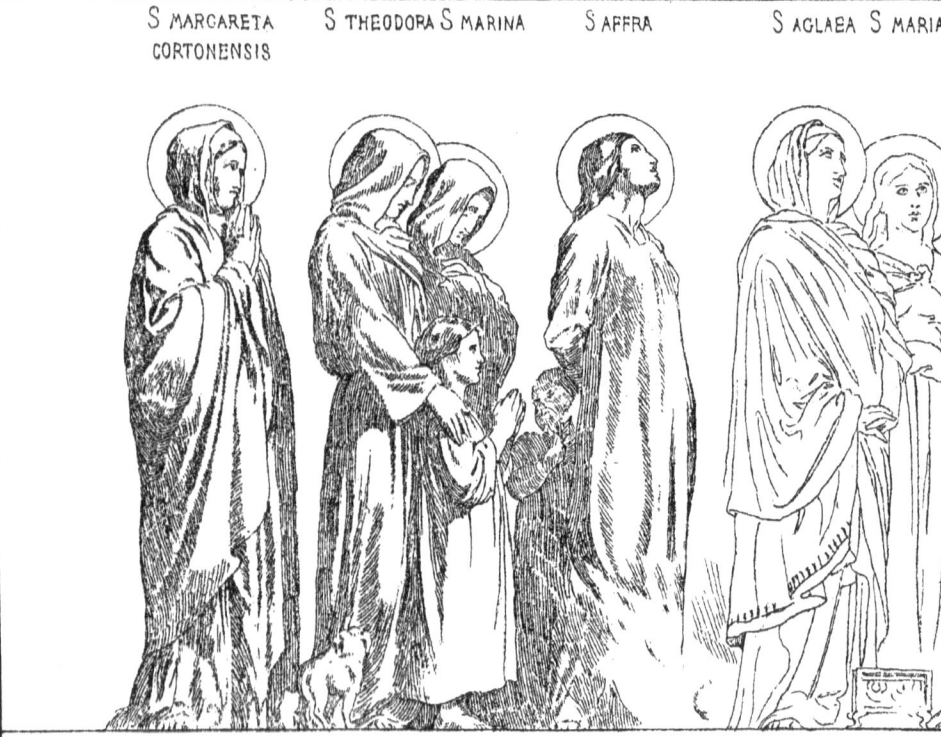

S MARGARETA   S THEODORA S MARINA   S AFFRA   S AGLAEA S MARIA
CORTONENSIS

Mur

Frieze of the Nave of the Church of S. Vincent de 9

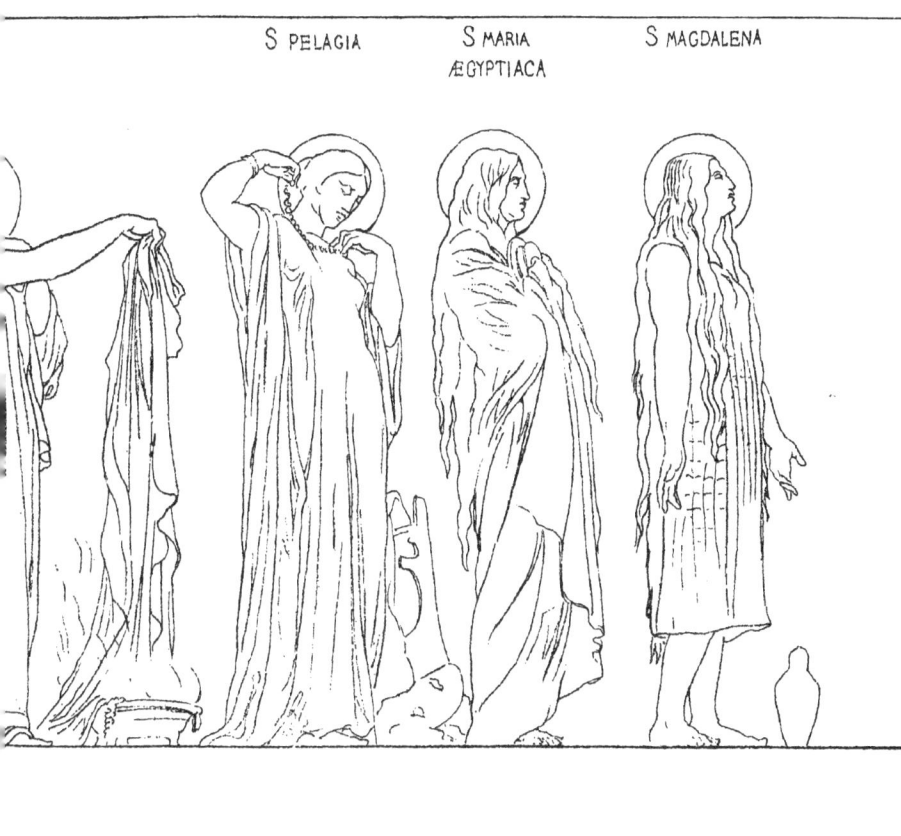

S PELAGIA   S MARIA   S MAGDALENA
ÆGYPTIACA

...ting.

...ippolyte Flandrin. —— "Les Saintes Pénitentes."

England and France, and the seeming discouragements to the artists of London and Paris in particular, yet since the time Du Bos speaks of, France hath produced many eminent masters, both in painting and sculpture." After mentioning Nicholas Poussin (1594–1665), and Le Sueur (1617–1655), he cites "Charles Le Brun, born at Paris, in 1619, whose painting of the *Family of Darius*, which is at Versailles, is not surpassed by the coloring of the picture of Paul Veronese, which is placed over against it; but is greatly superior to it in design, composition, dignity, expression, and the justness of the *costume*. The prints from his pictures of the *Battles of Alexander* are even more esteemed than the *Battles of Constantine*, by Raphael and Julio Romano. He died in 1690."

" It is very remarkable, also, that even in countries capable of inspiring every kind of genius, there have been barren ages, in which the liberal arts, and the genius that produced them, declined to such a degree as to seem in the course of the next to be wholly lost."

"History mentions only three *ages* in which they have arrived to a degree of perfection : That to which we owe their first rise, and commenced ten years before the reign of Philip, the father of Alexander the Great, in which they obtained their highest perfection ; the age of Augustus ; and that of Julius the Second and Leo the Tenth; unless that which commenced with Poussin, and continued to the end of the reign of Louis XIV, he reckoned as a *fourth*, which it justly may, though not so general as any of the former. And *we* have reason now to flatter ourselves with the pleasing hope that the reign of his present Majesty will be the *era* of the *fifth*, and distinguished by the *Age of George the Third*. True Genius in the liberal arts seems now to have visited this island, and taken up her residence among us, which we apparently owe, and may justly be ascribed (physical causes, of which we can only judge by the effects, perhaps conspiring), to a *Liberal Society* formed among us, for the *encouragement of Arts*, and for other laudable and very valuable purposes, and the *patronage* and *munificence* of our *truly amiable Monarch*." [Who preferred Benjamin West to Joshua Reynolds !]

In his preface the translator remarks : "Altho' I wish to avoid mentioning living artists by name, that I may not give umbrage to any, yet, lest those who have not seen our exhibitions should esteem this only to proceed from partiality, and a desire of making the state of the Arts here appear other than it really is, I cannot help producing, as instances, the Regulus, Jacob blessing Joseph's children, Cleombrotus, &c., of Mr. West; an artist whose works would have done honor to Rome, even in the time of Raphael and Titian. The appeal might safely be lain with any person of taste and judgment, whether these and many other of our modern works do not fully prove this assertion."

ILLUSTRATIONS.

1.

2.

" The advent of the gothic style resulted in the overthrow of the Byzantine school and its congeners, and to substitute the study of life for the quest of pomp or grandeur. The master who stamped the new tendencies with the seal of perfection was an Italian, Giotto. This revivalist of genius, the greatest painter of the Middle Ages, based his reform on the imitation of nature. No more conventional scenes, no more pompous and empty formulas ! Without yet pushing realism so far as to give to Christ, to the apostles, to the saints, the features of his contemporaries, Giotto regenerates his types by a spirit of observation which forms a complete contrast to his predecessors' spirit of abstraction. He is the first to rediscover the structural laws of the human body, and those of its movement. We are no longer confronted by conventional figures, but by men, living the life that is peculiar to them. Landscape resumes its rights. Finally, the representation of the episodes of sacred history abounds in snatches from life, now spiritual, now pathetic. So many conquests would have sufficed to immortalize the name of Giotto. But the founder of the Florentine school has still greater claims. His compositions reveal a dramatic feeling which ought to have made Michael Angelo and Raphael jealous. Force of expression, eloquence of attitude and gesture have never been carried further. What could be more moving than Saint Francis defying the false doctors, than the sisters of Lazarus at the feet of Christ ! "

" Giotto was philosopher as well as dramaturgist ; I mean that he was an artist who knew how to translate into his own language the most abstract ideas. Through his instrumentality allegory enters into religious painting, and regenerates it. His frescos open the series of those grand compositions which for more than a century are to make the reputation of Italy, the Triumph of Faith and Poverty, the Triumph of Chastity and Fame, the Triumph of St. Francis, of St. Thomas Aquinas, of Charlemagne, etc., etc. By the power of their conception, the beauty of their arrangement, the richness of their details, these noble pages, that can be admired even to-day at Florence, Siena, Pisa, Assisi, Naples, Avignon, etc., etc., remained as inimitable models till the moment when Raphael created the Dispute of the Holy Sacrament and the School of Athens."

" In this *ensemble*, half theological, half philosophical, so vigorously conceived and elaborated under the direct influence of Giotto's friend, Dante, there was no place for secular representations; so that in the work of Giotto we must neither look for scenes borrowed from ancient or contemporaneous history, nor for *genre* subjects, nor for portraits. Even his easel pictures are rare. Such grandiose conceptions demand the repose and breadth of fresco."—Eugène Müntz, *Études sur l'Histoire de la Peinture.*

After this succinct and comprehensive estimate of Giotto's genius scarcely anything remains to be said. As a mere matter of detail, one cannot fail to be impressed by the beauty of the women in the Arena frescos. How sweet, in the accompanying illustration, is the woman-faced angel in the centre! Considering their age, these frescos are remarkably well preserved.

3.

' ÆNEAS PICCOLOMINI CREATED CARDINAL BY POPE CALIXTUS III'
(FRESCO) BY PINTURICCHIO (1454–1513). LIBRARY, SIENA.

This fresco forms one of a series by Pinturicchio, representing the principle events in the life of Pius II (Æneas Sylvius Piccolomini). Like many other Sienese frescos, they are still wonderfully fresh and sound, as the heliotype testifies, though it is less perfect than the photograph. [See chap. IX, p. 87.]

4.

' ERYTHRÆAN SIBYL ' (FRESCO) BY MICHAEL ANGELO (1474–1564).
SISTINE CHAPEL, ROME.

The genius of Michael Angelo and the Sistine frescos have been exhaustively treated by brilliant pens. Wilson, who has already been quoted several times, gives in his ' Life of Michael Angelo ' a luminous technical description, most valuable to the student, of the Sistine vault. This illustration is introduced, not only as a specimen of a giant's craft in the palmiest days of mural painting, but also to exemplify that nicety of adjustment between the real and the ideal, to which reference has been made in chapter XII. The forms are monumental — simple, rhythmical, and heroic — yet fundamentally true, and instinct with life. The head in particular is full of calm majesty, very broadly painted, but thoroughly natural and unconventional, almost a portrait.

[The term *conventional* is used sometimes in a good, sometimes in a bad sense. In its former acceptation all art is conventional; but the word is often employed disparagingly to indicate a stilted, false, and lifeless phase of art, generally the academic phase.]

5.

'THE TEMPTATION' (FRESCO) BY RAPHAEL SANZIO (1483–1520).
STANZE OF THE VATICAN, ROME.

It would have been possible to illustrate Raphael more comprehensively by such monumental compositions as the 'Jurisprudence' of the Vatican, the 'Heliodorus,' or the 'School of Athens,' which eloquently reveal his loftier and more stately moods. But these have been so frequently reproduced and can so readily be consulted that I have given the preference to a less familiar fresco, less completely illustrative of the master's widely-ranging genius, yet entirely characteristic of one side of it. Notwithstanding her "length of limb" could anything be more sweetly, divinely, *peculiarly* Raphaelesque than the Eve? In all his moods Raphael is supremely harmonious : he is the musician of the brush. For mere melody of line he has no peer, unless it be Andrea del Sarto (1487–1531), when he painted the 'Madonna del Sacco' in the cloister of the Annunziata — a fresco that I had hoped to include in my repertory. Such men as Raphael and Michael Angelo — if men they can be called — seem to give all the majesty of the best Byzantines and a great deal more, too. For the student who would study "composition," they are the authorities.

6.

'MANSUETUDO' (OIL-PAINTING) BY F. PENNI (1488 ?–1528), AND GUILIO ROMANO (1492 ?–1546). HALL OF CONSTANTINE, VATICAN.

This illustration is given to show the deterioration of oil painting on plaster, of which a description is given on p. 103, chap. X. The figure of Mansuetudo alone is painted in oil. The greater part of the back-ground, and the arm, drapery, book, and hand to the right are executed in fresco.

Crowe and Cavalcaselle, in assigning the motives that induced Raphael to substitute oil for fresco, remark that, "there was evidently an impression in Raphael's mind that Sebastian's revival of a system which had failed at Florence in the days of Alessio Baldovinetti, might now be attended with advantages which it would be desirable to try." *Life of Raphael*, vol. ii, p. 449.

"*Alessio Baldovinetti*. Born in 1422, he lived to the very close of the century [1499], gaining a name for the minuteness with which he studied still life in nature, the boldness, more than the success, with which he introduced the old tempera varnish amongst the mediums employed in wall painting." Vasari says of his wall paintings, that they were "sketched in (abbozzato) in fresco and retouched *a secco*, the colors being tempered with a mixture of yolk of egg, and heated *vernice liquida*. Baldovinetti thought that this tempera would guard the painting against wet, but it was in such a measure strong, that when too heavily laid on, it scaled off" [C. & C. Hist. of Paint. in Italy, vol. ii, p. 372]. There is but little left of these paintings to-day. They have greatly suffered by abrasion, darkening, blistering and scaling. Cennini is silent concerning the nature of *vernice liquida*. See Mrs. Merrifield's notes thereon, page 159. She thinks it "highly probable that the varnish consisted of some resin dissolved in linseed oil."

Cennini gives the following directions for painting in oil on walls:

"Cover your wall with mortar, exactly as you would do when painting in fresco, except that where you then covered but a small space at a time, you are now to spread it over your whole work. Make your design with charcoal and fix it with ink, or verdaccio [a mixture of white, ochre, red and black — a quiet greenish tone] tempered. Then take a little glue much diluted, — a whole egg well beaten in a porringer, with the milky juice of the fig tree, is still better. You must add to it a glassful of clean water. Then either with a sponge or a pencil without a point, very soft, go once over the ground on which you are going to paint, and leave it to dry for one day at least."

"Vasari, in his *Introduction to the Three Arts*, teaches, in chapter XXII, how to paint in oil on walls, but in a very different manner from this, for he requires that the wall should be dry, and that it should have a coat of linseed oil, and then a mixture of resin, of mastic, and of fat varnish. He also teaches another method, which he had tried and approved of, in which it was necessary to give the wall two coats of the intonaco, but he always recommends that the wall should be perfectly dry. Here, on the contrary, Cennini points out a very simple method of painting in oil on damp walls, which may be painted on the next day. It concerns the modern artist to determine by experiments which is the best mode." [Tambroni: from Mrs. Merrifield's translation of Cennini's *Treatise*, p. 141]. What may be the actual condition of wall paintings executed in either or both of these methods, I am not in a position to ascertain, but it has certainly fared very ill with oil mural paintings in general, for the reasons given in chapter X.

7.

'JUPITER AND JUNO' (FRESCO) BY ANNIBALE CARRACCI (1560–1609). FARNESE PALACE, ROME.

This is another specimen of a well preserved series of frescos. Though nominally executed by the Carracci and their pupils, by far the larger portion of the work is attributable to Annibale. Here and there it betrays symptoms of academism, which grew apace and subsequently proved so baneful. The generation of immortals had passed away, and art was on the wane. But propinquity to the great epoch, the vitality of its traditions, and inherited faculties gave to their successors all that can be given — save genius. (And yet the church was as influential, as prodigal, and far less *pagan* than in the days of Julius and Leo). Among their successors the Carracci took their stand as reformers. Even during the life-time of Michael Angelo, anatomical exaggeration and the pedantic "mock heroic" were rampant. It was the aim of Ludovico Carracci (1553–1619), assisted by his kinsmen Agostino (1557–1602), and Annibale, to neutralize these bombastic tendencies by reverting to the best models of the past, to the works of Leonardo, Michael Angelo, Raphael, Titian, Correggio, etc., to extract their peculiar essence from each, and to combine them in a faultless whole. On these principles they founded their celebrated academy at Bologna. The result of this learned eclecticism, though a great improvement on what it sought to antagonize, was naturally convictionless academism.

Of the three Carracci, Annibale was the most independent and ablest. At one time, and before his style was definitely formed, he leaned towards the sect then known as *naturalisti*. The composition of the 'Jupiter and Juno' is irreproachable — rythmical, well-balanced, and scholarly.

8.

'RECOMPENSE' (OIL PAINTING) BY PAUL VERONESE (1528–1588).
CEILING, SALA DEL COLLEGIO, DUCAL PALACE, VENICE.

No colorless reproduction can adequately represent this sumptuous painter. Not that his forms are without dignity or style; for his draughtmanship is both easy and noble, and his figures have a grand mien; but the Venetians were not the champions of form, as were the Florentines; they were the apostles of color. Veronese was neither "deep thinker nor moralist," and therefore less heroic than Michael Angelo, Raphael, or even Titian, but he was essentially a painter. Couture (*Entretiens d'Atelier*) in estimating Veronese, says : " Let us speak of his method of painting. It is not that of Titian. I do not hesitate to say that it is *the* painting *par excellence;* there is nothing beyond it; it is the apogee. He paints with a full brush (*En pleine pâte*) and *alla prima ;* he employs the so-called Venetian processes only for certain draperies, and with so much frankness that there is no doubt about it." He is not only a great painter, but a great decorator as well, — some hold the greatest. His color is blonde and splendid; his effects are obtained by a learned distribution of the local colors — the true decorative method — not by chiaro-oscuro. In his time when Italian painting was moribund, the Venetian school was still vital. Nevertheless the germs of decadence are apparent even in Veronese.

The accompanying illustration is not subject to the reproach made in page 106, chapter X, that many of the Venetian mural paintings have the character of easel-pictures.

9.

CEILING IN CHURCH OF S. MARIA DEL ROSARIO, OR 'I GESUATI,'
VENICE, (FRESCO). TIEPOLO (GIOVANNI BATTISTA, 1697–1770).

There is a descent from Veronese to Tiepolo. The former, sumptuous and luxuriant in his *mise en scène*, is contained withal. His foreshortenings are bold, but less violent than they were subsequently, for he lived in the grand era. Tiepolo is all execution, all *chic*, all scintillation. His color is not splendid and learned like Veronese's, but rather commonplace, though sparkling. He depended largely for his effects on his brilliant, sharp, and *scenic* touch. (See p. 125, chap. XII.) His handling was that of the theatre. Yet in spite of his startling foreshortenings, his agitated forms, and his barocco taste, we cannot but admire his consummate facility, his inexhaustible fancy, his splendid *bravura*. This unlicensed reveler, this violent masquerader of the brush paints as his people sing, as other people talk. Tiepolo once made a wager — and won it — that he would paint in ten hours the twelve apostles receiving the communion from Christ, the figures to be half the size of life. [For a scholarly estimate of Tiepolo, the reader should consult Charles Blanc's *Venetian Painters*.]

Tiepolo has made many converts among modern painters. Fortuny, who was unmoved by the Sistine Chapel, greatly admired him. I once heard a group of the Roman-Spanish artists discuss the paintings of the Vatican. They preferred the 'Communion of St. Jerome,' by Domenichino to all others.

10.

OIL PAINTINGS FOR THE DECORATION OF THE LUXEMBOURG PALACE (NOW IN THE LOUVRE) BY PETER PAUL RUBENS (1577–1640).

These compositions are intended to illustrate a statement made on page 106, chapter X. But whether or not, from the quality and distribution of their light and shade, they are rather easel pictures than mural paintings, they testify that Rubens was gifted with that exuberant creative power, that broad and generous handling, that feeling for ample and eloquent forms which are the requisites for decorative painting. His work is a striking exemplification of native genius, strengthened and developed by a free and intelligent study of Italian precedent.

11.

'MINERVE ÉLEVANT LE GÉNIE VERS L'EMPYRÉE.' DRAWING IN BLACK AND WHITE FOR A CEILING, BY PRUD'HON (PIERRE, 1760–1825).

This simple, poetic, lovable artist was a contemporary of David and the classic school. In the words of Charles Blanc, "he observed this great movement with a smile," though protesting against the methods of the men who studied statues till they forgot how to paint. Enabled to travel in Italy by a prize gained at Dijon, "he understood Raphael, loved Leonardo, but studied Correggio by preference," as his works clearly evince. He was not uninfluenced by the classicism of his day, but extracted only the good and the assimilable from the antique. He is a sort of Greek Correggio; but not merely that, for his own pure, sad, and tender soul, which shunned the garish light of day, and sought expression in a subdued atmosphere, is embodied in his creations. He is a chiaro-oscurist, sees by light and shade, and therefore not a great decorator in the strict sense of the word; yet the nobility, purity and simplicity of his style, eminently fitted it for the wall.

12.

' LES SAINTES PENITENTES.' CHURCH OF S. VINCENT DE PAUL,
PARIS. BY HIPPOLYTE FLANDRIN (1809–1864).

Flandrin left Lyons, where he was born, in 1829, and entered the atelier of Ingres at Paris. The relations between the two were as close as that of master and pupil in the days of Cennini. Flandrin admired and venerated Ingres, who was sincerely proud of his *élève.* The Italian masters most sympathetic to him were Giotto, Angelico, and Raphael. "While the stanze of the Vatican [were] to his mind the most absolute expressions of pictorial perfection; while, as he repeatedly would affirm, Giotto's frescos in S. Maria del Arena, or those of Fra Angelico in the Chapel of Nicholas V, ought to be ' the very breviary' of the painter of religious subjects, Flandrin none the less sought daily to study on his own account, and adapt the lessons of the past to the requirements of his personal feeling and the wants of the present day." (*Life of Flandrin,* London, 1875.) His reverence for the antique, and an inborn feeling for the beautiful tempered the expression of Christian austerity with grace. Flandrin did not resemble other men; so sweetly patient was he, so serene, and even humble, yet by no means devoid of character or convictions, for he stoutly championed the tenets of his school. The reply of a sharp-tongued female model to the fellow student who asked why she spared Flandrin is all significant. "*O in quanto a lui, pare proprio la Madonna.*" (Oh, as to him, he appears to be the very Madonna herself).

" He neither attained the masculine grandeur of Poussin (1594–1665) nor the profound and pathetic tenderness of Le Sueur (1617–1655); but if the extent of his works is considered, their character and their unity; if a comparison is made of a labor so vast and a fervor so sustained; if the number of churches he has decorated and glorified is reckoned, we cannot but justly call the artist who has decked his country in such attire, *the religious painter* of France." (Pierre Larousse, *Dictionnaire Universel*).

The frieze of St. Vincent de Paul was christened by his contemporaries the " Panathénées Chrétiennes."